FREEDOM AND SOCIETY

MERCER UNIVERSITY PRESS

Endowed by

TOM WATSON BROWN
and
THE WATSON-BROWN FOUNDATION, INC.

FREEDOM AND SOCIETY

Essays on Autonomy, Identity, and Political Freedom

Edited by

Yi Deng
Creighton Rosental
Robert H. Scott
Rosalind S. Simson

MERCER UNIVERSITY PRESS
Macon, Georgia
MMXXI

MUP/ P624

© 2021 by Mercer University Press
Published by Mercer University Press
1501 Mercer University Drive
Macon, Georgia 31207
All rights reserved

25 24 23 22 21   5 4 3 2 1

Books published by Mercer University Press are printed on acid-free paper
that meets the requirements of the American National Standard for
Information Sciences—Permanence of Paper for Printed Library Materials.

Printed and bound in the United States.

This book is set in Adobe Caslon Pro.

Cover/jacket design by Burt&Burt.

Library of Congress Control Number: 2021933059

ISBN   978-0-88146-787-1
Cataloging-in-Publication Data is available from the Library of Congress

Contents

FREEDOM AND SOCIETY

Introduction:

The Task of Freedom

Robert H. Scott

The idea for this volume arose from discussions at the annual meeting of the Georgia Philosophical Society that took place at Mercer University in February of 2019. Drafts of most of the chapters included here were first presented at the conference, and the editors of this volume were the officers of the Georgia Philosophical Society at the time. The chapters included here are tied together by questions about the nature of political freedom and autonomy in a democratic society and of the ways in which the enactment of democratic freedom depends on awareness of and engagement with the underlying conditions of freedom, which include social responsibility, creative innovation, and strong democratic institutions.

In order to preserve and ensure the vitality of freedom and democracy in the US and in all democratic societies, it is important that we, as democratic citizens and agents, periodically take time to reflect deeply on what freedom means and on what are the necessary conditions that sustain it.[1] As I write, we, as an international community, are in the throes of a global pandemic. Along with the international community, much of the US has been, for several weeks, sheltering in place, practicing social distancing, and wearing masks when making necessary excursions to stores. After more than ten weeks of largely sheltering in place, many regions in the US and around the world are beginning to partially reopen (with some restrictions), but it remains uncertain what the coming months will bring, as the development of a vaccine, while promising, remains months away. In addition to the health crisis, the pandemic has led to the sudden onset of a global economic crisis, the repercussions of which are sure to be far-reaching. One lesson to be learned about freedom from these events is that

---

[1] As David Wood writes, "Autonomy is made possible by receptive engagement with conditions of possibility, rather than their denial or refusal....It might be said that this is not real autonomy. But what could be more fictional than an autonomy that presupposes background conditions it cannot acknowledge!" David Wood, *Deep Time, Dark Times: On Being Geologically Human* (New York: Fordham University Press, 2019), 23.

absolute demands, claimed in the name of individual freedom, to reopen without first engaging in rigorous public debate and heeding the guidance of health experts, must be resisted. Such absolute claims to individual freedom exhibit a lack of recognition or denial of the social dimension of freedom—a distortion that exaggerates the rights of atomized individuals and discounts the importance of social responsibility to freedom. The question of whether or not to wear a mask in public provides an instructive illustration of the social conditions of freedom. In the absence of a vaccine or widespread testing and contact tracing, failure to wear masks in public places and to practice social distancing will surely accelerate the spread of the virus and result in more deaths, especially among the most vulnerable. Echoing J.S. Mill, free individuals are not free to pose a definite risk of harm to others;[2] behaviors such as not practicing social distancing or not wearing a mask in public are likely to do such harm. It is because of the social risk, not only the risk to personal health, that following such directives is crucial to the enactment of freedom during the pandemic. Further, not only is following such directives necessary to minimize the spread of the virus, following such measures is also necessary to protect the freedom of healthcare workers to do their vital jobs without undergoing unnecessary personal risks that would result from shortages in hospital beds, medical staff, and personal protective equipment (PPE).[3]

Another lesson to be learned from the pandemic, which points to social responsibility as a condition of freedom, is the importance of public health as a necessary, basic condition of a free society. In addition to the suffering of the sick, businesses, workers, and society as a whole are also suffering profoundly from the health crisis.[4] In order to maximize freedom for both individuals and society, the pandemic has made it clear that public

---

[2] In *On Liberty* Mill writes, "Whenever, in short, there is a definite damage, or a definite risk of damage, either to an individual or to the public, the case is taken out of the province of liberty, and placed in that of morality or law." J.S. Mill, *On Liberty and Other Essays* (Oxford: Oxford University Press, 2008), 91.

[3] For information on PPE shortages during the pandemic and strategies for addressing them, see "Strategies to Optimize the Supply of PPE and Equipment," Centers for Disease Control and Prevention, May 18, 2020. https://www.cdc.gov/coronavirus/2019-ncov/hcp/ppe-strategy/index.html.

[4] Applications for unemployment benefits from March to May 2020 surpassed 38 million, and in April 2020 the jobless rate rose above 14%. See Patricia Cohen, "Many Jobs May Vanish Forever as Layoffs Mount," *The New York Times*, May 21, 2020, https://www.nytimes.com/2020/05/21/business/economy/coronavirus-unemployment-claims.html

health must be prioritized ahead of monetary goals, and this includes not only ensuring adequate staffing of healthcare personnel and provision of medical supplies and PPE, but also the provision of strong institutions that guarantee the broad accessibility of healthcare for all and support for collaborative, scientific work devoted to the prevention and containment of future pandemics and health crises. Yet, in the response to the pandemic, in many instances, monetary values have taken precedence over public health, as is evident in incidences of price-gouging on essential medical supplies, for example.[5] Further, a recent study,[6] suggests that if the U.S. had implemented the lockdown one week earlier, over 35,000 lives could have been saved. With David Byrne, many of us may be wondering, "How did I [or we] get here?"[7]

To answer this question, it is important to understand the idea of freedom associated with neoliberalism, an economic model of freedom that has had a broad and morally flawed influence on the general understanding of democratic freedom in recent decades. Over the past forty years the prevailing model of freedom in the west has been neoliberalism, which places emphasis on the freedom of entrepreneurs and consumers to participate in markets with minimal restraints imposed by the state.[8] Neoliberalism defines freedom in economic terms and assumes that political freedom coincides with market freedom. An important problem with the

---

[5] From the early weeks of the pandemic there have been reports of price-gouging on products ranging from hand sanitizer to ventilators. See Michael Levenson, "Price-gouging Complaints Surge Amid Coronavirus Pandemic," *The New York Times*, March 27, 2020, https://www.nytimes.com/2020/03/27/us/coronavirus-price-gouging-hand-sanitizer-masks-wipes.html.

[6] Sen Pei, Sasikiran Kandula, and Jeffrey Shaman, "Differential Effects of Intervention Timing on COVID-19 Spread in the United States," *Science Advances* (November 2020), https://doi.org/10.1126/sciadv.abd6370.

[7] The reference is to the song by David Byrne, "Once in a Lifetime," track 4 on Talking Heads, *Remain in Light*, Sire Records, 1980, www.songfacts.com/lyrics/talking-heads/once-in-a-lifetime.

[8] While neoliberal theorists differ in their views and range from radical (e.g., Milton Friedman) to moderate (e.g., Friedrich Hayek), all forms of neoliberalism tout the self-organizing rationality of markets and actively seek to orient all aspects of civil society around market principles, including "the media, schools, families, science, churches, unions, and the corporate estate." William Connolly, *The Fragility of Things: Self-organizing Processes, Neoliberal Fantasies, and Democratic Activism* (Durham, NC: Duke University Press, 2013), 22, 52. For a virtue ethics based critique of neoliberalism, see Todd May, *Friendship in an Age of Economics: Resisting the Forces of Neoliberalism* (Lanham, MD: Lexington Books, 2014).

neoliberal definition of freedom is, as political theorist William Connolly points out, that it "expresses inordinate confidence in the unique, self-regulating power of markets."[9] That is, neoliberalism fails to take adequate notice of self-organizing processes external to and interacting with markets that function as limiting conditions on markets and carry significant moral implications for both entrepreneurs and consumers. One example of such a self-organizing process, starkly evident in the pandemic, is the self-organizing capacity of infectious diseases such as the coronavirus. Other examples of self-organizing processes that impinge on markets, the significance of which neoliberalism downplays or discounts, are the climate system and the nonhuman natural environment as a whole.[10]

The invitation to recognize the "multiple sites of self-organization"[11] that interact with and impinge on markets evokes the moral importance of responsibility, both in its attributive and responsive dimensions, to the realization of a free society. In relation to the attributive sense of responsibility, careful stewardship of political freedom entails that democratic societies cultivate strong institutions that hold accountable bad actors who damage, threaten, or undermine political freedoms, the epistemic parameters of public discourse,[12] or the common good. The responsive dimension of responsibility calls for recognition of and open dialogue with the underlying bodily and social conditions of freedom.[13] Paying due attention

---

[9] Connolly, 20.

[10] Connolly notes that the multiple (perhaps innumerable) self-organizing processes that impinge on the self-organizing process of markets have differential capacities, time-scales, and degrees of predictability, but the main point here is that neoliberal theory does not give due attention to the effects of external self-organizing processes on markets. See Connolly, 8-9.

[11] Connolly, 14.

[12] Social epistemology is the area of philosophy that studies the social character of parameters for knowledge. Viable epistemic parameters for public discourse include a commitment to truth without pre-determining it, affirming freedom of the press and expression while, through engaged, open public dialogue, prioritizing the best supported views, e.g., empirically verifiable positions and the considered views of discipline-specific experts over others. I am indebted to J. Aaron Simmons for pointing out how those who undermine epistemic parameters for public discourse, for example, by dismissing empirical evidence or discounting the considered views of experts, threaten the viability of democracy. For more on social epistemology, see Alvin I. Goldman and Matthew McGrath, *Epistemology: A Contemporary Introduction* (Oxford: Oxford University Press, 2014), 203-248.

[13] Underlying conditions of freedom, noted above, include the social condition, which entails basic epistemic parameters for public discourse and harm to others as a

to the social dimension of freedom not only answers the call to social responsibility, such attentiveness also provides the impetus for a discursive process that facilitates the creative formulation of innovative solutions to socio-economic problems that arise.[14] In an age which tends to place undue confidence in impersonal market forces to solve socio-economic problems, cultivation of responsiveness to the underlying bodily and social conditions of freedom, and to self-organizing processes that impinge on markets, facilitates the development of virtues integral to maintaining the vitality of democratic freedom: creative responsiveness and what Connolly calls awareness of "the fragility of things."[15]

Connolly makes a strong case that, as the bankruptcy of the neoliberal model of freedom that focuses exclusively on the freedom of markets becomes increasingly apparent, the need to rethink the concept of freedom and to articulate "an image of freedom that challenges neoliberal orthodoxy" is becoming urgent.[16] In order to take up this challenge, I have inquired briefly into the underlying conditions of political freedom, focusing on three key elements for the enactment of political freedom: social responsibility, creativity, and institutional integrity. I have already touched on the importance of social responsibility to political freedom, and several chapters in this volume engage with this theme, challenging an atomistic picture of autonomy and illustrating ways in which autonomy depends on basic social conditions for its realization. In a discussion of the debate in military ethics over standards for the use of Autonomous Weapons Systems (AWSes), Matthew Lee, in chapter 5, challenges the possibility of calling such weapons systems autonomous. Lee argues that true autonomy is not possible without meeting the conditions of moral agency and responsibility, neither of which is met by current AWSes. In chapter 6, Tony Chackal highlights several basic, underlying conditions for autonomy, including intersubjectivity, embodiment, and the surrounding environment. Chackal goes on to show how race-based obstructions to autonomy feed

---

limit on freedom, and public health, which the pandemic has shown, in stark terms, to be a condition of freedom of movement and commerce in society. Other underlying conditions of freedom, discussed in the following paragraphs, include institutional integrity, creativity, and the situatedness of free agency and free societies in relation to time and to multiple self-organizing processes.

[14] Connolly, *The Fragility of Things*, 135.

[15] Connolly, 14.

[16] Connolly, 39 and 72.

on selective and inconsistent applications of conflicting models of autonomy. In chapter 9, through a critical evaluation of the ideal of impartiality as a guideline for moral obligation, Rosalind Simson considers the implications for the ideal of impartiality of the differential weight owed to local versus global conditions of autonomy.

I now turn to the integral relation between political freedom and creativity and chapters that touch on this aspect of freedom. In considering the importance of creativity to the enactment of freedom, it is important to note first that the prevailing neoliberal conception of freedom prioritizes what is called negative freedom which conceptualizes human desires and preferences as static and places emphasis on minimizing obstructions to the free expression of supposedly static desires and preferences. Negative freedom, however, is shown to be only a partial way of realizing political freedom through the recognition that the formation of desires and preferences is dynamic, not static, and involves creative engagement with surrounding circumstances, history, and present possibilities as integral to the enactment of freedom.[17] The creative dimension of freedom draws on the dynamic temporal and social conditions of autonomy, which facilitate the malleability of desires and preferences. The historical and temporal aspects of autonomy refer to the temporal context of action—that one always acts in the present in a manner that draws on the past with an eye towards the future. The intersubjective (or social) aspect of autonomy refers to the social context of action which continually invites discursive engagement with others, as well as with one's surrounding circumstances and the inflow of verifiable, new information. By way of receptive engagement with the temporal and social conditions of freedom, desires and preferences are composed, modified, and refined, and this creative dimension of freedom entails that the enactment of political freedom involves more than the removal of hinderances to static desires, or negative freedom. Rather, the enactment of political freedom involves recognition of and attentiveness to surrounding circumstances and the underlying temporal and social conditions of agency, accompanied by active, creative engagement. The creative dimension of freedom often leads to something new—a new idea or a new social dynamic and new sensibilities which may be short-lived or may prove to have a lasting, positive impact on society, such as the civil rights movement in the US has had.

---

[17] Connolly, 74.

Several chapters in the volume take up the theme of the creative dimension of freedom in a variety of ways and contexts. In chapter 7, Osman Nemli addresses the creative aspect of freedom in his discussion of W.E.B. Du Bois's book, *Black Reconstruction in America*, on the unfinished project of social reconstruction in the post-Civil War US. The integral importance of creativity to the enactment of political freedom is again taken up by Susan Bredlau in chapter 8 in a discussion of creative modifications made by the Navajo community to align their implementation of US jurisprudence with the Navajo community court system. In prior chapters, the importance of the creative dimension of freedom is developed in chapter 3 by William Parkhurst in his discussion of Nietzsche on the role of creativity in language use, and it is further developed in chapter 4 by Pablo Munoz Iturrieta in a discussion of Hannah Arendt's concept of creative public action as a model for political freedom.

The third and final concept I want to discuss as intertwined with political freedom is institutional integrity. The integrity of democratic institutions is of fundamental importance to the preservation of free, democratic societies. Democratic institutions, starting with a nation's constitution, are established by democracies in order to guarantee basic political freedoms and individual and social rights, including the rights to freedom of the press, freedom of religion, and to non-discrimination. Today, many of these institutions are under threat, in various countries, from anti-pluralistic populist movements. In chapter 1, Steven Lee addresses in detail the dangers that anti-pluralistic populism poses to democratic societies, and, in chapter 2, Gary Simson highlights the importance of effective democratic legal institutions in the US for adjudicating conflicts between laws designed to promote the general welfare and individual claims of religious liberty. In chapter 4, Pablo Munoz Iturrieta extends further the thread of the importance of democratic institutions in his discussion of Arendt's proposal for the institution of a system of local governing councils as a means of ensuring the vitality of citizen involvement and creative public action in democracies. Each of these chapters points to the fundamental value of institutional integrity for the preservation of political freedom, for as Steven Lee points out in Chapter 1, it is through democratic institutions and the procedures and rights they uphold, not through any single individual, that the will of the people is reliably expressed.

Chapter Summaries

In the opening chapter, Steven P. Lee brings into focus the fragility of democracy and considers ways in which it is threatened by the rise of populism, in particular, anti-pluralistic versions of populism. Lee probes the nature and causes of populism, noting that its salient features include anti-elitism along with anti-pluralism (in cases of right-wing populism), which he argues is the most dangerous element of populism. Anti-pluralism runs counter to the ideals of liberal democracy in its allowance for expressions of xenophobia, racism, and other forms of discrimination. Lee suggests that in order to counter the threat of populism, it is important to understand how populist movements originate. He agrees with many commentators that economic inequality and racism contribute to anti-pluralistic populism. But an underlying basis of anti-pluralistic populism, he argues, originates from a confusion or category mistake on the part of the citizens. This mistake involves equating the will of the people with the will of a single individual, embodied in the populist leader. In an effective democracy, Lee points out, the will of the people cannot be equated with the will of any single individual; the belief that it can is based on a bad analogy. Rather, the will of the people is constructed historically through democratically established institutions and procedures which guarantee basic rights. The will of the people does not exist prior to those institutions or their operations. Through the cultivation and preservation of its institutions and greater attention to public education, liberal democracy has the capacity to protect individual rights and to uphold pluralism in society.

In chapter 2, Gary J. Simson, a legal scholar, builds further on themes Lee discusses by examining, from the perspective of American constitutional law, the kinds of clashes of fundamental values that arise with increasing frequency in our pluralistic society. Simson's point of departure is *Masterpiece Cakeshop v. Colorado Civil Rights Commission*, a highly publicized case decided by the US Supreme Court in 2018. The case involved a baker who refused to make a custom wedding cake for a same-sex couple because, as a devout Christian, he believed that creating the cake would make him complicit in what he considers the sin of same-sex marriage. The baker claimed that his First Amendment right to free exercise of religion entitled him to an exemption from a Colorado law that outlaws discrimination based on sexual orientation. The Supreme Court essentially punted on the issue, ruling in favor of the baker on a narrow ground with little significance for future cases. However, Simson uses the religious liberty claim raised, but not decided, in the Masterpiece Cakeshop case as a vehicle to explore more broadly when, in a society as religiously pluralistic as ours, religious liberty claims must give way to laws designed to protect other important values, including a commitment to pluralism of other sorts.

In chapter 3, William A. B. Parkhurst presents a compelling interpretation of the political implications of Nietzsche's philosophy of language, challenging prevailing views among Nietzsche scholars who frame Nietzsche's philosophy as apolitical and tending toward a form of extreme individualism. Through a close reading of Nietzsche's work, especially the *Genealogy of Morals* and other texts that relate to philosophy of language, Parkhurst argues that Nietzsche conceptualizes the individual as deeply social and political, tied to others through language. Meticulously grounding his argument in Nietzsche's texts, Parkhurst draws out a necessary consequent of Nietzsche's philosophy: that the inherently social and linguistic character of Nietzsche's epistemology affords a path, accessible for all, to the enactment of political freedom through careful and creative choices in language use.

In Chapter 4, Pablo Munoz Iturrieta extends reflection on the relation between political freedom and language, shifting the focus from language *per se* to its innovative application in public action. Munoz Iturrieta traces Hannah Arendt's conceptualization of political freedom, highlighting the importance of creative expression and public action in Arendt's account. In order for genuine political freedom to be possible, Munoz Iturrieta emphasizes with Arendt that a democratic society must have effective institutions in place that guarantee a public space for creative expression and public action. In addition to recalling the discussion in the previous chapter of the link between political freedom and language use, the emphasis in this chapter on the importance of effective democratic institutions as conditions for political freedom resonates with prior discussions of the fundamental importance of institutional structures as guarantors of political freedom.

In chapter 5, Matthew Brandon Lee takes a critical approach to the commonly invoked "Better-than-Human" (BTH) standard as a viable ethical guide for the use of autonomous weapons systems (AWSes). A key problem in the debate over AWSes, other than the question of just what a "better-than-human" standard would look like, is the equivocal use of the term "autonomy" in relation to AWSes. In modern philosophy, the idea of autonomy carries a sense of moral agency and membership in the moral community, neither of which apply to AWSes. Hence, it would be more accurate, Lee argues, to consider AWSes simply as weapons systems whose operators are alone subject to moral and legal evaluation. By removing the idea of autonomy from the conceptualization of such weapons, the relevance of the BTH standard falls away as the moral responsibility for their implementation must rest on the moral agents (the officers and soldiers) who have them at their disposal. The guidelines of Just War Theory, which serve as the ethical standard for war time ethics, are to be applied only to the actions of the human wielders of AWSes. In place of the elusive "better that human" standard, Lee proposes what he calls the "question-of-advantage-harm-balance" (QAHB). In keeping with the criteria of Just War Theory, those implementing the QAHB standard must use only AWSes that are discriminating enough that the users can seriously claim to intend harm only to combatants and military objects (even if, as with many weapons, some harm to protected persons and objects is inevitable), and AWSes may replace human soldiers only where AWSes confer an increased military advantage without a comparable increase in harm to protected persons and objects.

In chapter 6, Tony Chackal extends the discussion of autonomy and distinguishes two models of the individual and autonomy: the modern, atomistic, space-based model, and his ecological, place-based model. Chackal highlights the manner in which the ecological conception of autonomy is more descriptively accurate than the atomistic model, by virtue of accommodating the necessary social and environmental conditions of autonomy. He also demonstrates its greater effectiveness in accounting for external obstructions to autonomy, including those brought about by racism. Further, Chackal lucidly shows how racist actors apply the two models selectively in ways that inflate the achievements of white actors by applying the atomist model to them, while undermining the achievements of nonwhite actors by applying the ecological model to them and emphasizing the role of enabling social conditions in their achievements. Conversely, he shows how blame for crimes by whites gets diminished by citing the role of social conditioning factors (in line with the ecological model), while blame for crimes committed by nonwhites gets inflated by emphasizing individual responsibility (in line with the atomistic model). Drawing on Charles Mills's *The Racial Contract*, Chackal traces racist perception to binary forms of racial essentialism that took root in the early modern period and, despite having been falsified, continue to have influence today.

In chapter 7, Osman Nemli takes a close look at W.E.B. Du Bois's 1935 work *Black Reconstruction in America*, bringing into focus the claim that if democracy is to live up to its ideal of government by the people, it must continually critique and reconstruct itself in ways that are more inclusive of *all* people. Recalling obstructions to autonomy that nonwhites continue to face in the US (discussed also by Chackal in chapter 6), Nemli brings to the fore Du Bois's insights into multiple ways in which the colorline has played a role in unjust political and economic arrangements that, despite movements for equality and efforts at social reconstruction, persist in the post-Civil War US.

In chapter 8, Susan Bredlau analyzes the political problem of autoimmunity, drawing from Jacques Derrida's work on this concept. The metaphor of autoimmune disease is a way of conceiving of the danger a society poses to itself when it attempts to isolate itself from surrounding conditions and communities. As does Nemli in Chapter 7, Bredlau brings out the importance for political freedom of ongoing reconstruction and creative engagement with surrounding conditions and highlights ways in which such creative engagement has led to greater realizations of community identity and political freedom for oppressed communities. Bredlau focuses in particular on two cases: the response of Algerian subjects under French colonial rule to laws against wearing the haik and the integration, by Navajo society, of elements of the traditional Navajo courts system in compliance with US jurisprudence. Through these examples Bredlau shows how communities cannot avoid being changed by their surroundings, and she suggests that political communities are much more able to maintain their identity and expand their political freedoms by creatively engaging with surrounding conditions than by isolating themselves from them.

In the final chapter, Rosalind S. Simson raises an ethical question regarding the relationship between freedom, impartiality, and moral obligations. Her analysis focuses on recent work by Peter Singer on "effective altruism," a social movement aimed at ensuring that charitable efforts do "the most good" possible. As explained by Singer, effective altruism holds that, after meeting one's own basic needs, one has a duty not only to be benevolent, but also to ensure that the resources one donates are impartially directed towards projects or organizations that will maximize their probable impact. Simson argues that, because of the importance of interpersonal relationships in building self-esteem, confidence, and a sense of personal identity, there are often strong moral reasons to prioritize the needs of relatives, friends, and members of one's local community. She then offers proposals for deciding whether and when special obligations to those with whom one shares relationships should take precedence over impartial obligations to promote the general good.

Works Cited

Byrne, David. "Once in a Lifetime." Track 4 on Talking Heads. *Remain in Light*. Sire Records. 1980. www.songfacts.com/lyrics/talking-heads/once-in-a-lifetime.

Centers for Disease Control and Prevention. "Strategies to Optimize the Supply of PPE and Equipment." May 18, 2020. https://www.cdc.gov/coronavirus/2019-ncov/hcp/ppe-strategy/index.html.

Cohen, Patricia. "Many Jobs May Vanish Forever as Layoffs Mount." *New York Times*. May 21, 2020. https://www.nytimes.com/2020/05/21/business/economy/coronavirus-unemployment-claims.html.

Connolly, William. *The Fragility of Things: Self-organizing Processes, Neoliberal Fantasies, and Democratic Activism*. Durham: Duke University Press, 2013.

Glanz, James and Campbell Robinson. "Lockdown Delays Cost at Least 36,000 Lives, Data Show." *New York Times*. May 20, 2020. https://www.nytimes.com/2020/05/20/us/coronavirus-distancing-deaths.html.

Goldman, Alvin I. and Matthew McGrath, *Epistemology: A Contemporary Introduction*. Oxford: Oxford University Press, 2014.

Levenson, Michael. "Price-gouging Complaints Surge Amid Coronavirus Pandemic." *New York Times*. March 27, 2020. https://www.nytimes.com/2020/03/27/us/coronavirus-price-gouging-hand-sanitizer-masks-wipes.html.

May, Todd. *Friendship in an Age of Economics: Resisting the Forces of Neoliberalism*. Lanham: Lexington Books, 2014.

Mill, J.S. *On Liberty and Other Essays*. Oxford: Oxford University Press, 2008.

Pei, Sei, Sasikiran Kandula, and Jeffrey Shaman. "Differential Effects of Intervention Timing on COVID-19 Spread in the United States." *Science Advances*. https://doi.org/10.1126/sciadv.abd6370.

Wood, David. *Deep Time, Dark Times: On Being Geologically Human*. New York: Fordham University Press, 2019.

1

The Populist Threat

Steven P. Lee

We have entered a dark time politically, not just in the US, but in much of the West, and in large parts of the developing world as well. It is not, of course, the darkest time the world has faced in the past century, but it is dark enough, especially coming after the hope of the 1990s with the end of the Cold War, when democracy seemed to be on the march. Bill Galston notes: "In just twenty-five years, the partisans of democracy have moved from triumphalism to near despair."[1] We now realize how fragile democracy is, how dependent it is on norms or "guard rails," which are easily trampled or ignored.

What has darkened our political time is the phenomenon of populism and the threat it poses to liberal democracy. I have been led to investigate populism in a personal effort to understand the political times we are going through, which many find deeply distressing. It seems like the arc of the moral universe is no longer bending toward justice. Note that this essay is not specifically about populism in the US and the reign of Donald Trump, though he will appear as an example (and while he may no longer be in power when this is published, the threat of populism will remain). He is but one instance of this global phenomenon, though given America's influence and power in the world, he is perhaps the most dangerous instance. On the other hand, the protean character of populism indicates that not all that can be said about populism in general will apply equally to any particular populist movement. There are many different sorts of populist regimes and programs.

In the paper below, I seek to explain what populism is, to distinguish the currently surging right-wing populism (what this paper is mainly about) from left-wing populism, to consider explanations for why populism is surging now, and to discuss the opposition between populism and

---

[1] William A. Galston, *Anti-Pluralism: The Populist Threat to Liberal Democracy* (New Haven, CT: Yale University Press, 2018), 1.

liberal democracy. While there are a number of factors leading to the current surge of populism, I explore one of these, which I argue has to do with a mistaken analogy that supporters of populism often hold.

I. What is populism?

Let me begin by offering a general characterization of populism based on the work of a number of authors and theorists. Populism has two basic features. The first and foremost is *anti-elitism*. Populism is a Manichean view of politics in which the elites are opposed to the people.[2] While the elites to which the people are opposed are mainly political, they may also be economic, cultural, or intellectual. As populist politician George Wallace used to say, "there is not a dime's worth of difference" between the two main political parties in the US. In the populist view, the division between the elites and the people is a moral one. Populism is a "moralistic imagination of politics."[3] The people are pure and virtuous, while the elites are corrupt. Populist leaders advocate (or so they say) for the virtuous people in their opposition to the debased elites.[4] Certainly, many people see the political world in this way. Populist leaders are the voice of the people. Only they can understand the people and the will of the people; only they can successfully battle the elites on behalf of the people.

The second feature of populism considered in the essay is its *anti-pluralism*. Populism's anti-pluralism is seen in the answer it gives to the question, who are "the people"? The populist answer is that they are those opposed to the elites. The people are assumed to be homogenous in their opposition to the elites, and so, not plural. Populists understand the people to be "homogeneous and unitary, which contradicts the pluralism that characterizes all free societies in modernity."[5] Populists "speak and act *as if* the people could develop a singular judgment, a singular will....They speak *as if* the people were one."[6] Because the people are as one in their opposition to the elites, those who do not share the views of the people regarding the elites are considered *not* a part of the people.[7] They are, let us say, the

---

[2] Cas Mudde and Christóbal Kaltwasser, *Populism—A Very Short Introduction* (Oxford University Press: 2017), 97, 99.

[3] Jan-Werner Müller, *What is Populism?* (Philadelphia: Pennsylvania University Press: 2016), 19.

[4] Mudde and Kaltwasser, 6.

[5] Galston, *Anti-Pluralism*, 5.

[6] Müller, *What is Populism?*, 77.

[7] Trump quote in Müller, 22.

Other, a third theoretical category in addition to the people and the elites. A populist leader uses the people's opposition to the Other, sometimes the result of their inherent anti-pluralism (for example, in their racism), to solidify the leader's own power and to mobilize the people against the elites. The elites are portrayed by the populists as in league with the Other against the people. The elites give special favors to the Other in exchange for their political support. For example, populists often see the elites as redistributing the wealth of the people in the form of "welfare measures" to the Other. Populists claim that this occurs through the elites practicing "identity politics," dispensing favors derived from taxes paid by the people on "identity groups" among the Other. But, in fact, populism is itself a form of identity politics, based on an *exclusive* form of identity, e.g., as in its advocacy of white nationalism.[8] In fact, populism is sometimes referred to as "white identity politics." The identity politics populists oppose is *inclusive* in its respect for multiple identity groups. Because it represents multiple identity groups, the politics populists oppose is a form of pluralism.

Populism has been referred to as a "thin-centered ideology."[9] It lacks the substance of a thicker ideology, such as fascism or communism. Included among thicker ideologies would be religions or religious ideologies, which historically have probably been the most common thick ideologies with which populism has been connected. It is more a strategy for gaining and holding political power than for pursuing the goals specified by a thicker ideology. Populism itself, in contrast with thick ideologies, as one commentator notes, has no idea of the *good life*, as thick ideologies do. Populism is often adopted in the context of a thicker ideology to achieve the goals of that ideology. A populist leader recognizes that a populist approach is a good way to achieve personal power, and this may be the main or only reason for which it is pursued. As a strategy for gaining and holding power, populism often involves a paranoid style of politics, trading in conspiracy theories, a convenient way of dismissing facts inconsistent with the populist worldview.[10] Populist leaders use conspiracy theories in order to blame their own shortcomings and failures on the elites (or the Other, or on both).[11] The anti-pluralist dimension of the populist world-view is one

---

[8] Müller, 2-3.
[9] Mudde and Kaltwasser, *Populism*, 6.
[10] Mudde and Kaltwasser, 82
[11] Müller, *What is Populism?*, 43

way in which populist leaders seek to take advantage of (and foster) racist, misogynist, and xenophobic tendencies among the people.

The ideological thinness of populism has been on display during the Trump administration. For example, an important feature of his 2016 campaign was a commitment to fully support Medicare and Social Security. That feature was touted as a political commitment that set him apart from his Republican primary opponents and identified him as a populist instead of a standard Republican. But he has since abandoned a strong commitment to these social programs, putting his political capital at the service of the traditional conservative ideology of the Republican Party, such as tax cuts benefiting the wealthy. Populism seems to be a stance or strategy adopted by Trump not to advance a coherent governing program, but for some non-ideological reason, to enhance his family's wealth and power, perhaps. He seems to have no overriding ideological commitments beyond his own dominance, to which he sees populism as a means.

In general, the "thin-centered" nature of populism means that there are different forms of populism. Populist regimes of the sort I am discussing can vary, due, for example, to differences in national political cultures. One large difference is the role of religion in defining the people and the Other. This is the root of the protean character of populism, mentioned earlier.

II. Right-wing and left-wing populism

There is, however, one other form of populism, different from that discussed above, that should be mentioned. So far, I have discussed populism as characterized by three key elements, namely, *the people*, *the elites*, and *the Other*. Because there is a dynamic of these three elements, we may refer to this as *triadic populism*. But a different form of populism is characterized by only two of these elements, *the people* and *the elites*. This is *dyadic populism*.[12] Practitioners of dyadic populism do not use the *Other* as part of a political strategy in opposing the elites.[13] So, dyadic populism is not antipluralist. The difference between dyadic and triadic populism is roughly the difference between left-wing populism and right wing-populism, so

---

[12] John Judis, *The Populist Explosion* (New York: Columbia Global Reports, 2016), 15. See also Galston, 126-27, who understands the distinction in a different way.

[13] Müller sees the third element as necessary for populism (20), as apparently does Galston (127).

understanding the former difference will help us understand the latter difference.

Movements on the left are often called populist. Indeed, theorists identify the historical beginnings of populism in the U.S. with the left-wing People's Party in the 1890s.[14] But left-wing populist movements, in general, are not triadic; while anti-elitist, they are generally not anti-pluralist. Left-wing movements are usually pluralist and inclusive, or strive to be so. Populist leaders on the left generally do not base their efforts to achieve political power on their exercise of an anti-pluralist agenda. They do not engage in racist, misogynist, or xenophobic appeals, or, if they do, they are subject to the same moral criticisms as triadic populism. Indeed, dyadic populists often advocate anti-discrimination legislation and other administrative measures for that purpose. Some may see anti-pluralism as intrinsic to populism,[15] but it better corresponds to how we talk about our political world to regard populism as also having a left-wing, pluralistic form. The key feature of populism in general is its opposition to the elites, but this may take a dyadic or a triadic form. It is the "thin-centered" character of populism that allows it to take either form, and, more generally, allows it to vary in other ways across a range of historical and regional cases.

The contrast between triadic and dyadic populism represents a crucial moral difference, for what marks populism as subject to special moral opprobrium is its anti-pluralism. Its basis in racist, xenophobic, and misogynistic policies is the principal moral objection to populism. The reason is that anti-pluralism is opposed to the foundational liberal idea of equality, to the anti-discriminatory idea that all individuals are to be considered equal before the law.[16] (To be more precise, anti-pluralism involves discrimination against individuals due to factors for which they are not responsible, though the anti-pluralist may have a more expansive view about the conditions for which one is responsible.[17]) To the extent that a system of government is anti-pluralistic, it should be strongly condemned morally on those grounds alone. This is the key moral objection to triadic populism. Populism may, apart from its form, have some moral value as a form of government. For example, as populists claim, elites are often out of

---

[14] Müller, *What is Populism?*, 3

[15] Barry Eichengreen, *The Populist Temptation* (Oxford University Press, 2018), 2; also Galston, *Anti-Pluralism*, 127.

[16] On this point in general, see Galston, *Anti-Pluralism*.

[17] I owe this point to Rosalind Simson.

touch with the interests of the people, requiring the political mobilization of the people to combat them. The elites sometimes deserve to be attacked; often they are oppressing the people or ignoring their needs. They may need to be brought more thoroughly under democratic control, and populism might help in achieving this. Populism can be a "democratic corrective."[18] There may be moral objections to populism that apply to it in either form, such as its tendency to concentrate power in the hands of the populist leaders and open the door to authoritarianism. But the anti-pluralist objection applies to all cases of triadic populism, so that triadic populism may, as a rule, be rejected out of hand, while dyadic populism should be considered case-by-case. But it is triadic populism, the form of populism that challenges us today, that is my subject.

III. What explains the current eruption of populism?

What is the explanation for the current upwelling of triadic populism? This question has been much discussed. In briefly addressing it here, I will consider general forms of explanation, not necessarily specific explanations of particular historical episodes or eruptions of populism. Speaking generally, there are two types of explanation that might be given for the rise of populism: psychological and political-institutional. The first focuses on the psychology of individuals that makes populism attractive to them, while the second focuses on the context, that is, the political-institutional setting facilitating the rise of populism. Psychological explanations include, for example, an appeal to the idea of the authoritarian personality, claiming that some individuals are naturally attracted to populist leaders who promise the order, stability, and political clarity such personalities crave.[19] Stenner and Haidt offer one example of this sort of explanation. They argue that there is a psychological feature common to individuals who are inclined to populism, namely, "a multifaceted demand for less diversity and difference in society, a lack of openness to experience." This feature (or the tendency for it) is "substantially heritable" and is characteristic of about one-third of the population.[20] An individual's desire for less diversity and difference in society would incline that person to support the

---

[18] Mudde and Kaltwasser, *Populism*, 79, 82
[19] Karen Stenner and Jonathan Haidt, "Authoritarianism is Not a Momentary Madness, but an Eternal Dynamic within Liberal Democracies," in *Can it Happen Here*, ed. Cass Sunstein (New York: Harper Collins, 2018), 175-219.
[20] Stenner and Haidt, 183

anti-pluralism of a triadic populist leader.[21] Political-institutional explanations find the genesis of a populist upwelling in a constellation of particular conditions in society, for example, in a high degree of economic inequality or serious unemployment among certain sectors of the population. Under such conditions it may be easy for populist leaders to convince individuals that it is the elites (and the Other) who are responsible for their economic suffering. For some commentators, a specific example of such an explanation is to be found in the effects of the devastating economic impact of the great recession of 2008.[22]

These two modes of explanation are not mutually exclusive. On the contrary, it seems that a combination of a psychological predisposition in a large number of individuals and an appropriate political-institutional situation must come together (along perhaps with other factors) in explaining any particular instance of a populist eruption. One example of this question is the debate about whether the victory of Donald Trump in 2016 was due to economic insecurity among his voters (a political-institutional explanation) or to their inherent anti-pluralism (a psychological explanation). There have been a number of studies of this issue, but perhaps the safest thing to say is that there are multiple interactive factors, including psychological and political-institutional ones, explaining Trump's victory.[23]

Bill Galston argues that the opposition we are interested in is not that between populism and democracy in general, but rather that between populism and liberal democracy. The opposition is straight-forward: democracy is liberal when it enforces a range of individual rights, while populism's anti-pluralism involves a denial or an ignoring of those rights. For example, liberal democracy supports freedom of the press, which is the chief vehicle for allowing the expression of different points of view that represent the pluralism of a society. Populism does not support freedom of the press because populism assumes that all persons among the people (not among the Other) share the same point of view regarding political matters. The expression of multiple points of view and criticism of the leadership is a threat to a populist regime. The press can, in challenging a populist movement, be the enemy of the people.

---

[21] According to Müller (15-16), to focus on a psychological explanation is to condescend to supporters of populism, to suggest that they cannot be reasoned with and that the only form of treatment is therapy. This is, he says, a form of paternalism.

[22] Galston, *Anti-Pluralism*, 9.

[23] Galston, 76-77.

There is another composite explanation worth noting that adds a third factor to psychological and political-institutional factors, namely, *tribalism*. For Galston, one explanation of populism is that there is "an element of tribal thinking inherent in the human condition."[24] Tribalism is, roughly, the tendency of individuals to strongly identify with other members of their particular social group (or the group itself) and to treat those outside the group as less worthy of consideration. "Populism is unambiguously and unashamedly tribal. It legitimates sentiments that liberal democratic principles seek to suppress."[25] The implication seems to be that racism, for example, has a kind of natural purchase in human nature. Populist leaders seek to sharpen these differences by stoking members of the population's fear of the Other, and individuals, because of their tribal identities, are naturally susceptible to such anti-pluralist fearmongering. All of this is at odds with the prospects for a successful liberal democracy, but it does not make liberal democracy impossible. According to Galston, though the "basic structure of liberal democracy creates tensions that can never be expunged,…they can be managed in response to ever-changing circumstances."[26] When we fail to put into place proper policies of management, this failure becomes a political-institutional factor that is part of the explanation for the eruption of populism.

Shortly, I will suggest another explanation.

IV. The will of the people

Populism, seeks to enact "the will of the people." In this respect, populism is akin to, or is said by some even to be a form of, democracy. But the opposition I am concerned with, as mentioned, is not between populism and democracy, but between populism and liberal democracy. For the sake of this discussion, I will treat democracy as liberal democracy, so that populism and democracy are opposed forms of government. Populism and democracy differ in two basic ways: (1) they differ in what each counts as the will of the people and (2) they differ in how they believe the will of the people is to be determined. Müller observes: "At least in theory, populists claim that the people as a whole not only have a common and coherent

---

[24] Galston, 77.

[25] Galston, 132.

[26] Galston, 5-6. In discussing what the proper policies might be, Galston focuses mostly on policies that would ameliorate the sorts of economic conditions and inequalities that are for him part of the discontent on which populism feeds (see Chap. 6.)

20

will but also can rule in the sense that the right representatives can implement what the people have demanded."[27] The two points are closely related, so discussions of them overlap.

Consider (2) first. How is the will of the people to be determined? This is mainly an epistemological issue. If democratic theory and populist theory claim that society should be guided by the will of the people, each must include a mechanism for determining what that will is. Recall that a crucial assumption of populism is that the *people* are in some sense unified in their views about the *elites* (and the *Other*). This unified view of the will of the people is referred to by Mudde and Kaltwasser as the "monist core of populism."[28] The unified will of the people is sometimes referred to by populists as "common sense," something that is evident and clear to the people, even in the absence of education and expertise. Again, Mudde and Kaltwasser: "Rather than a rational process constructed via discussion in the public sphere, the populist notion of the general will is based on the notion of 'common sense'."[29] The right representatives are the populist leaders, who can perceive what this common sense is, apparently on an intuitive basis. Populist leaders, Galston claims, "often claim legitimacy and authorization based on their special insight into the values and desires of their people." For example, Galston says regarding the rule of Vladimir Putin of Russia: "The deeper truth, Putin insists, is that his regime rests on his people's conviction that he understands them, an intuitive bond that cuts deeper than more formal systems of public authorization."[30]

So, the populist response to (2) is that the will of the people, ideally at least, is determined intuitively by populist leaders, who have a special form of insight into the needs and desires of the people. Galston observes: "Contemporary autocrats, for example, often claim legitimacy and authorization based on their special insight into the values and desires of their people."[31] Following the populist assumption, the needs and desires of the people are unitary. In contrast, in the case of democracy, the will of the people is determined by an apparatus of representative government, without an assumption that that wishes of the people are unitary (in fact, with the opposite assumption), and the will is determined by a political process involving voting.

---

[27] Müller, *What is Populism?*, 76.
[28] Mudde and Kaltwasser, *Populism*, 18.
[29] Mudde and Kaltwasser, 18.
[30] Galston, *Anti-Pluralism*, 22, 23.
[31] Galston, 22.

This leads to a discussion of (1), what do populism and democracy count as the will of the people? The important difference here is captured by Müller. According to the populist, "a majority in parliament is not 'the people' and cannot speak in the name of the people." On the other hand, democracy "presumes precisely the opposite."[32] Democracy presumes that the will of the people is the outcome of a representative process, a complex electoral, legislative, and judicial procedure. The will of the people is an institutional construct, a construct which results from following a (constitutional) procedure for aggregating diverse individual ballot-box choices. It does not exist prior to that construct, capable of being discovered in some other way, such as by the intuition of a populist leader. It is nothing apart from such a construct. The will of the people under democracy is *mediated rather than immediate*. The point of politics for the democrat is not to discover an existing will of the people, as something that might be knowable in some other way. *That* idea of the will of the people is a fantasy.[33] The will of the people is an institutional fact, not a non-institutional nor pre-institutional fact. This is what populists fail, or pretend to fail, to understand. Populist leaders represent people not in an empirical sense, but only in a moral or symbolic sense.[34]

V. Populism and liberal democracy

Populism has the *form* of democracy, but without its *substance*. Elections are the form of democracy, but respect for individual rights is its substance. Populist regimes, by and large, have elections, but the elections don't mean a great deal. Populist leaders often ensure their victory in elections by engaging in political activities designed to ensure their preferred outcome. Populist leaders have tried and true ways to manipulate voting outcomes in their favor, for example, by determining who constitutes the electorate, controlling what information is available to the electorate, choosing the wording of referenda and the lists of candidates, and by means even more nefarious. Populist leaders are, in general, autocrats. But, under the populist view, this is as it should be because the populist leaders have insight into what is genuinely in the people's interest, and it is their responsibility to act in the people's interest, requiring autocratic control.

---

[32] Müller, *What is Populism?*, 78.
[33] Müller, 31.
[34] Müller, 40.

The form of democracy that populism places itself in opposition to, as mentioned earlier, is *liberal* democracy. Populism places itself in opposition to the recognition of the sorts of individual rights that are necessary to the expression of the political differences among members of society, that is, it places itself in opposition to pluralism. Victor Orbán, the current populist leader of Hungry, has referred to his government as an "illiberal democracy," partly to tweak his EU colleagues, but accurately, nonetheless. He is an autocrat, and while he may claim to be a democrat, he is not a liberal democrat. "Populism holds that nothing should constrain 'the will of the (pure) people' and fundamentally rejects the notions of pluralism and, therefore, minority rights as well as the 'institutional guarantees' that should protect them."[35]

As many have pointed out, liberal democracy exists in a permanent tension between its two principal components, majoritarianism and respect for individual rights. If a government is to achieve both of these, and be a full-fledged liberal democracy, it must find a "harmonious equilibrium between majority rule and minority rights."[36] Populism abandons an effort to achieve such an equilibrium and goes all in with majority rule, but it is *guided* majority rule, a majority rule that assumes that there is a unity to the will of the people, a unity divined by the populist rulers. Because there is such a unity, the vote must be guided in order to achieve it. So, for example, administrative guidelines may be put in place making voting more difficult for those who are thought likely to vote against the populist rulers' perception of the will of the people (as in various forms of voter suppression).

There is another important relationship between populism and democracy. Müller says: "Populism is something like a permanent shadow of modern representative democracy, and a constant peril."[37] Populism and democracy are sometimes referred to as two sides of the same coin, the former being parasitic on the latter. Populism is said to be the mirror image of democracy,[38] or perhaps its evil twin. What this image suggests is that populist eruptions are not one-off events but are more or less endemic to liberal democracies. Given the right set of psychological predispositions

---

[35] Mudde and Kaltwasser, *Populism*, 81.

[36] Mudde and Kaltwasser, 82.

[37] Müller, *What is Populism?*, 11.

[38] Francisco Panizza, ed., *Populism and the Mirror of Democracy* (London: Verso, 2005).

among a sufficient portion of the population and a favorable political-institutional context, populism is likely to erupt. Liberal democracy can never completely avoid the risk of a populist eruption. In the US, prior to the current populist eruption, there was McCarthyism, Huey Long, the post-World War I Red Scare, and others such situations and individuals. All that can be done is to lessen the risk. But how? There have been a number of suggestions made in this regard, but let me offer another by considering one psychological factor in the rise of populism.

VI. "He says what I think."

It has become a cliché of TV journalism in the U.S. to have reporters standing outside a Trump rally and asking those waiting to get in why they support Trump. One answer, which I have heard reported many times, is "he says what I think." One supporter is quoted as saying, "he speaks like me and he talks like me."[39] Such remarks may be explained by the observation that many Trump supporters feel intimidated by what they call "political correctness" from expressing their anti-pluralist (for example, racist) thoughts, and Trump's giving voice to such thoughts provides them with the freedom to indulge in these thoughts (and this talk). They are excited with Trump that he has given them permission to utter such forbidden thoughts. They no longer feel under the oppressive weight of the elitist liberal culture (the source of political correctness). In the past they felt under that weight and worried about being accused, for example, of racism, should they say what they think. But now, Trump has given them permission to say such things out loud, at least at his rallies. They can go to his rallies and say or shout those things along with many others who feel so liberated. More importantly, they can now vote in affirmation of such beliefs. They love Trump and will never forsake him. He is their leader and protector. As a part of their gratitude toward Trump, they have developed a tribal-like, almost unconditional, attachment to him. (However, Trump's relationship to them is transactional, not unconditional, as is theirs to him, which is unconditional.)

Such a tribal attachment accords with the populist idea that supporters of a populist regime should relate to their leaders directly, not in terms of a political apparatus. According to Müller, this is part of the "logic" of

---

[39] Astead W. Herndon, "With the Faithful at Trump's North Carolina Rally: 'He Speaks Like Me'," *New York Times*, September 20, 2019, https://www.nytimes.com/2019/09/10/us/politics/trump-voters-supporters-policies.html.

populism. He says there is "a populist incentive to 'cut out the middleman' and to rely as little as possible on parties as intermediaries between citizens and politicians."[40] This partly explains the *frequency* of the slogan, "he says what I think," offered by Trump's supporters as the reason for their support. There is, in that remark, no hint of mediation between the supports and the object of their support. This kind of support is distinct from the more common kind of political support, such as: "I support him because his stance on issues X and Y, are like my own, even though we disagree on Z." In the latter case, it is understood that the support is mediated by a political apparatus that takes account, through voting, of the diverse interests of citizens. (Though it is certainly true that some support populist leaders for this kind of standard political reason as well.) But the true believers think: "I am with him all the way, we are completely at one in our thinking." To that extent, there is no need for institutional or other forms of mediation. The same is evident in two slogans used by an Austrian populist party to promote their leader, as cited by Müller: "he is like you" and "he says what Vienna thinks."[41]

As onlookers to this political drama, what should we say about such an attitude, which seems to characterize the tribalistic tendencies among supporters of populist leaders? I believe we can get a handle on this by returning to the question of what *explains* eruptions of populism. Recall what we are looking for in an explanation. Like any important social or political phenomenon, an eruption of populism is likely to have many interacting causes. We try to find major underlying or background causes, seeking to understand at the general level a phenomenon that erupts periodically in the political life of representative democracies. With an understanding of such causes, we can hope to have a guide for the actions we might take to ameliorate eruptions or to minimize their likelihood. Earlier, we discussed two general families of explanations, the psychological and the political-institutional, on the assumption that an eruption of populism results when many citizens are psychologically disposed to accept populist leaders (for example, in cases where there is a high level of anti-pluralism in the population) and the political-institutional conditions are ripe for an eruption (for example, in cases where there is a high level of economic distress in a society).

---

[40] Jan-Werner Müller, "'The people must be extracted from within the people': Reflections on Populism," *Constellations* 21 (2014),14.

[41] Müller, "Reflections on Populism," 15.

While psychological explanations of populism seem to be largely matters of affect, such as the prevalence of racism, they also involve cognitive elements: beliefs about the world. For example, an individual's racism, when this is a matter of that person's conscious reflection, is likely to include the belief that the group that is the subject of the racist attitude is inferior in some way to the group to which the racist belongs. Should this belief change, this would likely affect the attitude as well (though they may not be so closely tied that the change in cognition would guarantee a rapid change in affect).

I argue that there is a false cognition of a different sort that is part of the explanation of populism. It is a kind of logical mistake, a fallacy, a form of equivocation. It involves the acceptance of a false analogy between "the will of the people" and a person's individual will. More specifically, part of the explanation of the appeal of populism is the mistaken belief on the part of supporters of populism that "the will of the people" should be understood as being in important ways like my own individual will. I discussed earlier the nature of this mistake, namely, that populist supporters tend not to recognize or accept the fact that "the will of the people" is necessarily institutional, the product of a complex political-institutional procedure. On the contrary, the populist supporter may believe that "the will of the people" should be as transparent and intuitable as an individual will is (or at least seems to be) to the individual whose will it is. The mistake is to think that "the will of the people" is like an individual's will writ large.

In virtue of accepting this faulty analogy, an individual is more likely to become a supporter of populism. This is illustrated by an interpretation of "he says what I think": "My political beliefs emanate from the mouth of Trump. As our leader, he must be representing "the will of the people," and he must have correctly divined this will because, assuming the faulty analogy, the will of the people is as transparent to him as my will is to me." The supporter shifts from "he says what I think" to "we think what he says."[42]

This point of view jibes with the suspicion that populist supporters direct toward the political elites. Political elites serve as the intermediaries between the people and government policy, which is an implication of understanding "the will of the people" as the result of a complex political-institutional procedure. But supporters of populism see such a mediation

---

[42] Supporters of the right-wing radio host Rush Limbaugh refer to themselves affectionately as "dittoheads," meaning, apparently, that they believe everything he says. His will is theirs.

conducted by the political elites as a mechanism by which "the will of the people" can be distorted or subverted. They can come to feel oppressed by the elites who they perceive as ignoring what the people want while what the elites may be doing, if they are playing their proper role, is simply working to accommodate the diverse views of a diverse society. (Of course, the elites may also be taking advantage of their position for their own benefit at the expense of the citizens, which shows the some-time value of left-wing populism.) The result, under normal political times (that is, when society is not in the midst of a populist eruption) is that people who adopt political beliefs of this sort under the sway of the faulty analogy feel alienated from politics and often do not vote or otherwise participate, or they may "participate" in a way further destructive of democratic institutions, for example, by forming hate groups or joining right-wing militias. But should the time be ripe, a candidate who "says what they think" may lead them to participate as part of a populist eruption, where they might otherwise have simply remained alienated from the political process.

Those under the sway of the faulty analogy fail, as a result, to fully understand the inherent complexity and contestable nature of political relations in a large and diverse society, which requires an appreciation of the way in which "the will of the people" is achieved. This relates to the anti-pluralistic nature of populism. One who does not understand that "the will of the people" is a matter of institutional contestation is unlikely to appreciate those who offer the following sort of argument as a criticism of the faulty analogy: we live in a large and diverse society, which must, as a result, be governed by mutual accommodation, and there must be an apparatus to achieve this accommodation, and this apparatus must be a political-institutional intermediary between the people and policy. To ignore the inherent diversity of interests of the people is part of the element of anti-pluralism that characterizes populism. The charge of "political correctness" arises from populists when they think that political policy in a diverse society must represent their interests, but not those of the Other. The language labeled as "politically correct" by the populists is language that seeks to be inclusive rather than exclusive.

This explanation, that populism involves the cognitive mistake of confusing the nature of the individual will with the nature of "the will of the people," need not be true of all supporters of populism. All I claim is that it is one among other significant causes that would characterize a fuller explanation of populist eruptions. Certainly, another significant (and closely related) cause is tribalism. The rough but familiar argument for the sway of tribalism over our behavior is that, because humans evolved in small groups where survival would best accrue to groups with a collective suspicion and hatred of outsiders, this general attitude is selected for and is "in our genes." But whatever the source of tribalism, it is clearly a feature of our existence. Stenner and Haidt discuss this sort of attitude, relating it to the human desire for "oneness and sameness." These authors claim that the openness of liberal democracy, pulling against the inherent desire for "oneness and sameness," may now have come to the point where it has "exceeded many people's capacity to tolerate it."[43] So populism erupts. Galston has an important discussion of tribalism and comes to effectively the same conclusion.[44] He argues that there are human needs of communal solidarity that liberal democracy by itself cannot satisfy. All of these authors suggest measures that could mitigate the pull of tribalism, "manage it" as Galston suggests, for example, creating and supporting public rituals and collective experiences that would provide sources of unity even in a large and diverse society. One thinks here of the way in which Nelson Mandela used the activity of the South African rugby team as a national unifying experience to help transcend black-white tribalism after apartheid.

The faulty-analogy explanation also provides suggestions about better management, that is, actions to ameliorate the impact of the eruptions or reduce their likelihood. The sort of better management suggested by faulty-analogy explanation is *an improved and more widely available educational system*. There are other arguments that a better educational system would lessen the likelihood of populist eruptions, for example, because it would save individuals from the kind of economic despair (through poor job prospects, and so forth) that is an institutional-political explanation of populist eruptions.[45] But the suggestion to adopt a better educational system that flows from the faulty-analogy explanation provides a narrower prescription, focusing primarily on *civics education* and improved *critical thinking skills*. Better instruction in civics would help people better understand the diverse nature of society and the mediation role that must be fulfilled (by political elites) to determine "the will of the people." In addition, a better civics education should include more exposure in school to members of a range of different socio-economic groups, in the role of both students and instructors, to make it less likely that the students, when

---

[43] Stenner and Haidt, "Authoritarianism Is Not a Momentary Madness," 216.
[44] Galston, chap. 8, esp. pp. 132-33.
[45] Galston, 64-65, 77.

grown, would see these groups as part of the Other.[46] The role of stronger critical thinking would be to help students not only to avoid the faulty analogy discussed above, but also to avoid the other fallacies by which populist demagogues seek to seduce citizens. Like other measures of management, these educational changes would not eliminate the risk of populist eruptions, but, if my argument is sound, they should reduce this risk (and bring other positive side-effects).

VII. Conclusion

Populism poses a serious problem to the progress (and perhaps existence) of liberal democracy in the West and elsewhere. The danger is posed by right-wing populism, which in addition to being anti-elitist, is also anti-pluralist. It is the latter property that makes populism inimical to liberal democracy and its fundamental principles of equality and anti-discrimination. It is important to consider the causes of the current surge of populism in order to develop proposals for limiting and reversing the populist advance. One cause of the surge of populism is the mistaken analogy held by some populist supporters that "the will of the people," an idea which plays an important role in populist thinking, is like an individual's will in its transparency to consciousness. This view misunderstands the fact that in a democracy, the will of the people is a complex institutional construction, necessarily overseen by the political elites.[47]

Works Cited

Eichengreen, Barry. *The Populist Temptation.* New York: Oxford University Press, 2018.

Galston, William. *Anti-Pluralism: The Populist Threat to Liberal Democracy.* New Haven: Yale University Press, 2018.

Herndon, Astead W. "With the Faithful at Trump's North Carolina Rally: 'He Speaks Like Me'." *New York Times.* September 20, 2019. https://www.nytimes.com/2019/09/10/us/politics/trump-voters-supporters-policies.html.

Judis, John. *The Populist Explosion.* New York: Columbia Global Reports, 2016.

---

[46] I owe this point to Rosalind Simson.

[47] For valuable comments on earlier drafts of this essay, I would like to thank Creighton Rosental, Rosalind Simson, and Yi Deng. Incoherencies, errors, mistakes, and malapropisms are, of course, purely my own fault.

Mudde, Cas and Christóbal Kaltwasser. *Populism—A Very Short Introduction.* New York: Oxford University Press: 2017.

Müller, Jan-Werner. *What is Populism?*. Philadelphia: Pennsylvania University Press, 2016.

Müller, Jan-Werner. "'The people must be extracted from within the people': Reflections on Populism." *Constellations* 21 (2014): 483-93.

Panizza, Francisco, ed. *Populism and the Mirror of Democracy.* London: Verso, 2005.

Stenner, Karen, and Jonathan Haidt. "Authoritarianism is Not a Momentary Madness, but an Eternal Dynamic within Liberal Democracies." In *Can it Happen Here?*, edited by Cass Sunstein, 175-220. New York: Harper Collins, 2018.

Constitutional Law and the Culture Wars:
When Religious Liberty and the Law Conflict,
Which Should Prevail?

Gary J. Simson

Clashes between individual claims of religious liberty and laws designed to promote health, safety, and other general welfare objectives are nothing new in the United States. As far back as colonial times, for example, Quakers insisted that they must be exempted for religious reasons from military conscription laws. They also maintained that their religion prohibited them from complying with laws requiring anyone testifying in court to take an oath swearing to give truthful testimony.[1]

As a result of two long-term trends, clashes of this sort have occurred with greater and greater frequency over the years. First, the range of people's activities governed in some way by state or federal law has expanded enormously. Broadly speaking, as technological and other advances have made everyone and everything more interconnected, activities once local in their effects increasingly have had more far-reaching effects that invite, if not demand, government regulation to serve the common good.[2] Sec-

---

[1] *See* Michael W. McConnell, *The Origins and Historical Understanding of Free Exercise of Religion*, 103 HARV. L. REV. 1409, 1467-69 (1990).

[2] *Wickard v. Filburn*, 317 U.S. 111 (1942), a well-known Supreme Court decision on the scope of Congress's power to "regulate Commerce...among the several States" (U.S. CONST. art. I, § 8, cl. 3), offers a vivid illustration. The owner of a small farm in Ohio resisted a limitation imposed pursuant to the federal Agricultural Adjustment Act on the acreage that he could devote to growing wheat and on the number of bushels of wheat that he could produce per acre. In particular, he questioned whether the federal government could fine him for exceeding those limits when he regularly sold only a small portion of the wheat grown on his farm and instead used most of it to feed his animals, to make flour to help meet his family's food needs, and to provide future seeding at his farm. In rejecting the farmer's argument, Justice Jackson explained for a unanimous Court:

ond, the number of religions in the United States has grown exponentially.[3] As more belief systems find a place among the populace, the likelihood of conflict between religious liberty and the law can't help but increase as well.

A highly publicized case decided by the U.S. Supreme Court in 2018, *Masterpiece Cakeshop, Ltd. v. Colorado Civil Rights Commission,*[4] illustrates the special potential today for such conflicts to end up in court. In July 2012 a Colorado couple, Charlie Craig and David Mullins, visited Masterpiece Cakeshop, a bakery located in a Denver suburb. The two men asked the owner, Jack Phillips, to make a custom wedding cake for the wedding reception that they were planning to have in Denver. They were not planning to have the wedding itself in Denver because Colorado was not one of the small group of states that as of 2012 allowed a same-sex couple to marry.[5] Instead, their plan was to get married in Massachusetts–an especially inviting locale for the wedding, because almost a decade earlier Massachusetts had become the first state to legalize same-sex marriage.[6]

The effect of the statute before us is to restrict the amount which may be produced for market and the extent, as well, to which one may forestall resort to the market by producing to meet his own needs. That appellee's own contribution to the demand for wheat may be trivial by itself is not enough to remove him from the scope of federal regulation where, as here, his contribution, taken together with that of many others similarly situated, is far from trivial....

317 U.S. at 127-28.

[3] The census does not gather statistics on people's religious affiliations, but according to a nonprofit nonpartisan research organization, there were approximately 313 religions and denominations represented in the U.S. populace as of 2008. *Religions and Denominations in the U.S.*, PROCON.ORG, https://www.procon.org/religious-and-denominations-in-the-us/ (last updated Oct. 24, 2008). For an excellent, brief overview of the increase in religious diversity in the United States over the years, see Columbia University historian Randall Balmer's *Religious Diversity in America*, TEACHERSERVE, http://nationalhumanitiescenter.org/tserve/twenty/tkey info/reldiv.htm (last visited Dec. 12, 2020).

[4] 138 S. Ct. 1719 (2018).

[5] *See A Timeline of the Legalization of Same-Sex Marriage in the U.S.*, GEORGETOWN.EDU, https:/guides.II.georgetown.edu/c.php?g=592919&p=4182201 (last updated Dec. 7, 2020).

[6] Massachusetts's legalization of same-sex marriage was the product of judicial decision. The state's high court held that the Massachusetts Constitution guarantees

Phillips immediately turned down Craig and Mullins's request. He explained that, as a devout Christian, he deeply believes that same-sex marriage is wrong and that he shouldn't be engaged in an activity–designing and making a wedding cake for a same-sex couple–that God would see as affirming the value of such marriages.[7] Not long after, Craig and Mullins filed a formal complaint against Phillips under the Colorado Anti-Discrimination Act.[8] The Act prohibits discrimination on the basis of race, national origin, sex, sexual orientation, and other specified characteristics in "places of public accommodation"–essentially, any place where goods are sold, or services offered, to the public. The Act clearly covers bakeries, and it says nothing to suggest that a bakery owner's discrimination on any of the forbidden bases is acceptable if done to avoid violating the owner's religious beliefs.

The Colorado Civil Rights Commission ruled in favor of the complainants. It held that Phillips's practice of making custom wedding cakes for opposite-sex, though not same-sex, couples constituted discrimination on the basis of sexual orientation and violated the Act. The Commission also rejected Phillips's arguments that the Free Exercise and Free Speech Clauses of the First Amendment required that he be granted an exemption from the Act.[9] A Colorado intermediate appellate court affirmed the Commission's decision, and the Colorado Supreme Court declined to hear the case on appeal. The U.S. Supreme Court agreed to hear it, and almost a full year later, handed down a remarkably anticlimactic decision. The Court avoided even addressing the clash of interests that lay at the heart of the case and that, by all indications, was the reason the Court had agreed to hear the case in the first place. Instead, predicating its decision on a

---

a right to same-sex marriage. *See* Goodridge v. Dep't of Pub. Health, 798 N.E.2d 941 (Mass. 2003).

[7] Phillips offered to sell them brownies or cookies, but said he needed to draw the line at creating a custom wedding cake. *See Masterpiece Cakeshop*, 138 S. Ct. at 1724.

[8] COLO. REV. STAT. §24-34-601 (2016).

[9] It is beyond the scope of this Essay to examine Phillips's free speech argument, which relied on Supreme Court cases interpreting the Free Speech Clause as affording protection against compelled speech. *See* Petition for Writ of Certiorari at 13-18, Masterpiece Cakeshop, Ltd. v. Colo. Civil Rights Comm'n, 138 S. Ct. 1719 (2018) (No. 16-111). My focus throughout the Essay will be religious liberty and the Free Exercise Clause.

narrow ground of little consequence for future cases, the Court ruled in Phillips's favor.[10]

Although the Supreme Court ultimately decided to pass on the hard questions posed by *Masterpiece Cakeshop*, the case offers a prime opportunity to explore a type of clash between religious liberty and the law that has fueled a great deal of public debate in recent years. The religious liberty claim in the case epitomizes what Yale Law Professors Douglas NeJaime and Reva Siegel have called "complicity-based conscience claims."[11] As Professors NeJaime and Siegel have explained, such claims are based on "religious objections to being made complicit in the assertedly sinful conduct of others," and they are especially worthy of close examination today because they are "asserted by growing numbers of Americans about some of the most contentious 'culture war' issues of our day."[12]

To help answer when, if ever, today's complicity-based conscience claims should take precedence over conflicting law, this Essay closely examines the religious liberty claim raised, but not decided, in *Masterpiece Cakeshop*. Part I lays the groundwork for that examination with a brief account of the Supreme Court's approach to the Free Exercise Clause of the

---

[10] Writing for a 7-2 majority, Justice Kennedy maintained that the order directing Phillips to treat same-sex couples no differently than opposite-sex couples as customers was constitutionally defective because the tribunal that first entered the order—the Colorado Civil Rights Commission—was not the fair and neutral decisionmaker to which any litigant is entitled by the Due Process Clause and other constitutional guarantees. Instead, according to Kennedy, the Commission included members biased against Phillips because of his religious views. *Masterpiece Cakeshop*, 138 S. Ct. at 1729-31.

The evidence cited by Kennedy in support of his ground for decision was unimpressive, to put it mildly. For a number of reasons—how very little the parties said in their Supreme Court briefs to suggest that a biased tribunal was truly a concern, how very little the Justices said during oral argument to suggest such a concern, how very controversial any ruling on Phillips's religious liberty and free speech claims was apt to be, and more—I find it difficult to understand the Court's opinion as anything other than a means of disposing of a controversial case that the Justices (or at least the one Justice, Kennedy, widely assumed to hold the decisive fifth vote) no longer had the appetite to decide. If I'm right, this certainly was not the first time the Court has seized on a narrow ground to dispose of a case they ultimately wished they had not agreed to hear, and it won't be the last.

[11] Douglas NeJaime & Reva B. Siegel, *Conscience Wars: Complicity-Based Conscience Claims in Religion and Politics*, 124 YALE L.J. 2516 (2015)

[12] *Id.* at 2519-20.

First Amendment over the years. In particular, after discussing a 1990 Supreme Court decision, *Employment Division v. Smith*,[13] that interpreted the Clause in a manner that rendered it much less protective of religious liberty than it had been under the Court's prior interpretation of the Clause, I call attention to several post-1990 developments that have diminished *Smith*'s practical significance and breathed new life into the Court's pre-*Smith* approach.

Part II uses Phillips's free exercise claim in *Masterpiece Cakeshop* to illustrate the shortcomings of complicity-based conscience claims when analyzed from the perspective of the Court's approach to claims for free exercise exemptions prior to *Smith*. I maintain that Phillips's claim should fail under the Court's pre-*Smith* approach, but I add a caveat: The Court appears likely to revisit its decision in *Smith* in the not too distant future. If it does revisit *Smith*, and if it decides to overrule it, there is reason to believe that the Court may adopt a more lenient approach to claims for free exercise exemptions than its pre-*Smith* approach.

The Essay concludes in Part III by turning briefly to a question not implicated by the facts of *Masterpiece Cakeshop* itself but readily presented by a variation on those facts: If a *legislature* decides to create a religious exemption, is the Free Exercise Clause's companion provision in the First Amendment–the Establishment Clause–a significant constraint?

I.

The Free Exercise Clause of the First Amendment provides that "Congress shall make no law...prohibiting the free exercise [of religion]."[14] For many years, it, like the rest of the first ten amendments, was interpreted as applicable only to federal, not state or local, lawmaking.[15] However, in 1940, as part of a process of "selective incorporation" that began fifteen

---

[13] 494 U.S. 872 (1990).

[14] U.S. CONST. amend. I. The First Amendment provides in full: "Congress shall make no law respecting an establishment of religion, or prohibiting the free exercise thereof; or abridging the freedom of speech, or of the press; or the right of the people peaceably to assemble, and to petition the Government for a redress of grievances."

[15] In *Barron v. Mayor & City Council of Baltimore*, 32 U.S. (7 Pet.) 243 (1833), the Court in an opinion by Chief Justice Marshall established that the first ten amendments—the Bill of Rights—were intended as a limitation only on the federal government.

years earlier with the Free Speech Clause and ultimately encompassed almost all the rights in the first ten amendments, the Supreme Court held
that the Free Exercise Clause is best understood as applying to state and
local lawmaking as well.[16] With that expansion of the Clause's applicability
beyond federal lawmaking, claims predicated on the Clause came to the
lower courts and the Supreme Court with far greater frequency. As a practical matter, the important developments in the Supreme Court's interpretation of the Clause began in 1940.

From 1940 to 1990, the great majority of free exercise claims litigated
in the courts were ones seeking an exemption from a broadly applicable
law that, on its face, made no mention of religion. Free exercise claimants
typically maintained that a law was substantially burdening their ability to
practice their religion and asked the court to relieve them of that burden
by declaring them exempt from the law's requirements. Although *Masterpiece Cakeshop* came well after this era, Phillips's free exercise claim nicely
illustrates the form that such claims would take. His objection to Colorado's Anti-Discrimination Act was limited to its being applied to require
him to treat same-sex couples asking for a custom wedding cake no differently than he treats opposite-sex couples. He had no objection to the Act
in general. He simply wanted the court to carve out an exemption for him
so that he would not be penalized for refusing, in accordance with his religious beliefs, to make custom wedding cakes for same-sex couples.

Under the approach in place from 1940 to 1990, claimants who could
persuade the court that holding them to the terms of a broadly applicable

---

[16] In *Gitlow v. New York*, 268 U.S. 652, 666 (1925), the Court held that the
Fourteenth Amendment's Due Process Clause made the First Amendment's Free
Speech Clause applicable to state and local government. The Court did not disclaim
its longstanding view that, as initially adopted, the first ten amendments were intended to apply only to the federal government. It maintained, however, that the Fourteenth Amendment's Due Process Clause, which was adopted in 1868 and which prohibits "any State" from "depriv[ing]" any person of life, liberty, or property, without
due process of law," U.S. CONST. amend. XIV, § 1, had effected a major change in
the constitutional constraints on state and local government. In *Cantwell v. Connecticut*, 310 U.S. 296, 303 (1940), the Court held that the "fundamental concept of liberty
embodied in" the Fourteenth Amendment's Due Process Clause "embraces" the liberty "guaranteed" by the Free Exercise Clause. By the late twentieth century, the Court
had incorporated, one by one, almost all the protections in the Bill of Rights, and in
the current century, the Court in *McDonald v. City of Chicago*, 561 U.S. 742, 791
(2010), added the Second Amendment's right to bear arms.

law would place a substantial burden on their ability to practice their religion would be granted a court-ordered exemption from the law unless the government could prove that denying them an exemption was necessary to serve–or, as the Court often phrased it, was the least drastic (or restrictive) means of serving–a compelling state interest.[17] If Phillips had litigated his claim during that era and had succeeded in persuading the court that the Colorado Anti-Discrimination Act was a substantial burden on his practice of Christianity, he would have been entitled to an exemption unless the government could show that requiring him to comply with the Act was necessary to serve a compelling governmental interest.

The event in 1990 that marked the beginning of a new era for exemption claims was the Supreme Court's 5-4 decision in *Employment Division v. Smith*.[18] In an opinion by Justice Scalia widely criticized as sorely deficient in both logic and candor,[19] the Court replaced its longstanding free exercise approach with one that, except for a few relatively narrow categories of claims,[20] essentially eliminated the possibility of court-ordered free exercise exemptions. According to the Court in *Smith*, the Free Exercise Clause generally does not authorize courts to grant religious exemptions from broadly applicable laws that on their face are neutral as to religion. People whose religious liberty is burdened by such a law are welcome, the Court explained, to lobby the lawmaker to amend the law and

---

[17] *See, e.g.,* Wisconsin v. Yoder, 406 U.S. 205 (1972); Sherbert v. Verner, 374 U.S. 398 (1963).

[18] 494 U.S. 872 (1990).

[19] Not surprisingly, scholars who disagreed with the Court's abandonment of its prior approach were highly critical of Justice Scalia's opinion for himself and four of his colleagues, *see, e.g.,* Douglas Laycock, *The Remnants of Free Exercise*, 1990 SUP. CT. REV. 1; Michael W. McConnell, *Free Exercise Revisionism and the* Smith *Decision*, 57 U. CHI. L. REV. 1109 (1990); Gary J. Simson, *Endangering Religious Liberty*, 84 CALIF. L. REV. 441, 442-45 (1996), but even scholars who agreed with the Court's change in approach were highly critical of the Scalia opinion as well, *see, e.g.,* William P. Marshall, *In Defense of* Smith *and Free Exercise Revisionism*, 58 U. CHI. L. REV. 308 (1991).

[20] The exceptions are catalogued in Laycock, *supra* note 19. In general, they are probably best understood as reflecting a desire on the part of at least some of the five Justices in the majority to avoid a large-scale overruling of precedent in the course of adopting a dramatically different free exercise approach. For example, but for the Court's recognition in *Smith* of an exception for "hybrid" claims–ones involving "not the Free Exercise Clause alone, but the Free Exercise Clause in conjunction with other constitutional protections," *Smith*, 494 U.S. at 881-82–*Wisconsin v. Yoder*, 406 U.S. 205 (1972), discussed Part II.A *infra*, was almost certainly doomed.

carve out an exemption for them, but court-ordered exemptions are generally out of bounds. Litigating during the *Smith* era, Phillips understood that his only hope of getting a court-ordered free exercise exemption from the Colorado Anti-Discrimination Act lay in arguing that his religious liberty claim fell within one of the exceptions recognized in *Smith*.[21] He actually argued that it fell within two,[22] but his effort to circumvent *Smith* failed in the Colorado proceedings; and in reversing the Colorado judgment against Phillips, the U.S. Supreme Court made no mention of his argument based on the *Smith* exceptions.

It is difficult to overstate the unpopularity of *Smith* when it was handed down. Shortly after, a broad coalition of religious and civil liberties groups spanning the political spectrum was hard at work intensely lobbying Congress to undo by statute the Court's interpretation in *Smith* of the Free Exercise Clause.[23] With near unanimity, Congress in 1993 passed the Religious Freedom Restoration Act (RFRA), and President Clinton promptly signed it into law.[24] In RFRA, Congress unambiguously expressed its dissatisfaction with *Smith*. It included as "findings" that "laws 'neutral' toward religion may burden religious exercise as surely as laws intended to interfere with religious exercise" and that the Court in *Smith* "virtually eliminated the requirement that the government justify burdens on religious exercise imposed by laws neutral toward religion."[25] In addition, Congress made clear in RFRA that reinstating the Court's pre-*Smith* approach was the remedy it had in mind. It provided in RFRA that "[g]overnment may substantially burden a person's exercise of religion only if it demonstrates that application of the burden to the person–(1) is in furtherance of a compelling governmental interest; and (2) is the least restrictive means of furthering that compelling governmental interest,"[26] and it broadly defined "government" to include any "branch, department,

---

[21] I use "court" in "court-ordered" broadly to include any adjudicatory body or tribunal. Phillips unsuccessfully sought a free exercise exemption from both the Colorado Civil Rights Commission and the Colorado Court of Appeals.

[22] Craig v. Masterpiece Cakeshop, Inc., 370 P.3d 272, 289-93 (Colo. App. 2015).

[23] *See* David E. Anderson, *Signing of Religious Freedom Act Culminates 3-Year Push*, WASH. POST, Nov. 20, 1993, at C6.

[24] *All Actions H.R. 1308–103ʳᵈ Congress (1993-1994)*, CONGRESS.GOV., https://www.congress.gov/bill/103rd-congress/house-bill/1308/all-actions.

[25] Religious Freedom Restoration Act of 1993 § 2(a), 42 U.S.C. § 2000bb(a) (2020).

[26] *Id.* § 3(b), 42 U.S.C. § 2000bb-1(b).

agency, instrumentality, and official (or other person acting under color of law) of the United States, a State, or a subdivision of a State."[27] Furthermore, to avoid any possible misunderstanding of its intention to return the Court's pre-*Smith* approach to full force, Congress in RFRA specifically named two of the Court's leading free exercise decisions prior to *Smith* as exemplifying the approach that it was putting in place.[28]

Several years later, the Supreme Court in *City of Boerne v. Flores*[29] held that Congress had overstepped its constitutional authority in enacting RFRA. According to Justice Kennedy's opinion for the Court, Congress had tried in RFRA to substitute its understanding of the proper interpretation of the Free Exercise Clause for the Court's understanding as expressed in *Smith*, and that is something Congress simply had no power to do.[30] In no uncertain terms, Justice Kennedy maintained that the Court, not Congress, is the ultimate authority on what the Constitution means.

Boerne clearly was a setback for those seeking to reinstate the pre-*Smith* approach to free exercise exemptions. For a number of reasons, however, the pre-*Smith* approach has great practical significance today nonetheless. First of all, the Court in *Boerne* struck down RFRA only as applied to state and local law. Because it left RFRA standing as to federal law, the approach to individual religious liberty codified in RFRA–i.e., the pre-*Smith* approach–continues to apply to federal law.[31] Second, the state

---

[27] *Id.* § 5(1), 42 U.S.C. § 2000bb-2(1).

[28] *Id.* § 2(b), 42 U.S.C. § 2000bb(b) (citing *Sherbert v. Verner*, 374 U.S. 398 (1963) and *Wisconsin v. Yoder*, 406 U.S. 205 (1972)).

[29] 521 U.S. 507 (1997).

[30] The source of power on which Congress had relied in passing the Act was the enforcement clause of the Fourteenth Amendment. U.S. CONST. amend. XIV, § 5. By its terms, section 5 gives Congress power to "enforce" by "appropriate legislation" the other parts of the Fourteenth Amendment, which include, most notably, the Equal Protection and Due Process Clauses in section 1. In relying on section 5 as authority for displacing the *Smith* Court's interpretation of free exercise, Congress clearly had in mind the Court's discussion of section 5 in a well-known Warren Court decision, *Katzenbach v. Morgan*, 384 U.S. 641 (1966). Although that discussion in *Morgan* reasonably–and, in my view, *most* reasonably–may be understood as recognizing that Congress has at least *some* power to substitute its understanding of the proper interpretation of a constitutional provision for the Court's understanding, the Court in *Boerne* essentially denied that the Court in *Morgan* had said anything of the sort.

[31] Although I question whether the Court in *Boerne* was right in striking down the Act as applied to state and local law, I agree that the validity of the Act as applied to federal law presents an easier and very different case. To make the pre-*Smith* balancing test a limitation on federal laws, Congress did not need to rely on any power

courts of more than half the states essentially apply the pre-*Smith* approach
as a matter of *state* law to any claim for a religious exemption from state or
local law. Most do so pursuant to a state religious freedom statute modeled
after RFRA, but a number do so based on judicial interpretation of a religious liberty clause in the state constitution.[32] Third, when Congress, a
few years after *Boerne*, enacted the Religious Land Use and Institutionalized Persons Act (RLUIPA),[33] it adopted the pre-*Smith* approach as the
measure of whether a claim for an exemption under RLUIPA should be
granted. RLUIPA, which Congress enacted on the basis of a different
source of constitutional authority than it had invoked in enacting RFRA,[34]
has been upheld as applied to state and local, as well as federal, law.[35] Although RLUIPA is considerably narrower in scope than RFRA, the two
areas that it addresses–basically, church zoning and prisoners' religious
rights–are ones where religious liberty issues frequently arise. Fourth and
lastly, as noted earlier, *Smith* itself explicitly recognized some exceptions
to its general rule that the Free Exercise Clause does not provide authority
for court-ordered exemptions, and it indicated that, in a case falling within

---

to override the Court's interpretation of the Constitution and establish as the law of
the land a constitutional interpretation of its own. Instead, because federal law, unlike
state or local law, generally is either made by Congress or subject to revision by Congress, Congress had the authority to adopt, simply as a matter of policy, an across-the-
board exception to the scope of all federal laws.

[32] The total number appears to be in the low thirties. Twenty states have statutes
modeled after RFRA, and one (Alabama) has incorporated a provision based on
RFRA into its constitution. *See* National Conference of State Legislatures, *State Religious Freedom Restoration Acts*, NCSL.ORG, May 4, 2017, www.ncsl.org/
research/civil-and-criminal-justice/state-rfra-statutes.aspx. Less certain is the number
of states whose courts have interpreted a religious liberty provision in the state constitution not modeled on RFRA as implicitly offering RFRA-like protection. It appears
to be roughly ten to twelve. *See* Juliet Eilperin, *31 states have heightened religious freedom
protections*, WASH. POST, Mar. 1, 2014 (stating that 13 states have RFRA-like protection based on judicial interpretation); *State Religious Freedom Restoration Acts*,
WIKIPEDIA, Aug. 28, 2019 (listing ten such states).

[33] Religious Land Use and Institutionalized Persons Act of 2000, 42 U.S.C. §§
2000cc to 2000cc-5 (2020).

[34] In enacting RLUIPA, Congress relied on its taxing and spending power, U.S.
CONST. art. I, § 8, cl. 1, and its interstate commerce power, *id.* cl. 3. *See* Religious
Land Use and Institutionalized Persons Act of 2000 §§ 2(a)(2), 3(b), 42 U.S.C. §§
2000cc(a)(2), 2000cc-1(b) (2020).

[35] Cutter v. Wilkinson, 544 U.S. 709 (2005).

an exception, the court would be expected to apply the pre-*Smith* exemptions approach.

In short, despite *Smith*, understanding the key ingredients of the pre-*Smith* approach remains important today. The resolution of many clashes between religious liberty and the law turns on what those ingredients mean. What counts as a "substantial" burden on religious liberty? What kinds of government interests deserve to be called "compelling"? What constitutes a "necessary" relationship between denying an exemption and serving a compelling interest (or, to frame the question somewhat differently, what makes a means the "least drastic (or restrictive)" means of serving a compelling interest)?

Generalizing about the answers to those questions in cases where the religious liberty claimant is seeking an exemption is complicated by the fact that the claimant may predicate his or her exemption claim on one or more of several different sources: RFRA; a state statute modeled after RFRA; RLUIPA; a state-court interpretation of a religious liberty provision in the state constitution; and, in cases falling within a *Smith* exception, the federal Free Exercise Clause. Strictly speaking, the last of these sources–the federal Free Exercise Clause–is the only one of the five where a court is bound by Supreme Court precedent to answer those questions as the Court would have answered them prior to *Smith*.[36]

Absent concrete evidence to the contrary, however, a court has good reason to assume that the answers to those questions for any of the first four sources named are the same as for the fifth source. The key terms in the various sources–substantial burden, compelling government interest, and necessary means-end relationship (or least drastic (or restrictive)

---

[36] Although RFRA and RLUIPA borrow the terms of the Court's pre-*Smith* free exercise case law, they are federal *statutes* and therefore derive their meaning from Congress's intent. If Congress, for example, intended "substantial" to mean something different in RFRA than it meant in the Court's pre-*Smith* free exercise case law, then the different meaning intended by Congress is what "substantial," as used in RFRA, means. By the same token, although a state statute or a state-court interpretation of the state constitution may use the same terms in their religious exemptions approach as the Court used in its pre-*Smith* free exercise case law, the terms appearing in the state statute or state constitutional interpretation mean what the state legislature or state court intended them to mean. If the state legislature or state court did not intend them to have the same meaning as they have in the pre-*Smith* free exercise case law, then they don't.

means)–do not simply *happen* to be virtually identical. As discussed earlier,[37] Congress in enacting RFRA very deliberately borrowed the terms
from the pre-*Smith* free exercise case law and made clear that the scope of
the religious freedom that it was seeking to restore was the scope that religious freedom enjoyed under that case law. Under the circumstances, it
is very difficult to defend an interpretation of the terms that RFRA borrows from the pre-*Smith* free exercise case law that does *not* equate the
terms' meaning in the two sources, and the Supreme Court in interpreting
RFRA has expressly relied on *Sherbert*, *Yoder*, and other pre-*Smith* decisions.[38] Although there may be more room to argue that those terms when
used in RLUIPA, state RFRAs, and state courts' state constitutional interpretations were not intended to mean the same thing as they meant in
the pre-*Smith* free exercise case law, a strong presumption of congruence
is surely in order.[39]

---

[37] *See supra* text accompanying notes 24-28.

[38] In *Gonzales v. O Centro Espirita Beneficente Uniao do Vegetal*, 546 U.S. 418
(2006), the Court's first decision applying RFRA, Chief Justice Roberts's opinion for
a unanimous Court relied not only on *Sherbert* and *Yoder* but on three other of the
Court's pre-*Smith* decisions as well. Justice Alito's majority opinion in *Burwell v.
Hobby Lobby Stores, Inc.*, 573 U.S. 682 (2014), relied heavily on two pre-*Smith* decisions in holding that Hobby Lobby and two other closely held for-profit corporations
qualified as "persons" under RFRA and therefore could seek a religious exemption
from the Affordable Care Act.

[39] More specifically, although RLUIPA, unlike RFRA, does not include explicit
citations to pre-*Smith* cases, it was plainly an effort by Congress to reclaim some of
the ground lost when the Supreme Court in *Boerne* struck down RFRA as applied to
state and local law. A strong presumption that Congress intended its use of terms in
RLUIPA to mean the same as its use of those same terms in RFRA readily follows.
Similarly, a strong presumption that the terms in state RFRAs mean the same as those
terms as used in RFRA readily follows from the fact that the state RFRAs came after
RFRA's enactment and were consciously modeled on RFRA. In interpreting particular provisions in their state constitutions, state courts often have relied heavily on the
U.S. Supreme Court's interpretation of comparable provisions in the U.S. Constitution. If, in interpreting a religious liberty provision in its state constitution, a state
court essentially reiterates the terms in the U.S. Supreme Court's free exercise exemption test, a strong presumption of congruence in meaning is in order. For a defense of
the meaning that the Court prior to *Smith* gave to the key ingredients of its free exercise approach, see Gary J. Simson, *Permissible Accommodation or Impermissible Endorsement? A Proposed Approach to Religious Exemptions and the Establishment Clause*, 106
KY. L.J. 535, 572, 588-91 (2018).

II.

I now return to *Masterpiece Cakeshop* and consider how Phillips's exemption claim would fare under the Supreme Court's free exercise approach prior to *Smith*. Under that approach, the success of Phillips's claim turns on the following questions:

> Does requiring Phillips to abide by Colorado's Anti-Discrimination Act place a substantial burden on his freedom to practice his religion?

> If so, is requiring Phillips to abide by the Act necessary to serve a compelling state interest?

For Phillips to prevail, the answer to the first question must be "yes," and the answer to the second must be "no." As explained below, I believe that the first question should be answered "no" and that Phillips's claim should be denied without even reaching the second question. Furthermore, even assuming that the first question should be answered "yes," Phillips should fare no better. His claim would fail to survive the second question, which should also be answered "yes."

A.

To answer the first question, I should begin by disposing of an argument that may sound probative but that ultimately is not. According to Phillips, filling the gay couple's order for a custom wedding cake would violate his beliefs as a Christian because it would send a message affirming same-sex marriage that would displease God. But wasn't it a stretch for Phillips to assume that people would interpret his filling the order as a statement on his part that same-sex marriage is a good thing? Even more importantly– because displeasing God was Phillips's concern–wasn't it even more of a stretch for him to assume that *God* would interpret his actions that way? Even if some *people* might not recognize the importance of the fact that Phillips is running his bakery in a state that by statute prohibits bakery owners from discriminating on the basis of sexual orientation, surely *God* would recognize it and wouldn't interpret Phillips's making a custom wedding cake for a gay couple as any sort of pro-same-sex-marriage statement on Phillips's part.

That may sound like pretty good logic, but religious beliefs don't have to pass any sort of logic test in order to count for free exercise purposes. As the Supreme Court stated in *Thomas v. Review Board* in reversing a state court decision that had denied a free exercise claim on the ground that the claimant was seeking protection for a belief that was not genuinely "religious":

> The determination of what is a "religious" belief or practice is more often than not a difficult and delicate task.... However, the resolution of that question is not to turn upon a judicial perception of the particular belief or practice in question; religious beliefs need not be acceptable, logical, consistent, or comprehensible to others in order to merit First Amendment protection.[40]

By the same token, there is no requirement that, to count for free exercise purposes, Phillips's beliefs as a Christian must conform to most, or even a significant proportion of, Christians' understanding of their religion. "Intrafaith differences," the Court explained in *Thomas*, "are not uncommon among followers of a particular creed, and the judicial process is singularly ill-equipped to resolve such differences in relation to the Religion Clauses."[41] The Court in *Thomas* allowed for the possibility that a free exercise claimant might make a claim "so bizarre, so clearly nonreligious in motivation, as not to be entitled to protection under the Free Exercise Clause."[42] However, even if one assumes that Phillips's claim is predicated on an understanding of Christianity that most, or even an overwhelming majority of, Christians do not share, his claim is hardly so tenuously related to the Christian religion as to fail for that reason to deserve free exercise protection.

The question whether the burden on Phillips's religious liberty is substantial therefore can't fairly be answered "no" simply by characterizing his claim as not sufficiently religious for free exercise purposes. The substantiality of the burden itself, however, remains to be seen, and I suggest that Phillips's claim falls short in that regard. In trying to persuade the Supreme Court to hear his case, Phillips argued that Colorado was offering him a "stark choice." He could "[e]ither use [his] talents to create expression that

---

[40] Thomas v. Review Bd., 450 U.S. 707, 714 (1981). The free exercise claimant in *Thomas* was a Jehovah's Witness. The case turned on whether the personal beliefs that led him to quit work qualified as "religious" for purposes of the Free Exercise Clause. In denying that the beliefs counted as "religious," the Indiana Supreme Court had emphasized that it found the beliefs inconsistent with one another and not shared by some Jehovah's Witnesses.

[41] *Id.* at 715. (The First Amendment's Establishment and Free Exercise Clauses are often referred to together as the "Religion Clauses.")

[42] *Id.*

conflicts with [his] religious beliefs about marriage, or suffer punishment under Colorado's public accommodation law."[43] The choice, though, was not as stark as Phillips claimed. Colorado was not telling him that, to avoid running afoul of Colorado law, he must make a custom wedding cake for any same-sex couple who wishes to order one. Colorado's message to Phillips was "stop discriminating," not "start violating your religious beliefs." As far as Colorado was concerned, it was fine for him not to start making custom wedding cakes for same-sex couples as long as he stopped making them for opposite-sex couples.

Was that an option that appealed to Phillips? Obviously not. But the relevant question for free exercise purposes is not whether Phillips liked the idea of eliminating custom wedding cakes from his bakery business. Instead, it is whether Colorado placed a substantial burden on his religious liberty by telling him that if, in keeping with his religious beliefs, he didn't want to start making custom wedding cakes for same-sex couples, then he needed to stop making them for opposite-sex couples. And the key to answering that question lay in practicalities and legal precedent, not abstract logic: How much pressure was Colorado placing on Phillips to act contrary to his religious beliefs, and was that as much pressure as the Supreme Court in its pre-*Smith* cases typically required to find a substantial burden on free exercise?

Most obviously, the pressure that Colorado was placing on Phillips was significantly less than the pressure that a state places on religious liberty claimants when it flatly forbids them from acting in conformity with their religious beliefs or requires them to act in a way that conflicts with those beliefs. The well-known free exercise case, *Wisconsin v. Yoder*,[44] illustrates the point. Wisconsin law required all parents to send their children to school until age sixteen or else face a fine or imprisonment or both. Jonas Yoder and the other Amish parents who were defendants in the case were convicted of violating the law for refusing to send their children to school beyond eighth grade. As Chief Justice Burger explained in his opinion for a nearly unanimous Supreme Court,[45] the defendants saw high school as very different from the schooling that precedes it. In their view,

---

[43] Petition for Writ of Certiorari, *supra* note 9, at 2.

[44] 406 U.S. 205 (1972).

[45] In a partial dissent, Justice Douglas wrote that the case could not be decided without consulting the children whose parents were the defendants in the case and ascertaining whether the children shared their parents' religious opposition to their attending high school. *See id.* at 241–46 (Douglas, J., dissenting in part).

sending their children to high school would be fundamentally at odds with their religious beliefs:

> They object to the high school, and higher education generally, because the values [taught] are in marked variance with Amish values and the Amish way of life; they view secondary school education as an impermissible exposure of their children to a "worldly" influence in conflict with their beliefs....
>
> The Amish do not object to elementary education through the first eight grades as a general proposition because they agree that their children must have basic skills in the "three R's" in order to read the Bible, to be good farmers and citizens, and to be able to deal with non-Amish people when necessary in the course of daily affairs. They view such a basic education as acceptable because it does not significantly expose their children to worldly values or interfere with their development in the Amish community during the crucial adolescent period....[46]

In holding that the Free Exercise Clause required Wisconsin to allow the defendants not to send their children to school after eighth grade, the Court found that the Wisconsin law's "impact" on the defendants' "practice of the Amish religion is not only severe, but inescapable.... [C]ompulsory school attendance to age 16 for Amish children carries with it a very real threat of undermining the Amish community and religious practice as they exist today."[47]

The difference between the Amish defendants' situation and Phillips's situation in *Masterpiece Cakeshop* was more than a difference in degree. It was a difference in kind. While Colorado law allowed Phillips an opportunity to satisfy simultaneously the dictates of the law and his religion–don't make custom wedding cakes for anyone–Wisconsin law gave the Amish parents no such choice. They could obey the law and violate their religion or disobey the law and face criminal punishment.

But how realistic an option was it for Phillips to forgo the custom wedding cake part of his business? Was it an option available to him only in theory? As a practical matter, could he opt for it only at great cost? If so, then even though the Colorado law did not burden his religious liberty

---

[46] *Id.* at 210-12 (opinion of the Court).
[47] *Id.* at 218.

as much as the Wisconsin law burdened the Amish parents' religious liberty, there was good reason to treat the burden on Phillips as "substantial" for free exercise purposes.

The cost to Phillips of availing himself of that option, however, was not as great as it may appear. He had several means fairly readily available to help make up for the financial loss that he would suffer by getting out of the custom wedding cake business. In his petition for Supreme Court review, he acknowledged that his custom cake business was not limited to weddings. He also made custom cakes for birthdays, anniversaries, graduations, holidays, and other occasions.[48] Without inordinate time and effort, couldn't he at least partly offset his losses from getting out of the custom cake business for weddings by expanding his custom cake business for other occasions? Phillips regularly sold at his bakery not only custom cakes but also cookies, cupcakes, brownies, and other baked goods.[49] Even if he couldn't *entirely* offset his losses from discontinuing his custom cake business for weddings by expanding his custom cake business for other occasions, couldn't he close the gap by building up his non-custom-cake sales?

Ultimately, whether the likely costs to Phillips of getting out of the custom wedding cake business constitute a "substantial" burden on his religious liberty depends not only on financial projections but on the operative definition of "substantial" in this realm. The pre-*Smith* Supreme Court decision most closely in point is almost certainly the Court's 1961 decision in *Braunfeld v. Brown*.[50] *Braunfeld* was a free exercise challenge by various Orthodox Jewish merchants to Pennsylvania's Sunday closing law—a criminal statute that barred the sale on Sundays of various kinds of items, including some that the challengers sold. The merchants claimed that the law had the practical effect of coercing them to work on Saturdays, the Jewish Sabbath, in violation of their religious precepts. According to the merchants, if they didn't work on Sundays to comply with the law and took off Saturdays to observe their Sabbath, they would "suffer substantial economic loss" and be put in a position of "serious economic disadvantage."[51] They maintained that they and their competitors typically worked six days a week and that if they could not work on Sundays, they

---

[48] Petition for Writ of Certiorari, *supra* note 9, at 1-2.

[49] *Masterpiece Cakeshop*, 138 S. Ct. at 1724, 1726.

[50] 366 U.S. 599 (1961).

[51] *Id.* at 602 (Warren, C.J., announcing the judgment of the Court and an opinion joined by Black, Clark, and Whittaker, JJ.).

not only would lose a much-needed day's earnings every week but also be at such a competitive disadvantage that their competitors would be able to drive down their profits and maybe even drive them out of business.

The Supreme Court rejected the free exercise claim by a 6-3 vote. There was no "Opinion of the Court"—no opinion supported by a majority of the Justices. Instead, the reasoning of the six who voted to reject the claim was set forth in two separate opinions—an opinion by Chief Justice Warren joined by three other Justices, and an opinion by Justice Frankfurter joined by another Justice. Though different in some respects, the two opinions took a similar view of the economic realities faced by the challengers and the implications of those realities for the magnitude of the burden on free exercise.

A recurrent theme of Chief Justice Warren's opinion was the difference between the Orthodox Jewish merchants' situation and that of individuals faced with a law that "attempts to make a religious practice unlawful." In his view, the merchants' situation was "wholly different."[52] The Chief Justice underlined that he was not saying that the only laws that can violate the Free Exercise Clause are ones that expressly target a religious practice. It would be a "gross oversimplification," he conceded, "to hold unassailable all legislation regulating conduct which imposes solely an indirect burden on the observance of religion."[53] He strongly cautioned, however, that "[t]o strike down, without the most critical scrutiny, legislation which imposes only an indirect burden on the exercise of religion...would radically restrict the operating latitude of the legislature."[54]

In essence, the Chief Justice allowed for the possibility that a law that incidentally affects some people's religious liberty may burden religious liberty enough to raise the type of constitutional concerns raised by laws that explicitly prohibit certain religious practices. He was careful to make clear, however, that in recognition of the importance of not unduly limiting legislative prerogatives, he was interpreting the Free Exercise Clause as setting a relatively high bar for the degree to which religious liberty must be burdened before the Court would recognize the burden as substantial.

The Court's ultimate rejection of the Orthodox Jewish merchants' claim confirmed that the Court indeed was setting a relatively high bar for substantiality. The Chief Justice and, even more clearly, Justice Frankfurter—the one Jew on the Court—expressly recognized that the burden on the

[52] *Id.* at 605-06.
[53] *Id.* at 607.
[54] *Id.* at 606.

merchants was very real. The Chief Justice acknowledged that "the alternatives open to [the Orthodox Jewish merchants]–retaining their present occupations and incurring economic disadvantage or engaging in some other commercial activity which does not call for either Saturday or Sunday labor–may well result in some financial sacrifice in order to observe their religious beliefs."[55] According to Justice Frankfurter, the closing law "create[s] an undeniable financial burden upon the observers of one of the fundamental tenets" of Judaism.[56]

In voting to reject the merchants' challenge to the law, Justice Frankfurter, like the Chief Justice, placed great importance on the fact that the Sunday closing law was not forcing the merchants to choose between their religion and the law. They could comply with both, and Frankfurter suggested that "the legislature may have concluded" that the "severity" of the "disadvantage" at which the law placed the merchants "might be offset by the industry and commercial initiative of the individual merchant."[57]

Like the Chief Justice, however, Frankfurter made no attempt to deny the reality that the law placed considerable pressure on the merchants to forgo observance of their religion's Sabbath and go to work on Saturdays instead. Rather than work on Saturdays, the merchants could tighten their (and their families') belts and learn to live on one fewer day's earnings per week, or perhaps they could work longer hours on weekdays than they had been working, or perhaps, as the Chief Justice noted, they could change careers somewhat and go into "some other commercial activity" where the norm is working weekdays only. And other possibilities could of course be hypothesized as well. Did any of them realistically promise to provide the merchants with a fairly painless means of avoiding violating their religious beliefs? I very much doubt it, and it was no accident that the Chief Justice and Justice Frankfurter suggested nothing of the sort.

If the burden on the Orthodox Jewish merchants was not weighty enough to qualify as "substantial" for purposes of the Court's free exercise case law,[58] I see little ambiguity as to whether the burden in *Masterpiece Cakeshop* on Phillips's religious liberty was. It simply was not. Phillips was

---

[55] *Id.* at 605-06.

[56] *Id.* at 521 (Frankfurter, J., joined by Harlan, J., concurring in the judgment).

[57] *Id.*

[58] Other Supreme Court cases helpful to understanding the Court's conception in its pre-*Smith* free exercise case law of a "substantial" burden include *Sherbert v. Verner*, 374 U.S. 398 (1963), and *Tony & Susan Alamo Foundation v. Secretary of Labor*, 471 U.S. 290 (1985).

in a significantly better position than the merchants to comply with both the relevant law and his religion. Compared to them, he could do so with relative ease.

B.

If, as argued above, requiring Phillips to comply with the Colorado Anti-Discrimination Act did not substantially burden his religious liberty, a court deciding his exemption claim under the pre-*Smith* approach would not have needed to address whether requiring his compliance was necessary to serve a compelling state interest. That inquiry only arises in cases in which the free exercise claimant has been able to show a substantial burden on his or her free exercise rights. Absent such a burden, a court should treat the Free Exercise Clause as simply not at issue. To prevail in such a case on constitutional grounds, the unsuccessful free exercise claimant would have to demonstrate a violation of some other constitutional guarantee.

Assume, however, for purposes of argument, that the Colorado Act substantially burdened Phillips's religious liberty. Under the circumstances, the court would be obliged to decide whether the necessary-to-a-compelling-state-interest test is met—a decision best made by focusing separately on the test's two components:

> Is a compelling state interest served by requiring Phillips to comply with the Act?

> If so, is requiring Phillips to comply with the Act a necessary means of serving that interest?

If indeed there were a substantial burden on Phillips's religious liberty, Phillips would be entitled to a free exercise exemption unless Colorado could show that both of the above questions should be answered "yes"—something that, as indicated below, I believe Colorado could do.

1.

Answering the first question, whether requiring Phillips's compliance with the Act serves a state interest of compelling importance, is relatively straightforward. Although some interests undoubtedly present borderline cases from the perspective of the Supreme Court's pre-*Smith* free exercise case law, the state interest at issue here—protecting against discrimination on the basis of sexual orientation—does not. It plainly is compelling.

In the abstract one perhaps might imagine that the Court would reserve the label of "compelling" for state interests of the utmost importance—ones so absolutely vital to the general welfare that the state would prioritize serving them above all else. In fact, however, the Court has used "compelling" in a significantly broader and less restrictive way. For example, in the course of carving out a free exercise exemption for the Amish from Wisconsin's requirement of school attendance to age 16, the Court in *Yoder* characterized as compelling both Wisconsin's interest in "prepar[ing] citizens to participate effectively and intelligently in our open political system" and its interest in "prepar[ing] individuals to be self-reliant and self-sufficient participants in society."[59] Consider also the interest that the Court treated as compelling in another free exercise case, *United States v. Lee*[60]—the federal interest in "assuring mandatory and continuous participation in, and contribution to, the social security system."[61] Though surely important, none of the governmental interests called compelling in *Yoder* and *Lee* are the sort that one would expect the government to stop at nothing to serve, whatever the costs.[62]

The Court, quite properly, hasn't simply treated as conclusive the government's characterization of an interest as compelling. After all, the question of an interest's relative importance for free exercise purposes is a part of the larger question of what the Free Exercise Clause requires—a question that the Constitution ultimately leaves to the courts to resolve. Nonetheless, for courts to give the government some degree of deference as far as the relative importance of an interest that it seeks to serve seems warranted as a concession to the legislative branch's greater claim to policymaking expertise.

---

[59] Wisconsin v. Yoder, 406 U.S. 205, 221 (1972).

[60] 455 U.S. 252 (1982). As discussed below, the Court in *Lee* rejected an Amish employer's claim for a free exercise exemption from the social security system.

[61] *Id.* at 258-59.

[62] The Court has given no indication that it has a different standard of "compelling" in free exercise cases than in free speech and other kinds of cases in which the Court has required the state to show a compelling state interest. The Court's characterization of certain interests as compelling in non-free-exercise cases supports the inference that may be drawn from the free exercise cases alone that the Court does not use "compelling" in a highly restrictive way. *See, e.g.,* Grayned v. City of Rockford, 408 U.S. 104, 119 (1972) (rejecting a free speech challenge to an anti-noise ordinance applicable to areas adjacent to schools, and citing the municipality's "compelling interest in having an undisrupted school session conducive to students' learning").

The compelling nature of Colorado's interest in *Masterpiece Cakeshop* in preventing discrimination based on sexual orientation in places of public accommodation follows easily from a combination of three factors: the Colorado legislature's inclusion of sexual orientation in the Anti-Discrimination Act alongside race and other statutorily proscribed bases of discrimination; the Court's strong affirmation on a number of occasions of the compelling importance of the government's interest in preventing racial discrimination by private actors;[63] and the Court's relatively deferential approach to the government in *Yoder* and other cases as far as what state interests qualify as compelling.

2.

Answering the second question–whether requiring Phillips to comply with the Anti-Discrimination Act is a necessary means of serving Colorado's interest in preventing discrimination based on sexual orientation in places of public accommodation–is more complicated. As a first step toward answering it, I would like to reformulate it in a way that I believe makes it more accessible without changing its meaning: Would exempting Phillips from the Act substantially detract from Colorado's ability to serve as well as possible its interest in preventing discrimination based on sexual orientation in places of public accommodation? That reformulation mirrors the way in which the Court on various occasions has approached application of the necessary-to-a-compelling-interest test.[64]

A strong argument can be made that, in and of itself, an exemption for Phillips would inflict enough harm on gay and lesbian Coloradans to call for an affirmative answer to the above question. The problem with Phillips's refusing to fill Craig and Mullins's custom wedding cake order

---

[63] *See, e.g.*, Bob Jones University v. United States, 461 U.S. 574, 604 (1983), where the Court, in the course of denying two private nonprofit schools a free exercise exemption from an Internal Revenue Service ruling that predicated tax-exempt status on not discriminating against students based on race, described as "compelling" the federal government's "fundamental, overriding interest in eradicating racial discrimination in education."

[64] *See, e.g.*, United States v. Lee, 455 U.S. 252, 259 (1982) ("The remaining inquiry is whether accommodating the Amish belief will unduly interfere with fulfillment of the governmental interest."); Wisconsin v. Yoder, 406 U.S. 205, 221 (1972) ("[W]e must searchingly examine the interests that the State seeks to promote by its requirement for compulsory education to age 16, and the impediment to those objectives that would flow from recognizing the claimed Amish exemption.").

isn't that it forces Craig and Mullins to get their custom wedding cake from someone who may not be as talented a cakemaker as Phillips. No, the problem is that Phillips is telling them to go elsewhere because of their sexual orientation. His refusal to make a custom wedding cake for Craig and Mullins and any other same-sex couple is an attack on who they are as persons. By granting Phillips an exemption from the Anti-Discrimination Act, the court, as an arm of the state, would in effect be putting the state's stamp of approval on Phillips's discriminatory practice. So doing, it would significantly compound the indignity, stigma, and other harm that Phillips inflicts on same-sex couples whom he rejects as customers and on other gays and lesbians who learn of his discriminatory practice. Under the circumstances, it seems entirely appropriate for a court to conclude that exempting Phillips from the Act would substantially detract from Colorado's ability to serve as well as possible its compelling interest in preventing discrimination based on sexual orientation in places of public accommodation and that therefore the exemption should not be granted.

Perhaps, however, this matter is more open to debate than I have suggested. It may be argued, for example, that, in and of itself, a court's granting Phillips an exemption wouldn't be all that harmful to the same-sex couples whom Phillips rejects as customers and to other gays and lesbians who learn of his discriminatory practice because they primarily would perceive the court's action as a show of respect for Phillips's religious liberty, rather than any sort of endorsement of discrimination on the basis of sexual orientation. I don't find that argument particularly persuasive. Even assuming, however, for purposes of argument, that it is persuasive, the problem remains that an exemption for Phillips can't reasonably be considered only in isolation, and when it isn't, the necessity of not granting him an exemption becomes very clear.

The Supreme Court's unanimous decision in 1982 in *United States v. Lee*[65] helps drive the point home. Edwin Lee, a member of the Amish faith, had several Amish workers on his farm and in his carpentry shop. Lee sought a free exercise exemption from the federal statute requiring employers to participate in the social security system. In seeking the exemption, Lee relied heavily on the *New Testament*'s admonition, "But if any provide not...for those of his own house, he hath denied the faith, and

---

[65] 455 U.S. 252 (1982). The Justices all agreed that Lee's free exercise claim should be denied. Chief Justice Burger's opinion for the Court was joined by everyone but Justice Stevens, who wrote a separate opinion concurring only in the result.

is worse than an infidel."[66] The Amish religion, Lee explained, interprets that language as a command to the Amish to care for their own, and his participation in the social security system would violate that command and be sinful.[67]

In his opinion for the Court, Chief Justice Burger rejected the government's attempt to characterize the statute's burden on Mr. Lee's religious liberty as less than substantial, but found that the government's requiring Lee to comply with the statute was necessary to serve a compelling state interest. As noted earlier,[68] the Court held that the government interest in maintaining a sound social security system was compelling. The Chief Justice's reasoning in finding a necessary means-end relationship between requiring Lee's compliance with the statute and serving that interest is worth quoting at length for the light that it sheds on applying the "necessary" means-end requirement of the Court's free exercise test:

> The Court has long recognized that balance must be struck between the values of the comprehensive social security system, which rests on a complex of actuarial factors, and the consequences of allowing religiously based exemptions. To maintain an organized society that guarantees religious freedom to a great variety of faiths requires that some religious practices yield to the common good. Religious beliefs can be accommodated...but there is a point at which accommodation would "radically restrict the operating latitude of the legislature." *Braunfeld*....
>
> ...[I]t would be difficult to accommodate the comprehensive social security system with myriad exceptions flowing from a wide variety of religious beliefs. The obligation to pay the social security tax initially is not fundamentally different from the obligation to pay income taxes.... There is no principled way...to distinguish between general taxes and those imposed under the Social Security Act. If, for example, a religious adherent believes war is a sin, and if a certain percentage of the federal budget can be identified as devoted to war-related activities, such individuals would have a similarly valid claim to be exempt from paying that percentage of the income tax. The tax system could not function if denominations

---

[66] 1 *Timothy* 5:8 (KJV).

[67] *Lee*, 455 U.S. at 255 & n.3.

[68] *See supra* text accompanying notes 60-61.

were allowed to challenge the tax system because tax payments were spent in a manner that violates their religious belief....[69]

For purposes of claims like Phillips's in *Masterpiece Cakeshop*, two related concerns articulated in the above excerpt deserve special emphasis: first, the concern, made most explicit when the Court quotes from Chief Justice Warren's opinion in *Braunfeld*, with unduly restricting legislative prerogatives; and second, the concern, expressed throughout the second paragraph, with the ripple effects of granting a free exercise exemption to the claimant in the case at hand. In essence, the Court in *Lee* was saying that, in deciding whether to grant an exemption to a claimant whose religious liberty is substantially burdened by the statute at hand, a court must be mindful of (a) its strong obligation to treat like cases alike[70] and (b) the repercussions that its fulfilling that obligation would be apt to have for the legislature's "operating latitude" to address effectively matters important to the general welfare. More specifically, if a court concludes that granting an exemption to the claimant before the court would obligate it to grant exemptions to enough others to detract substantially from the state's ability to serve as well as possible a compelling interest underlying the law, the court must deny the exemption.[71]

---

[69] *Lee*, 455 U.S. at 259-60.

[70] The Court in *Lee* did not make clear that this strong obligation of evenhandedness is based on the Constitution, but it plainly is. It readily follows from the Court's longstanding doctrine that the state's treating people differently on the basis of religion–which is precisely what a court's granting a religious exemption does–is "suspect" under the Equal Protection Clause of the Fourteenth Amendment and must be disallowed unless necessary to serve a compelling state interest. Furthermore, the Court has interpreted the Establishment and Free Exercise Clauses of the First Amendment as making much the same demand on the state for an exceptionally high level of justification when it makes people's religious adherence or nonadherence a basis for difference in treatment. *See* Simson, *supra* note 39, at 591-93.

[71] Although the Court in *Wisconsin v. Yoder*, 406 U.S. 205 (1972), discussed in detail *supra* Part II.A, granted the requested exemption, its emphasis on the minimal ripple effects of doing so was very much of a piece with the concern about ripple effects that led the Court a decade later in *Lee* to deny the exemption requested there. As Chief Justice Burger, the author of the Court's opinion in both cases, wrote in closing in *Yoder*:

Aided by a history of three centuries as an identifiable religious sect and a long history as a successful and self-sufficient segment of American society, the Amish in this case have convincingly demonstrated the sincerity of their religious beliefs, the interrelationship of belief with their mode of

If the Court's approach in *Lee* is applied to Phillips's free exercise claim, the necessity of denying Phillips an exemption becomes apparent. If a court were to grant Phillips an exemption from the Colorado Anti-Discrimination Act, the court obviously would have to be prepared to do the same for other Christian bakers in Colorado who share his understanding of Christianity as a bar on making custom wedding cakes for same-sex couples. But the court could hardly stop there. Orthodox Jews and Muslims, for example, commonly are opposed to same-sex marriage.[72] If an Orthodox Jewish or Muslim baker wanted an exemption like the one sought by Phillips, a court would have to be accommodating if it had granted an exemption to Phillips.

The ripple effects of granting Phillips an exemption, however, go far beyond bakers who make custom wedding cakes. The Colorado Act covers a wide variety of "places of public accommodation." The Act defines "place of public accommodation" to mean "any place of business engaged in any sales to the public and any place offering services, facilities, privileges, advantages, or accommodations to the public."[73] Then, while explicitly disclaiming any intent to be comprehensive, the Act offers numerous examples, including businesses as different as motels, restaurants, barber shops, retail stores, gyms, and movie theaters.[74] If a court were to grant Phillips

---

life, the vital role that belief and daily conduct play in the continued survival of Old Order Amish communities and their religious organization, and the hazards presented by the State's enforcement of a statute generally valid as to others. Beyond this, they have carried the even more difficult burden of demonstrating the adequacy of their alternative mode of continuing informal vocational education in terms of precisely those overall interests that the State advances in support of its program of compulsory high school education. In light of this convincing showing, one that probably few other religious groups or sects could make, and weighing the minimal difference between what the State would require and what the Amish already accept, it was incumbent on the State to show with more particularity how its admittedly strong interest in compulsory education would be adversely affected by granting an exemption to the Amish....

Id. at 235-36.

[72] *See Faith Positions,* HUMAN RIGHTS CAMPAIGN, https://www.hrc.org/faith-positions (last visited Dec. 12, 2020); *Religious Groups' Official Positions on Same-Sex Marriage,* PEW RESEARCH CENTER, Dec. 7, 2012, https://www.pewforum.org/2012/12/07/religious-groups-official-positions-on-same-sex-marriage/.

[73] COLO. REV. STAT. §24-34-601(1) (2016).

[74] *Id.*

an exemption in deference to his belief that making a custom wedding cake for a same-sex couple would make him complicit in their sin of marrying someone of the same sex, wouldn't the court become obliged to grant an exemption to a motel owner who, for similar reasons, is unwilling to allow a same-sex couple to reserve a block of rooms for out-of-town guests coming to their wedding? What about a restaurant owner who, in the belief that serving any married same-sex couple would send a message of approval of same-sex marriage that would displease God, has posted at the entrance a sign saying that married same-sex couples are not welcome? And so on. Keep in mind that, under the Court's definition of "religion,"[75] a court has no business treating some of these conscience-based complicity claims as more meritorious than others on the ground that, in the court's view, some make more sense than others.

In short, when a court takes into account, as it must, the ripple effects of granting Phillips an exemption from the Act, the deeply debilitating effect of such an exemption on Colorado's achievement of the compelling nondiscrimination interest underlying the Act becomes unmistakably clear. The question whether the Free Exercise Clause calls for an exemption for Phillips is not a close one. It simply doesn't. The Clause commands no less respect for Phillips's religious beliefs than for anyone else's. However, "we are," as Chief Justice Warren put it in *Braunfeld v. Brown*, "a cosmopolitan nation made up of people of almost every conceivable religious preference,"[76] and in such a nation, claims, like Phillips's, based on sincere religious belief often must give way to laws designed to serve the common good.

C.

Thus far in Part II, I have analyzed Phillips's free exercise claim as I believe a court should analyze it if the court were applying the approach to claims for free exercise exemptions that the Supreme Court was applying prior to *Smith*. As I explained in Part I, the pre-*Smith* approach has considerable practical importance today even though the Court in *Smith* clearly was intent on making it of marginal importance.[77] It obviously would take on

---

[75] *See* Thomas v. Review Bd., 450 U.S. 707 (1981), discussed *supra* text accompanying notes 40-42.

[76] Braunfeld v. Brown, 366 U.S. 599, 606 (1961) (Warren, C.J., announcing the judgment of the Court and an opinion joined by Black, Clark, and Whittaker, JJ.), discussed *supra* text accompanying notes 50-57.

[77] *See supra* text accompanying notes 31-39.

even more importance if the Court were to decide to revisit and overrule *Smith* and reinstate the pre-*Smith* approach. As discussed below, the likelihood is high that the Court will revisit *Smith* in the near future, but the likelihood that when it does so it will overrule *Smith* and reinstate the pre-*Smith* approach is much less certain.

A strong indication that the Court is very likely to revisit *Smith* before long came in 2019 in the unlikely form of an opinion concurring in the Court's denial of a petition to review an appellate court's rejection of a *free speech* claim.[78] In *Kennedy v. Bremerton School District*,[79] Joseph Kennedy sued the public school that had fired him as its football coach. He alleged that the firing violated his free speech rights because it stemmed from his refusal to obey the school superintendent's order to stop kneeling and praying at midfield after each game—a practice in which Kennedy was typically joined by players from both teams. Kennedy lost both in the trial court and on appeal, and the Supreme Court declined discretionary review.

As is customary in cases in which the Court declines discretionary review, the Court wrote no opinion explaining its reasons. However, in an opinion concurring in the Court's denial of review and joined by Justices Thomas, Gorsuch, and Kavanaugh, Justice Alito had quite a bit to say about the case and went well out of his way to sow doubts about his and

---

[78] Kennedy v. Bremerton School Dist., 129 S. Ct. 634, 635-37 (2019) (Alito, J., joined by Thomas, Gorsuch, and Kavanaugh, JJ., concurring). Most obviously, that opinion was an unlikely place to find any discussion by the Justices of free exercise and *Smith* because, as a matter of prudence and conservation of judicial resources, judges ordinarily stick to the issues presented by the matter before them. The petition that the Court voted to deny was addressed to a free speech issue and said nothing about free exercise. The opinion was also an unlikely place for a discussion of free exercise and *Smith* simply because the individual Justices are so very much *not* in the habit of writing opinions when they are in agreement with a decision by the Court to deny a petition for review. The Supreme Court must decide whether or not to grant review in *thousands* of cases each year. For a variety of reasons, including a recognition that granting review of a case almost invariably commits the Justices to devoting a substantial amount of time to the case, the Court denies the overwhelming majority of petitions for review. Four Justices must vote to grant review for review to be granted. With rare exception, if a case is denied review, there is no indication as to which, if any, of the Justices may have voted to grant review. On occasion, however, when a Justice feels strongly that review should have been granted but wasn't, the Justice will note his or her dissent from the denial of review and perhaps write a dissenting opinion as well. For a Justice who *agrees* with the Court's decision to deny review to write an opinion concurring in that denial, as happened in this instance, is especially rare.

[79] 129 S. Ct. 634 (2019).

the three other Justices' commitment to *Smith*. He noted that the Court's refusal to review the appellate court's rejection of Kennedy's free speech claim did not preclude Kennedy from suing for violation of his free exercise rights. He then speculated that Kennedy might not have pursued a free exercise claim previously "due to certain decisions of this Court. In *Employment Div. v. Smith*, the Court drastically cut back on the protection provided by the Free Exercise Clause."[80]

Justice Alito's characterization of *Smith* as having "drastically" cut back on the Clause's protection may well have been a more neutral characterization of *Smith* than if he had said *Smith* "wrongly" cut back on that protection. However, it surely was a very critical and unflattering thing to say. At a minimum, it was a none-too-subtle announcement by Justice Alito and his three colleagues that the approach to free exercise exemptions that the Court adopted in *Smith* is ripe for reevaluation.[81] In 2020 the Court in *Fulton v. City of Philadelphia*[82] granted a petition for review that expressly asked the Court to revisit *Smith*. Although the Justices' questions and comments when they heard oral argument in *Fulton* in the fall of 2020 suggested that they are apt to decide the case without reaching the question of whether *Smith* should be overruled,[83] the concurring opinion in *Kennedy* is potent evidence that the Court will be deciding that question in the not too distant future.

---

[80] *Id.* at 637.

[81] I'm hardly alone in interpreting the four Justices' characterization of *Smith* as a signal that they are looking for an opportunity to revisit *Smith*. *See, e.g.,* Joseph Davis, *Top Scholars, Diverse Religious Groups Ask SCOTUS to Reconsider* Employment Division v. Smith—*Again*, FEDERALIST SOCIETY (Aug. 16, 2019), https://fed soc.org/commentary/blog-posts/top-scholars-diverse-religious-groups-ask-scotus-to-reconsider-employment-division-v-smith-again.

[82] 922 F.3d 140 (3d Cir. 2019), *cert. granted,* 140 S. Ct. 1104 (Feb. 24, 2020) (No. 19-123).

[83] For example, see the following exchange between Justice Barrett and the attorney for the party who filed the petition asking the Court to revisit *Smith*:

> JUSTICE BARRETT:...[Y]ou argue in your brief that *Smith* should be overruled. But you also say that you win even under *Smith* because this policy is neither generally applicable nor neutral. So, if you're right about that, why should we even entertain the question whether to overrule *Smith*?
> MS. WINDHAM: Justice Barrett, you're exactly right that we can and should win this case even under *Smith*....

Fulton v. City of Philadelphia (No. 19-123), Oral Argument, Nov. 4, 2020, at 29-30 (Heritage Reporting Corp. Official Report).

For purposes of argument, let's assume both that the Court will be revisiting *Smith* relatively soon and that Justice Alito and the three Justices who joined his opinion in *Kennedy* are sure votes for overruling *Smith*. That still doesn't settle that a majority of the Court will vote to overrule *Smith*. A fifth vote to overrule *Smith* may well exist on the Court, but it's not a sure thing. Furthermore, if and when a majority agrees that *Smith* should be overruled, it's unclear what approach the Court will put in its place. One possibility, of course, is that the Court simply will reinstate the approach that prevailed on the Court prior to *Smith*. The Court's options, though, are by no means limited to returning to what it was doing before *Smith*.

As I have argued elsewhere,[84] the Court's recent case law includes several indications that if the Court were to abandon its approach in *Smith*, it may adopt a more exemption-friendly approach than the pre-*Smith* approach.[85] If the Court indeed adopts such an approach, a claimant, like Phillips, making a complicity-based conscience claim would have a greater chance of success than under the pre-*Smith* approach. How much greater would depend on the specifics of the approach.[86] Predicting what the

---

[84] Gary J. Simson, *The Uncertain Good of Overruling* Smith, CANOPY FORUM ON THE INTERACTIONS OF LAW AND RELIGION (Emory Univ. Center for the Study of Law and Religion, Oct. 2020), https://canopyforum.org/2020/10/16/the-uncertain-good-of-overruling-smith/.

[85] *See id.* (discussing Burwell v. Hobby Lobby Stores, Inc., 573 U.S. 682 (2014), Trinity Lutheran Church v. Comer, 137 S. Ct. 2012 (2017), and Espinoza v. Montana Dep't of Revenue, 140 S. Ct. 2246 (2020), and examining certain possible implications of *Kennedy* not discussed in this Essay). For a case to similar effect decided after publication of my abovementioned article, see Roman Catholic Diocese of Brooklyn v. Cuomo, 141 S. Ct. ___ (Nov. 25, 2020) (No. 20A87) (per curiam), a case in which newly appointed Justice Barrett's vote was decisive in favor of the free exercise claimant.

[86] A more exemption-friendly approach might, of course, look very different than the pre-*Smith* approach. However, it's also entirely possible that the Court would replace the *Smith* approach with one that, in form, looks very much like the pre-*Smith* approach but that the Court indicates should be applied in a more exemption-friendly way. For example, assume that the Court goes back to the same basic formulation as the pre-*Smith* approach: if the claimant can prove that the law places a substantial burden on the claimant's freedom to practice his or her religion, the court should grant the claimant an exemption unless the government can show that requiring the claimant to abide by the law is necessary to serve a compelling state interest. Then assume that the Court applies that approach in a way that signals to trial and appellate courts

Court will do, however, is an uncertain enterprise at best, particularly in an area like freedom of religion where the Justices tend to be sharply divided and where they more than a few times have reached surprising results.[87] Ultimately, for present purposes, it seems best simply to note the possibilities as I've done. In all likelihood, if the inferences that I draw from the *Kennedy* concurrence are correct, it won't be all that long before the Court fills in the blanks.

III.

My focus thus far has been courts' authority to carve out religious exemptions from generally applicable laws. In closing, I would like to provide a somewhat broader perspective on the problem of religious exemptions by considering a hypothetical case, loosely based on *Masterpiece Cakeshop*, in which the court is not being asked to carve out a religious exemption from a law. Instead, the court must decide whether the legislature stayed within the bounds of the Establishment Clause in creating a religious exemption itself.[88]

---

one or more of the following: (a) the threshold for finding the burden to be "substantial" is lower than the threshold reflected in the pre-*Smith* case law; (b) the threshold for finding the state interest to be "compelling" is higher than that reflected in the pre-*Smith* case law; and (c) the threshold for finding the means-end relationship to be "necessary" is higher than that reflected in the pre-*Smith* case law. Finally, with regard to the Court's possible adoption of a more exemption-friendly approach, consider my comments in the closing paragraph of Simson, *supra* note 84: "To overrule *Smith* but put in place a lenient standard for free exercise exemptions shortchanges Establishment Clause values. It also threatens to hobble the government's ability to pursue effectively a host of important general welfare objectives."

[87] The Court's dramatic departure in *Smith* by a 5-4 vote from its longstanding approach to free exercise exemptions seems to me a prime example of the Court's unpredictability in freedom-of-religion cases. Counterparts in the Establishment Clause area include the Court's 5-4 decisions in *Lee v. Weisman*, 505 U.S. 577 (1992), and *Aguilar v. Felton*, 473 U.S. 402 (1985).

[88] The Establishment Clause, which immediately precedes the Free Exercise Clause in the First Amendment, provides that "Congress shall make no law respecting an establishment of religion." U.S. CONST. amend. I. (The First Amendment is quoted in full *supra* note 14.) Not long after the Supreme Court held in *Cantwell v. Connecticut*, 310 U.S. 296, 303 (1940), that the Free Exercise Clause is a limitation not only on the federal government but on state and local government as well, it held the same for the Establishment Clause. *See* Everson v. Bd. of Educ., 330 U.S. 1, 8 (1947). For discussion of the "selective incorporation" doctrine that provided the basis for those holdings, see *supra* note 16.

Assume that a year from now the U.S. Supreme Court overrules *Smith* and reinstates the more religious-liberty-protective approach to free exercise that prevailed prior to *Smith*. Assume also that a few months later, the Colorado legislature amends the Colorado Anti-Discrimination Act to exempt from its coverage any bakery owners who, like Phillips, believe that making a custom wedding cake for a same-sex couple would violate their religion and be sinful. Lastly, assume that several months after the legislature amends the Act, a Colorado same-sex couple asks a bakery owner in Boulder, Colorado to make them a custom wedding cake; the owner, citing the recent amendment to the Act, refuses their request for religious reasons essentially the same as Phillips had offered; and the couple, maintaining that the amendment to the Act violates the Establishment Clause, brings suit to compel the owner to comply with their request.

In deciding this hypothetical case, a court reasonably can take as its starting point a proposition that the Supreme Court has affirmed time and again: The Establishment Clause does not forbid what the Free Exercise requires.[89] In keeping with that proposition, if the court were to conclude that in amending the Act, the Colorado legislature simply carved out an exemption that the Free Exercise Clause required and that the court itself therefore would have felt obliged to carve out if the legislature hadn't done so first, the court would reject the couple's claim of an Establishment Clause violation with no further ado. As I argued at length in Part II, however, Phillips would not be entitled to a court-ordered exemption under the Court's free exercise approach prior to *Smith*. Accordingly, if, as hypothesized above, the Court overrules *Smith* and reinstates the approach to free exercise that prevailed prior to *Smith*, the Boulder bakery owner in my hypothetical case wouldn't be entitled as a matter of free exercise to an exemption of the sort that the Colorado legislature put in place. Ultimately, then, the court would have to address the question: How far may a legislature, in enacting exemptions to accommodate people's religious beliefs, go beyond the demands of free exercise without overstepping the boundaries that the Establishment Clause sets?

Justice Scalia concluded his majority opinion in *Smith* with some observations that may be read as tacitly suggesting that the political process is the most important constraint on how far a legislature may go beyond the requirements of free exercise in legislating religious exemptions and that the Establishment Clause plays only a peripheral role:

---

[89] *See* Gary J. Simson, *The Establishment Clause in the Supreme Court: Rethinking the Court's Approach*, 72 CORNELL L. REV. 905, 913-14 & nn. 39-41 (1987).

Values that are protected against government interference through enshrinement in the Bill of Rights are not thereby banished from the political process. Just as a society that believes in the negative protection accorded to the press by the First Amendment is likely to enact laws that affirmatively foster the dissemination of the printed word, so also a society that believes in the negative protection accorded to religious belief can be expected to be solicitous of that value in its legislation as well.… It may fairly be said that leaving accommodation to the political process will place at a relative disadvantage those religious practices that are not widely engaged in; but that unavoidable consequence of democratic government must be preferred to a system in which each conscience is a law unto itself or in which judges weigh the social importance of all laws against the centrality of all religious beliefs.[90]

If Justice Scalia in the above passage indeed was suggesting that the Establishment Clause poses little obstacle to legislatures' carving out whatever religious exemptions they wish, his suggestion on behalf of a majority of the Court wasn't binding authority. Instead, it was what lawyers would call *dictum*—discussion in a judicial opinion having no bearing on the resolution of the issue at hand and therefore carrying no precedential weight.[91] The Court in *Smith* addressed and decided a quintessential free exercise issue—courts' authority under the Free Exercise Clause to carve out exemptions to relieve claimants of burdens on their religious exercise. No Establishment Clause issue was before the Court.

Even though Justice Scalia's apparent suggestion was only *dictum*, the issue that it raises of Establishment Clause limitations on courts' authority under the Free Exercise Clause to carve out exemptions is one deserving of serious attention. The Establishment Clause commands the government to "make no law respecting an establishment of religion." As that wording makes clear, the Establishment Clause does not simply prohibit the government from enacting laws to establish an official religion. It prohibits government from making laws "respecting" an establishment of religion. In a leading decision almost fifty years ago, Chief Justice Burger explained for the Court that a law "may be one 'respecting' the forbidden objective while falling short of its total realization."[92] He underlined that

---

[90] Employment Div. v. Smith, 494 U.S. 872, 890 (1990).

[91] *Obiter dictum*, BLACK'S LAW DICTIONARY (Bryan A. Garner ed., 10th ed. 2014).

[92] Lemon v. Kurtzman, 403 U.S. 602, 612 (1971).

a law "might not *establish* a state religion but nevertheless be one 'respecting' that end in the sense of being a step that could lead to such establishment,"[93] and he identified laws sponsoring religion as prime candidates to take us step by step down the road to establishment.[94] Picking up on that theme, the Court in later cases developed an "endorsement test" that calls for the invalidation of laws that have the purpose or effect of putting the government's stamp of approval on a particular religion or on religion in general over nonreligion.[95]

In the hypothetical case described above, is the Colorado legislature's creation of a religious exemption that it had no free exercise obligation to create best understood as government sponsorship of religion? Although the Free Exercise and Establishment Clauses, standing side by side in the First Amendment, only sensibly must be interpreted as not genuinely in conflict with one another, it can often be difficult to reconcile their very different demands. When the Justices ultimately address the constitutionality under the Establishment Clause of a legislative exemption designed to accommodate a complicity-based conscience claim like Phillips's in *Masterpiece Cakeshop*, they must be mindful of the high importance under our Constitution of not only individual religious liberty but the values underlying the Establishment Clause as well.[96]

---

[93] *Id.*

[94] *See id.* (characterizing "sponsorship" as one of the "three main evils against which the Establishment Clause was intended to afford protection").

[95] *See, e.g.*, Allegheny Cnty. v. ACLU, 492 U.S. 573, 592-94, 599-600 (1989). For discussion of the endorsement test, the harmful effects of government endorsement of religion, and the debate among the Justices on the validity of the test, see Gary J. Simson, *Religious Arguments by Citizens to Influence Public Policy: The Lessons of the Establishment Clause*, 66 MERCER L. REV. 273, 284-308 (2015).

[96] For a proposed approach for deciding Establishment Clause limitations on legislatively created religious exemptions, see Simson, *supra* note 39, at 549-54.

3.

Nietzsche on Freedom, the Evolution of Language, and Social Epistemology

William A. B. Parkhurst

> The longing for "freedom of the will" in the superlative metaphysical sense..., the longing to bear the entire and ultimate responsibility for your actions yourself and to relieve God, world, ancestors, chance, and society of the burden — all this means nothing less than being that very causa sui and,...pulling yourself by the hair from the swamp of nothingness up into existence.[1]

Nietzsche's ideas surrounding political choice and freedom have generated not only political upheaval through misinterpretation but also deep disagreements among scholars surrounding even the most basic of premises. I argue that Nietzsche is best understood as offering a form of political freedom through the careful use of language. I articulate a positive necessary consequent hidden within Nietzsche's philosophy that supports a democratic notion of political freedom.[2]

This paper is composed of three parts. Part one summarizes contemporary debates surrounding Nietzsche's conception of freedom. Contemporary interpretations tend to argue that Nietzsche's conception of freedom is an atomistic and individualistic autonomy, which is achievable only by a sovereign individual divorced from society. I argue that there are good

---

[1] Friedrich Nietzsche, *Beyond Good and Evil* in *Beyond Good and Evil/On the Genealogy of Morality, The Complete Works of Friedrich Nietzsche Vol 8.*, trans. Adrian Del Caro (Stanford: Stanford University Press, 2014), 21. [Following standard scholarly convention, each citation to Nietzsche's work cites text abbreviation, book number, and section number. Page numbers are occasionally provided where needed].

[2] It is important to note this essay is neither Nietzsche apologism nor pure historical reconstruction. The political possibilities I draw out are necessary consequences of Nietzsche's philosophy of language and social epistemology. These consequences, which Nietzsche himself seems to have seen, are not political ideals he would endorse freely. That is, Nietzsche must begrudgingly admit this consequent of his philosophy. However, he attempts to suppress its realization, and his elitism led him to try to actively undermine the possibility of their realization by advocating for illiteracy. In this sense, I am turning Nietzsche's own philosophy against him.

textual reasons that we ought to read the sovereign individual as a polemic against Kantian autonomy.

Part two takes a closer look at Nietzsche's philosophy of language and its relation to making choices. Nietzsche's philosophy of language dictates that even great individuals are necessarily conditioned by, and dependent on, society. This means the sovereign individual should be read ironically. Further, Nietzsche's philosophy of language necessitates, perhaps to his annoyance, a form of linguistic freedom which is democratically available to everyone in a linguistic community.

In part three I develop an account of this necessary consequent of Nietzsche's philosophy. I conclude that when we use our words carefully, we express a democratically available kind of political freedom.

I. Review of Literature

There is a tendency in scholarship to understand Nietzsche as endorsing a radically individualist philosophy. Walter Kaufmann and those following him argue that Nietzsche's philosophy stresses the goal of attaining absolute autonomy.[3] It is generally agreed upon by scholars that Kaufmann's influential research program sought to rehabilitate Nietzsche from European fascist interpretations and did so by suggesting that Nietzsche was apolitical and focused solely on individual and existential concerns.[4] In so doing, Kaufmann made Nietzsche palatable for the post-war American audience.[5] Marina Cominos aptly summarizes this history:

> Walter Kaufmann's classic study, *Nietzsche: Philosopher, Psychologist, Antichrist* (1974),…has been extremely influential in defining Nietzsche as a radical individualist. Kaufmann argues that Nietzsche is

---

[3] Walter Kaufmann, *Nietzsche: Philosopher, Psychologist, Antichrist* (Princeton: Princeton University Press, 1974), 297; Leslie Paul Thiele, *Friedrich Nietzsche and the Politics of the Soul: A Study of Heroic Individualism* (Princeton: Princeton University Press, 1990), 45.

[4] Kaufmann claims that "the leitmotif of Nietzsche's life and thought [was] the theme of the antipolitical individual who seeks self-perfection far from the modern world" with the goal of "becoming autonomous" (Kaufmann, *Nietzsche: Philosopher, Psychologist, Antichrist*, 418, 291; cf. Keith Ansell-Pearson, *An Introduction to Nietzsche as Political Thinker: The Perfect Nihilist* (New York: Cambridge University Press, 1994), 2; Peter Bergmann, *Nietzsche, "The Last Antipolitical German"* (Bloomington: Indiana University Press, 1987), 1.)

[5] Jennifer Ratner-Rosenhagen, *American Nietzsche: A History of an Icon and His Ideas* (Chicago: University of Chicago Press, 2012), 223-224.

basically *"antipolitical"* insofar as his teachings pertain to the radically individual pursuit of 'self-perfection'.[6]

Kaufmann's work has, to a large extent, framed the discussion surrounding Nietzsche's approach to autonomy and individualism. However, as Robert Ackermann argues, by presenting Nietzsche this way, Kaufmann presented "King Kong in chains [...] appearing under heavy sedation."[7]

Anglo-American scholars, working within the basic framework set up by Kaufmann, have relied greatly on the notion of "the *sovereign individual*" in contrast to the herd in Nietzsche's *Genealogy of Morality*.[8] This type of interpretation emphasizes individualism and sovereign autonomy.

These interpretations find support within a single section of the *Genealogy of Morality* where Nietzsche writes,

> [T]hen we find as the ripest fruit on its [morality's] tree the *sovereign individual*, like only unto himself, the autonomous, supermoral individual who has liberated himself from the morality of custom (for "autonomous" and "Moral" are mutually exclusive), in brief, a human being of his own independent long will who is *allowed to promise*....This individual who has become free, who is really *allowed* to promise, this master of the free will, this sovereign... The "free" human being,...who gives his word as something that can be trusted because he knows himself to be strong enough to keep it even against accidents, even "against fate."[9]

---

[6] Marina Cominos, "The Question of Nietzsche's Anti-Politics and Human Transfiguration," in *Nietzsche, Power and Politics: Rethinking Nietzsche's Legacy for Political Thought*, ed. Herman Siemens and Vasti Roodt (New York: Walter de Gruyter, 2009), 87-88.

[7] Robert Ackermann, "Current American Thought on Nietzsche," in *Nietzsche heute, Die Rezeption seines Werks nach 1968*, ed. Sigrid Bauschinger, Susan L. Cocalis und Sara Lennox (Bern, Switzerland: A. Franke Verlag 1986), 129.

[8] An example of this kind of interpretation can been found in Ruth Abbey's work *Nietzsche's Middle Period*. She writes, "One of the purposes of Nietzsche's genealogy of morals is practical; he strives to discredit or demote values whose only purpose is to serve the common interest, and he wants to clear the ground for the creation, resurgence, or justification of those which foster individualism" (Ruth Abbey, *Nietzsche's Middle Period* (New York: Oxford University Press, 2000), 36).

[9] [GM] Friedrich Nietzsche, *On the Genealogy of Morality in Beyond Good and Evil/On the Genealogy of Morality, The Complete Works of Friedrich Nietzsche Vol 8*, trans. Adrian Del Caro (Stanford: Stanford University Press, 2014), GM II 2.

The individual described here is completely liberated from others, culture, and custom and expresses an unrestricted autonomy, that is, the autonomous ability to make promises. This means that the sovereign individual is "the master of *free* will." This power of free will is so strong that the sovereign individual can maintain their choices in the face of accidents by controlling and having absolute power over the world and even fate itself.

Many scholars make use of the sovereign individual as an anchor point for understanding many philosophical ideas in Nietzsche's texts as Christa Davis Acampora points out.[10] The majority of contemporary Nietzsche scholars, including Leslie Thiele, Aaron Ridley, Randall Havas, John Richardson, Peter Poellner, and Ken Gemes, hold that the sovereign individual is the ideal of autonomous individualism to which we ought to strive.[11]

However, many scholars who suggest that the sovereign individual is a Nietzschean ideal of sorts are often skeptical about whether such an ideal has been, or even could be, achieved.[12] For example, Simon May holds that

---

[10] "Once I committed myself to this topic, I was surprised to discover just how rampant the problem is, and how frequently the 'sovereign individual' creeps into all manner of discussions of Nietzsche's works. Those who point to the sovereign individual as Nietzsche's ideal generally associate it with "the higher men," and sovereign individuality is often discussed in the context of clarifying what it means to 'Become who one is'" (Christa Davis Acampora, "On Sovereignty and Overhumanity: Why it Matters How We Read Nietzsche's Genealogy II, 2," in *Nietzsche's On the Genealogy of Morals: Critical Essays*, ed. Christa Davis Acampora (New York: Rowman & Littlefield Publishers, 2006), 151).

[11] Thiele, *Friedrich Nietzsche and the Politics of the Soul*, 45; Aaron Ridley, *Nietzsche's Conscience: Six Character Studies from the "Genealogy"* (London: Cornell University Press, 1998), 18; Randall Havas, *Nietzsche's Genealogy: Nihilism and the Will to Knowledge* (New York: Cornell University Press, 2000), 94-95; John Richardson, "Nietzsche's Freedoms," in *Nietzsche on Freedom and Autonomy*, ed. Ken Gemes and Simon May (New York: Oxford University Press, 2009), 128; Peter Poellner, "Nietzschean Freedom," in *Nietzsche on Freedom and Autonomy*, ed. Ken Gemes and Simon May (New York: Oxford University Press, 2009), 152; Ken Gemes, "Nietzsche on Free Will, Autonomy, and the Sovereign Individual," in *Nietzsche on Freedom and Autonomy*, ed. Ken Gemes and Simon May (New York: Oxford University Press, 2009), 37, 39, 40.

[12] For example, Ken Gemes writes, "It is typical of Nietzsche's deliberately confusing caginess that it is not at first clear whether the sovereign individual is a creature already achieved or one yet to come" (Gemes, "Nietzsche on Free Will, Autonomy, and the Sovereign Individual," 37).

the sovereign individual is both an ideal and unattainable. Simon May writes,

> The Sovereign individual is unattainable because in order to achieve perfect mastery over himself and circumstances (and thus perfect 'free will' in Nietzsche's sense of the term), he would need to be infallible in controlling the myriad drives and dependencies created by his nature, nurture, and life-circumstances. In other words, he would need to be a man-god, invested with precisely the absolute autonomy of the 'dead' God.[13]

May proposes four reasons why the sovereign individual is not feasible. First, the sovereign individual would have to be completely isolated from human relationships which are important for Nietzsche. Second, we can never attain such absolute autonomy because we are always dependent on food, shelter, and health. Third, the conditions of life involve complex social dependencies: absolute autonomy is only achieved by starving the individual of these. Fourth, such an absolute autonomy would necessitate a complete lack of normative constraints which would make the individual vulnerable to mob morality. May writes, "Nietzsche's radical individualism not only largely ignores such needs, but treats all demanding human entanglements, such as friendship or marriage, as at best distractions and at worst crippling."[14] I find May's analysis of difficulties astute. However, May's insistence that this is a positive ideal put forward and accepted by Nietzsche seems unwarranted given several important points May does not consider.

I hold there are at least five objections to the thesis that the sovereign individual is a positive idea of freedom put forward by Nietzsche. First, the *Genealogy of Morals* bears a telling subtitle about its contents: "A Polemic." In this work Nietzsche takes up many different moral views polemically and ironically such as those of Paul Rée, Hubert Spencer, Henry Thomas Buckle, Rudolf Virchow, Silas Weir Michell, and more generally English psychologists, social Darwinists and Utilitarians.[15] In all these cases Nietzsche proposes such views only to polemically lead them to absurdity. It is reasonable to suspect, as Lawrence Hatab, Christa Davis Acampora, Daniel Rynhold, and Michael Harris do, that the sovereign

---

[13] Simon May, *Nietzsche's Ethics and his War on 'Morality'*, (New York: Oxford University Press, 1999), 117.

[14] May, *Nietzsche's Ethics and his War on 'Morality'*, 118.

[15] GM pref. 4, 7, GM I 3, 4, 5, 6.

individual is a polemic against enlightenment notions of autonomy held by philosophers such as Kant.[16]

Second, in other published passages Nietzsche rejects the exact same qualities he ascribes to the sovereign individual, including free will, autonomy, and the ability to control fate. Given Nietzsche's rejections, the principle of charity suggests this is a polemic against the enlightenment ideal of autonomy that Nietzsche mocks elsewhere. For example, in *Beyond Good and Evil*, he writes, "The desire for 'freedom of the will,'...a desire to bear the whole and sole responsibility for one's actions and to absolve God, world, ancestors, chance, society from responsibility for them", is a belief that "is the best contradiction hitherto."[17] Nietzsche writes that longing for this kind of freedom is necessary to slave morality.[18] Nietzsche, of course, does not hold slave morality as his ideal.

Third, if the autonomous "Sovereign Individual" (*souveraine Individuum*) is a central concept for Nietzsche, one would expect it to play a substantial role in Nietzsche's writings. However, "*souveraine Individuum*" is found nowhere else in Nietzsche's published writings. Further, if such autonomy ("*autonom*" and "*autonome*") in the section on the sovereign individual were a positive part of Nietzsche's philosophy one would also expect it to play a substantial role in Nietzsche's writing. However, this section is the only time Nietzsche uses the phrase "*autonom*" or "*autonome*" in his published writings. The closely related word "*Autonomen*" is only used in one place in Nietzsche's published works and that is to mock contemporary European morality that wants an "*autonomous* herd" ("*Autonomen Heerde*").[19] Nietzsche rejects Kant's moral theory and his conception of the autonomous individuality in a number of places.[20] Nietzsche explicitly at-

---

[16] Lawrence Hatab, *Nietzsche's 'On the Genealogy of Morality': An Introduction* (New York: Cambridge University Press, 2008), 76; Acampora, "On Sovereignty and Overhumanity," 147-161; Daniel Rynhold and Michael J. Harris, *Nietzsche, Soloveitchik and Contemporary Jewish Philosophy* (New York: Cambridge University Press, 2018), 78n31.

[17] BGE 21.

[18] BGE 260.

[19] BGE 202.

[20] [HAH I] Friedrich Nietzsche, *Human, All-Too-Human. The Complete Works of Friedrich Nietzsche Vol 3,* trans. Gary Handwerk (Stanford: Stanford University Press. 1995), HAH I 25; BGE 5, 54; [GS] Friedrich Nietzsche, *The Gay Science: With Prelude in German Rhymes and Appendix of Songs,* trans. Josefine Nauckhoff (Cambridge: Cambridge University Press, 2001), GS 335.

tacks Kant for creating a morality that wants to obey, that is, a herd morality.[21] This all suggests that an autonomous sovereign individual is not Nietzsche's positive idea but Kant's. Further, this suggests Nietzsche is using the sovereign individual as an *ad absurdum* argument. To become autonomous, one must attain the absurd requirement of the power of God over the entire world and fate itself. In this context, May's points support, rather than reject, Nietzsche's position.

Fourth, Nietzsche makes it very clear that the sovereign individual is a result of the "morality of custom."[22] The ability to make promises is an ability generated through a long history of cruelty to embed within man conscience and guilt. The ability to make promises is based on the contractual relationship between debtor and creditor.[23] Nietzsche writes, "Precisely here *promising* takes place; precisely here what matters is making a memory for the one who promises; precisely here, we may suspect, there will be a trove of harsh, cruel, painful things."[24] The creditor deals cruel punishment upon human beings who were unable to remember their promises.

Nietzsche claims in the second essay that this debtor/creditor relation is the origin of moral conscience and guilt.[25] Nietzsche is clear that the sovereign individual is not free from society but is the very product of society's mores and punishments. For Nietzsche, in order to promise, humans must first become "*calculable, regular,* [and] *necessary.*"[26] This is done through the morality of customs. Nietzsche writes, "Human beings were really made predictable with the help of the morality of custom and the social strait jacket."[27] The conclusion of the long history of cruelty is a sense of responsibility and duty that the sovereign human being calls "his conscience."[28]

Further, Nietzsche explicitly associates conscience and duty with Kant later in the *Genealogy of Morals*. Nietzsche writes,

---

[21] BGE 187, 188.

[22] GM II 2.

[23] GM II 4, 6.

[24] GM II 5.

[25] GM II 3, 4; [EH] Friedrich Nietzsche, *Ecce Homo* in *The Anti-Christ, Ecce Homo, Twilight of the Idols and Other Writings*, eds. Aaron Ridley and Judith Norman, trans. Judith Norman (Cambridge: Cambridge University Press, 2005), EH GM 1.

[26] GM II 1; cf. GM II 2.

[27] GM II 2.

[28] GM II 3.

In *this* sphere, hence in legal obligations, the moral conceptual world of 'guilt,' 'conscience,' 'duty,' 'sacredness of duty' had its cradle...in blood. And might we not add that this world at bottom has never quite lost its odor of blood and torture? (not even in old Kant: the categorical imperative smells of cruelty...).[29]

This suggests that the sovereign individual is a Kantian ideal, not Nietzsche's.

Fifth, Nietzsche's explicit rejection of Kant's notion of freedom in the *Genealogy of Morals* at both the beginning and end supports the claim that the sovereign individual is a parody. In the beginning of *Genealogy of Morals* Nietzsche stakes out his position as explicitly "anti-Kantian."[30] At the end of the third essay, Nietzsche accuses Kant of working in the service of the ascetic ideal because he put "freedom" beyond the reach of reason and therefore secures it along with God, immortality, and the soul.[31] More generally, the third essay's critique of the abstract disinterestedness of the aesthetic ideal, as manifested in Kant, can be seen in the sovereign individual's need for freedom from all circumstances.

We can, therefore, discard the notion that Nietzsche is putting forward the sovereign individual as an ideal to strive for. If the history of Nietzsche scholarship has put undue weight on the notion of the sovereign individual as the foundation of Nietzsche's positive view of freedom, where might we locate a more substantial notion of choice necessary for political freedom in Nietzsche's philosophy?

II. Nietzsche's Account of Language and Choice

I propose we locate the nexus of Nietzsche's account of political freedom in his genealogical history of the social sphere of language and communication. I conclude that language, according to Nietzsche, fundamentally represents the world as it is important for our survival, not as it is in-itself. Language is, perhaps, exactly the wrong vehicle for considering what the world might be independent of us. However, it does allow for the possibility of "choice" between meanings. This kind of choice is not restricted to higher types, as is often argued, but is democratically available to everyone in a linguistic community.

---

[29] GM II 6.
[30] GM pref. 2.
[31] GM III 25.

There is a strong tendency in Nietzsche scholarship to think that it is only the strong masters and linguistic geniuses who are responsible for the words we use and the development of language. Nietzsche has made such interpretations of his philosophy of language textually supportable. Consider the following:

> The master's right to give names goes so far as to allow us to conceive of the origin of language itself as an expression of power on the part of the rulers; they say "this *is* thus and such," they seal everything and occurrence with a sound and thereby take possession of it, so to speak.[32]

Such passages have led some scholars to conclude that it is only the masters or higher types which are the sole and isolated origin of language.[33] However, in the next line it becomes clear that language is also constituted democratically. Nietzsche writes,

> It is only with a *decline* of aristocratic value-judgments that this whole opposition of "egoistic" and "unegoistic" imposes more and more on the human conscience—to use my language for it, it is *the herd instinct* that finally get a word in (also *words* plural).[34]

These changes in language reflect what Nietzsche calls "a truly *grand* politics of revenge."[35] Language is itself a political battlefield of "grand politics" in which both linguistic geniuses and everyday people can make choices in a complex dynamic process.[36]

According to Nietzsche, language and consciousness developed under pressure for the survival of the species.[37] Nietzsche writes,

> Consciousness in general has developed only under the pressure of the need to communicate...conscious thinking takes place in words, that is, in communication symbols; and this fact discloses the origin

---

[32] GM I 2.

[33] Nadeem J. Z. Hussain, "The Role of Life in the Genealogy" in *Nietzsche's On the Genealogy of Morality: A Critical Guide*, ed. Simon May (Cambridge: Cambridge University Press, 2011), 142-169, 250.

[34] GM I 2.

[35] GM I 8.

[36] Cf. BGE 208, 241.

[37] It is important to note that "developed under pressure for" is not the same as "completely determined by" ([OL] Friedrich Nietzsche, "On the Origin of Language," in *Friedrich Nietzsche on Rhetoric and Language*, ed. and trans. Sanders L. Gilman, Carol Blair and David J. Parent (New York: Oxford University Press, 1989), OL 211).

of consciousness. In short, the development of language and the development of consciousness…go hand in hand….My idea is clearly that consciousness actually belongs not to man's existence as an individual but rather to the community and herd aspect of his nature.[38]

Since language is only useful for survival if it is understood, those linguistic innovations that were not useful to the community or herd were, in Nietzsche's words, "*outvoted.*"[39]

For language to be useful, there needed to be agreement within linguistic communities about the use of language; a "peace treaty" for the legislation of language.[40] The outcome of such legislation was agreed upon designations that became the first laws of truth.[41] Nietzsche is very clear in his mature writings that these designations reflect the interests of the species, the herd-aspect of our nature, and the values of the community, not only those of great individuals.[42] He writes, "Language is neither the conscious work of individuals nor of a plurality….Language is much too complex to be the work of a single individual, much too unified to be the work of a mass; it is a complete organism."[43] Language functions as a condition for the possibility of consciousness but itself neither comes from the individual or a collective but through their dynamic interrelation.

For Nietzsche, identities in language are brought into use communally, not by the individual in isolation. These socially constituted identities often cover over and oversimplify the world.[44] In *Human, All-too-Human II* Nietzsche explicitly claims that the absolute freedom of the will is such a linguistic prejudice.[45] Nietzsche later developed this view arguing it

---

[38] GS 354.

[39] GS 354.

[40] It should be noted that in this early framework Nietzsche uses the phrase "state of nature" but in his later writings mocked such contract theories if taken literally ([TL] Friedrich Nietzsche, "Truth and Lying in a Non-Moral Sense," in *The Birth of Tragedy and Other Writings*, eds. Raymond Geuss and Ronald Speirs, trans. Ronald Speirs (Cambridge: Cambridge University Press, 1999), TL 1, cf. GM II 17).

[41] TL 1.

[42] GS 354.

[43] OL 209.

[44] GS 354.

[45] [HAH II] Friedrich Nietzsche, *Human, All-Too-Human II and Unpublished Fragments from the Period of Human, All Too Human II (Spring 1878-Fall 1879)*, The Complete Works of Friedrich Nietzsche Vol 4, trans. Gary Handwerk (Stanford: Stanford University Press, 2013), HAH II WS 11.

is only because of the unity, the singular identity in language, that we postulate the "will" ontologically. Willing, which is a complex process, "is a unity in word only."[46] These linguistic prejudices demonstrate how our thinking is guided and constrained ahead of time by the history of language.

More generally, Nietzsche argues that all metaphysics are directly linked to our history of language. In his early work *Dawn*, Nietzsche suggests that the words available to us put constraints on our thought. He writes,

> *Words present in us.* - We always express our thoughts with the words that lie ready to hand. Or to express my entire suspicion: we have at every moment only that very thought for which we have ready to hand the words that are roughly capable of expressing it.[47]

It is not only singular words, but our very grammar that constrains our thoughts and philosophical systems ahead of time. He writes in *Beyond Good and Evil*,

> The peculiar family resemblance of all Indian, Greek and German philosophizing is explained easily enough. Precisely where linguistic kinship is present it cannot be avoided at all, thanks to the common philosophy of grammar—I mean thanks to the unconscious rule and leadership of the same grammatical functions—everything lies ready from the beginning for a similar development and sequence of philosophical systems: just as the route to certain other possibilities of interpreting the world seem almost barred.[48]

This view is consistent through his late unpublished writings. He writes, "*we cease thinking when we no longer want to think within the constraints of language*, we just manage to reach the suspicion that there might be a boundary here."[49] Language itself constrains and limits the kinds of metaphysics or ontologies we can even think about.

If language was formed out of historical, biological, and social pressure for the survival of the species, then language is tuned to survival rather

---

[46] BGE 19.

[47] [D] Friedrich Nietzsche, *Dawn*, *The Complete Works of Friedrich Nietzsche Vol 5*, trans. Brittain Smith with afterword by Keith Ansell-Pearson (Stanford: Stanford University Press, 2011), D 257.

[48] BGE 20.

[49] [LN] Friedrich Nietzsche, *Writings from the Late Notebooks*, ed. Rüdiger Bittner, trans. Kate Sturge (New York: Cambridge University Press, 2003), 5[22].

than correspondence to the world as it is independent of us.[50] Simply because language has been a condition of conscious life does not mean that
it gets at the world in an objective, veridical way. Nietzsche writes, "Life
is no argument. The conditions of life might include error."[51] For Nietzsche this does not count as an objection to the value of language. He
writes in *Beyond Good and Evil*,

> The falseness of a judgment is for us not yet an objection to a judg-
> ment; perhaps our new language sounds strangest in this respect.
> The question is how far it is life-promoting, life-preserving, spe-
> cies-preserving.[52]

Early in Nietzsche's career he traces the genealogy of reason to logi-
cally invalid metaphors in human culture and language.[53] He writes, "But
there is no "real" expression and *no real knowing apart from metaphor.*"[54]
This metaphorical nature of language means that it is essentially rhetorical
and was simply not forged to "penetrate the realm of truth."[55] Language
was formed to communicate and represent aspects of our experience that
were important to survival and has no necessary relationship to the world
as it is independent of us.

In Nietzsche's early lecture notes on rhetoric he writes, "There is obviously no unrhetorical "naturalness" of language to which one could appeal; Language itself is the result of purely rhetorical arts....*Language is
rhetoric.*"[56] The suspicion that language does not capture some eternal and
natural truth of the world was later expressed in much more detail in his
published work, *Human, All-Too-Human.* He writes,

> *Language as a supposed science* -...people believed for long stretches
> of time in the concepts for and names for things as if they were
> *aeternae veritates*...they really believed that in language they had
> knowledge of the world....Long afterward—only just now—is it

---

[50] [PT] Friedrich Nietzsche, *Philosophy and Truth: Selections from Nietzsche's
Notebooks of the Early 1870's,* ed. and trans. Daniel Breazeale (New York: Humanity
Books, 1979), PT 31 ("The Philosopher" p. 79).
[51] GS 121.
[52] BGE 4.
[53] PT 48 ("The Philosopher" p. 142, 143).
[54] PT 50 ("The Philosopher" p. 149).
[55] PT 50 ("The Philosopher" p. 149).
[56] [DAR] Friedrich Nietzsche, "Description of Ancient Rhetoric," in *Friedrich
Nietzsche on Rhetoric and Language,* ed. and trans. Sanders L. Gilman, Carol Blair and
David J. Parent (New York: Oxford University Press, 1989), p. 21.

dawning on people that they have propagated a colossal error with their belief in language.[57]

This is a direct attack against one possible interpretation of the Theory of Names in Plato's *Cratylus* which was later adopted in theological debates concerning the names given to things by God or Adam.[58] This view holds that names express some eternal essence or truth about the world. In the *Cratylus,* Hermogenes states, "Cratylus says, Socrates, that there is a correctness of name for each thing, one that belongs to it by nature."[59] Nietzsche rejects such a view and holds that language itself, and names with it, are simply forms of convention.[60] This means there is no "pure" language that captures the world outside of social convention.

Language always abbreviates and simplifies rather than penetrating the realm of truth or the world as it is in-itself. He writes, "Language never expresses something completely, but stresses the most outstanding characteristic."[61] What language captures is what is most important to us and our survival. It never gets at the world itself but only at the "sign" or "image" presented in language. Nietzsche writes,

> The full essence of things will never be grasped....Instead of the thing, the sensation takes in only a *sign*....Language never expresses something completely but displays only a characteristic which appears to be prominent to it.[62]

This means that what is most outstanding is constrained within the biological and social history of a language and what has proved to be useful to the species.

This historical observation about language means that language contains opinion *[doxa]*, not knowledge *[epistēmē]*.[63] The tendency to express something like the theory of names in the *Cratylus* can be explained in terms of the *feeling* of "purity" which comes along with consistent language

---

[57] HAH I 11.

[58] [BT] Friedrich Nietzsche, *The Birth of Tragedy* in *The Birth of Tragedy and Other Writings*, eds. Raymond Geuss and Ronald Speirs, trans. Ronald Speirs (Cambridge: Cambridge University Press, 1999), BT 18; cf. GM II 21.

[59] Plato, "Cratylus," in *Plato Complete Works*, ed. John M. Cooper (Indianapolis: Hackett Publishing Company, 1997), *Cratylus*, 383a.

[60] TL 1.

[61] DAR p. 53.

[62] DAR p. 23.

[63] DAR p. 23.

use. This consistent use is something developed and formed socially based on consistent choices. Nietzsche writes,

> There is neither a pure nor an impure speech in itself. A very important question arises of how the feeling for purity gradually is formed, and how an educated society *makes choices [wählt]*, to the point at which the whole range has been defined. It evidently acts according to unconscious laws and analogies here: a unity, a uniform expression is achieved; "pure" sanctioned style corresponds to a high society in the same way that a dialect corresponds to a limited group of people.[64]

Here Nietzsche gives a genealogical analysis of why we feel we get at a pure essence when we use words consistently. If the feeling of a pure language is developed through consistent use, then how does language and meaning change?

One way highlighted by Nietzsche is through the creation and adoption of new words. As Benedetta Zavatta suggests, "Individuals with idiosyncratic taste will experience things in ways that differ somewhat from the standard. These are the individuals that can become language innovators, that is, invent new words to name things."[65] Nietzsche also argues that languages changes through the trope as metaphor. He writes, "It [metaphor] does not produce new words but gives new meanings to them."[66] For Nietzsche, meaning is not contained in the authorial intention of the individual speaker but how others take it to symbolize.

The specific expression does not contain the meaning. Rather, it is the complex relationship between language innovators and society at large. Nietzsche writes,

> 'Meaning' means no more than that: no expression determines and delimits its movement of soul with such rigidity that it could be regarded as the *actual* statement of the meaning. Every expression

---

[64] DAR p. 27.

[65] Benedetta Zavatta, "From Pure Reason to Historical Knowledge," in *Nietzsche's Engagement with Kant and the Kantian Legacy. Volume I. Nietzsche, Kant and the Problem of Metaphysics*, eds. Marco Brussotti, Herman Siemens, Joao Constancio, and Tom Bailey (New York: Bloomsbury, 2017), 60.

[66] DAR p. 23.

is just a symbol and not the thing; and symbols can be interchanged. A *choice [Wahal]* always remains possible.[67]

What becomes clear in Nietzsche's philosophy of language is that this "*choice [Wahal]*" is precisely the choice made by an educated society; it is "how an educated society *makes choices (wählt).*"[68] This suggests that it is not only language innovators who decide the future of language, but also the educated society which chooses to take up such innovations.

Nietzsche is very clear that new words and new meanings are created by individuals. However, he is also very clear that it is the larger social group that chooses to take up a new word or metaphor. Nietzsche writes,

> Language is created by the individual speech artist, but it is determined by the fact that the taste of the many makes choices *[Auswahl]*. Only a very few individuals utter *Schemata* [figures] whose *virtus* [virtue, worth] becomes a guide for many....A figure which finds no buyer becomes an error.[69]

If new words are chosen by a society, this allows for the constraints on thought and experience to change. Zavatta makes this point well though does not acknowledge the above quote. Zavatta writes,

> These new words, insofar as they will prove useful and be shared by more and more persons, will then become new 'habits of sensation'. In other words, these names then become the new matrix for the vision of the world shared by a certain linguistic community.[70]

Although language constrains what can be thought, our ability to change our language offers a way to change what is thinkable.

According to Nietzsche, shifts in meaning and language use are simply part of how language functions. Nietzsche quotes Horace as evidence that meaning is use,

> Many terms that have fallen out of use shall be born again, and those shall fall that are now in repute, if Usage [sic] so will it, in whose hands lies the judgment, the right and rule of speech.[71]

---

[67] DAR p. 67.

[68] This term is often used to discuss the "choice" in political elections in German.

[69] DAR p. 25.

[70] Zavatta, "From Pure Reason to Historical Knowledge," 60.

[71] DAR p. 49.

Language and meaning are therefore always in a continual process of changing forms. Nietzsche writes, "The wondrous process of choosing *[Auswahl]* new forms of language always continues."[72] The activity of choosing is something foundational to Nietzsche's philosophy of language. These choices are not made by a radically independent autonomous agent divorced from society. Rather, conditioned upon the genesis of language itself, choice exists within the complex social dynamics between language innovators and a linguistic community.

One concern we might have is that Nietzsche seems to be proposing an evolutionary causal determinism in tension with his social ontology. However, Nietzsche's claims about genesis of language are not causally determinist but, rather, are a form of genealogical argumentation against the doctrine of names.[73] His genealogical method gives a historical reconstruction of how something we assume to be universal and ahistorical came to be. For example, if one can historically explain how belief in God arose and came into existence, then one need not presuppose God's existence to be a universal *a priori* truth. If something came to be, like language, then it is not universal. Nietzsche considers these kinds of historical "refutations" definitive.[74] Nietzsche's genealogical refutation of the doctrine of names is not an embrace of causal determinism. The tension between his genealogical method and his social epistemology only remains if one maintains, as some scholars do, that Nietzsche is some sort of causal determinist.

---

[72] DAR p. 51.

[73] Although Nietzsche sometimes uses quasi-Darwinian language, he clearly does not accept an evolutionary biological determinism that excludes social processes. Nietzsche's relationship to Darwin is much too complex to explicate here but discussions of this relationship can be found in Dirk Johnson, John Richardson, and George Stack (Dirk R. Johnson, *Nietzsche's Anti-Darwinism* (New York: Cambridge University Press, 2010); John Richardson, *Nietzsche's New Darwinism* (New York: Oxford University Press, 2004); George J. Stack, *Lange and Nietzsche* (Berlin: Walter de Gruyter, 1983), 156-194 [Chapter VII: Darwin and Teleology]; cf. GS 110, 112, 349; GM Pref. 7).

[74] D 95

Some scholars, such as Brian Leiter and Robin Small, simply suggest that Nietzsche is a causal determinist.[75] However, Nietzsche explicitly rejects this view as reification and misuse of cause and effect.[76]

In response to determinist interpretations of Nietzsche's philosophy, some have argued that Nietzsche offers various kinds of compatibilism including: fatalistic compatibilism, middle-voice compatibilism, Aristotelian compatibilism, and even Humean compatibilism.[77] The large number of compatibilist views ascribed to Nietzsche is due, at least in part, to Nietzsche's reluctance to join a debate he sees as fundamentally misguided. Aaron Ridley writes, "Nowhere...does Nietzsche even hint at what sort of compatibilism he might have in mind."[78] Ridley argues convincingly that Nietzsche is not particularly interested in the constraints of physical causation but rather other things which constrain our lives.[79] A serious lack in Ridley's argument is that he does not consider how such constraints developed out of Nietzsche's philosophy of language.

For Nietzsche, the whole debate between free will and determinism functions mythologically based upon our laws of agreement within our linguistic culture; our sign-world. The debate mistakes our social linguistic world, our "sign-world", for the world as it is in-itself. Nietzsche argues that when we engage in such a debate, "we're still doing things as we've

---

[75] Brian Leiter, *Nietzsche on Morality* (New York: Routledge, 2002), 83; Robin Small. *Nietzsche and Rée: A Star Friendship* (New York: Oxford University Press, 2005), 92.

[76] BGE 21.

[77] Fatalistic compatibilism: R. Lanier Anderson, "Nietzsche on Autonomy," in *The Oxford Handbook of Nietzsche*, eds. Ken Gemes and John Richardson (New York: Oxford University Press, 2013), 431-460; Robert Solomon, *Living with Nietzsche: What the Immoralist Has to Teach Us* (New York: Oxford University Press, 2003), 178; cf. Ivan Soll, "Reflections on Recurrence: A Re-examination of Nietzsche's Doctrine, *Die Ewige Wiederkehr des Gleichen,*" in *Nietzsche: Critical Assessments, Vol II: 'The World as Will to Power and Nothing Else?': Metaphysics and Epistemology*, eds. Daniel W. Conway and Peter S. Groff (New York: Routledge, 1998), 379. Middle-voice compatibilism: Lawrence Hatab, *Nietzsche's Life Sentence: Coming to Terms with Eternal Recurrence* (New York: Rutledge, 2005), 127,133. Aristotelian compatibilism: Daw-Nay Evans, *Nietzsche and Classical Greek Philosophy: Beautiful and Diseased* (New York: Lexington Books, 2017), 80f. Humean compatibilism: Maudemarie Clark, *Nietzsche on Ethics and Politics* (New York: Oxford University Press, 2015), 76.

[78] Aaron Ridley, "Nietzsche on Art and Freedom," *European Journal of Philosophy* 15, no. 2 (2007): 206.

[79] Ridley, "Nietzsche on Art and Freedom," 206-208.

always done them, namely *mythologically.*[80] That is, the debate between free will and determinism claims to be about the world as it is in-itself. Nietzsche, on the other hand, sees this debate as presupposing certain linguistic prejudices, such as cause and effect, and treating them as if they are accessible *a priori.*

This opens Nietzsche to criticism that he is flirting with linguistic determinism or a linguistic idealism and leaves no room for choice at all. However, most scholars concur that while Nietzsche argues language constrains our thought and actions, it does not completely determine our choices.[81]

Nietzsche rejects the canonical debate between free-will and causal determinism and is more interested in the historical constraints and social pressures that influence our actions. A closer analysis of Nietzsche's philosophy of language reveals that these social constrains function within the "sign-world" of linguistic practice.

Nietzsche's philosophy of language necessitates that there is "choice" that is made democratically within linguistic communities. This choice necessitates some notion of freedom, within the social and political realm of meaning creation within language.

III. "Choice" as Political Freedom

At the end of the first essay of *Genealogy of Morals* Nietzsche suggests a question for an academic prize-essay contest: "What light does linguistics, and especially the study of etymology, throw on the history and evolution [*Entwicklungsgeschichte*] of moral concepts?"[82] This question asks to what

---

[80] BGE 21.

[81] Cf. John Llewelyn, *Margins of Religion: Between Kierkegaard and Derrida* (Bloomington: Indiana University Press, 2009), 115; Zavatta, "From Pure Reason to Historical Knowledge," 60; Alex Pichler, "'Kant: or Cant as Intelligible Character," in *Nietzsche's Engagement with Kant and the Kantian Legacy. Volume I. Nietzsche, Kant and the Problem of Metaphysics,* eds. Marco Brussotti, Herman Siemens, Joao Constancio, and Tom Bailey (New York: Bloomsbury, 2017), 247; David McNalley, *Bodies of Meaning: Studies on Language, Labor, and Liberation* (New York: State University of New York Press, 2001), 32-33; Will Dudley, *Hegel, Nietzsche, and Philosophy: Thinking Freedom* (New York: Cambridge University Press, 2004), 223.

[82] GM I 17. "Entwicklungsgeschichte" might be better translated as "developmental history" rather than "history and evolution" (Matthew Meyer, *Nietzsche's Free Spirit Works: A Dialectical Reading* (Cambridge: Cambridge University Press, 2019), 54).

extent the history of language tells us something about the history of morality.

Nietzsche, of course, already has an answer in mind. For Nietzsche, a change in language points to a conceptual transformation in morality. Nietzsche argues, "The signpost to the *right* road was for me the question: what was the real etymological significance of the designations for "good" coined in various languages? I found they all led back to the *same conceptual transformation.*"[83] This implies that a change in concepts prompts a change in language.

However, for Nietzsche this relationship between concepts and language is not one-directional. The language, words, and grammar available to us change, and this changes the constraints on our possible forms of thought and concepts. Throughout Nietzsche's career he struggled with the boundary conditions language placed on thought and he strove to create a "new language."[84] This is what all "artists of language" strive to do.[85] By creating new languages, new form of expression, linguistic geniuses open the possibility to new kinds of thinking.

These new languages are clumsy and tend to fall back into old prejudices.[86] However, Nietzsche is clear that the creation of a new kind of language allows for a new kind of thinking and vice versa. The development of language and thinking are dynamically intertwined or, to use a Nietzschean phrase, "go hand in hand."[87]

For Nietzsche, language use is a battleground for what is thinkable. A battleground where the exceptional individuals propose new languages and the rest of society express their choices. The changes in language Nietzsche investigates in the *Genealogy of Morals* reflect what Nietzsche calls

---

[83] GM I 4.

[84] BGE 4.

[85] Friedrich Nietzsche, *Unpublished Fragments (Spring 1885-Spring 1886), The Complete Works of Friedrich Nietzsche vol. 16*, trans. Adrian Del Caro (Stanford: Stanford University Press, 2020), 34[124] (p. 36); Friedrich Nietzsche, *Unpublished Fragments from the Period of Thus Spoke Zarathustra (Summer 1882-Winter 1883/84), The Complete Works of Friedrich Nietzsche vol. 14*, trans. Paul S. Loeb and David F. Tinsley (Stanford: Stanford University Press, 2019), 9[23] (p. 313).

[86] [TI] Friedrich Nietzsche, *Twilight of the Idols* in *The Anti-Christ, Ecce Homo, Twilight of the Idols and Other Writings*, eds. Aaron Ridley and Judith Norman, trans. Judith Norman (Cambridge: Cambridge University Press, 2005), TI 5, BGE 24.

[87] GS 354.

"a truly *grand* politics."[88] Nietzsche is clear that individuals do not work in isolation when he writes,

> Language is neither the conscious work of individuals nor of a plurality....Language is much too complex to be the work of a single individual, much too unified to be the work of a mass; it is a complete organism.[89]

He reiterates this when he suggests the invention of the individual speech artist must be taken on board by a linguistic community in order to have an impact. He writes,

> Language is created by the individual speech artist, but it is determined by the fact that the taste of the many makes choices *[Auswahl]*. Only a very few individuals utter *Schemata* [figures] whose *virtus* [virtue, worth] becomes a guide for many....A figure which finds no buyer becomes an error.[90]

History and thought are not changed through the creation of new metaphors in isolation but through the adoption of new metaphors by a linguistic community. If a new metaphor is not picked up by anyone, if it finds no buyers, it cannot have a political impact at all.

Nietzsche is very clear that agreement within language is essentially a political kind of agreement; a kind of "peace treaty" about the meaning of words.[91] Nietzsche argues that the origin of language is itself an expression of power.[92] He writes about naming things, "they say 'this *is* thus and such,' they seal everything and occurrence with a sound and thereby take possession of it so to speak."[93] To name something is a form of power and a form of "grand" politics. To have the freedom and power to name, to choose names, is therefore a kind of political power over one's world.

Nietzsche assigns artists of language and linguistic geniuses a kind of political power through naming. However, these innovators have no power unless their innovations are taken up by linguistic communities. Even though our experiences are unique, when we place them into words they become "governed" or "outvoted" [*majorsirt*] by the linguistic perspective

---

[88] GM I 8.
[89] OL 209.
[90] DAR 25.
[91] TL 1, cf. "law of agreement" GS 73, "great politics of revenge" GM I 8.
[92] GM I 2.
[93] GM I 2.

of the many.[94] It is of course true that linguistic geniuses can create a new turn of phrase, a new name, or a new figure that molds language to their world view. However, whether that new expression is integrated into our language, and thus our thinking, "is determined by the fact that the taste of the many makes choices [Auswahl]."[95] This is the democratic flipside of Nietzsche's philosophy of language. The political freedom to decide which linguistic innovations stick is simply not in the hands of a few masters but is constituted democratically within a linguistic community.

Nietzsche's elitism leads him to nausea regarding this possibility and he even advocates illiteracy to avoid it.[96] It is nevertheless a necessary consequence of his philosophy of language that there is a form of linguistic political freedom democratically available to everyone in a linguistic community.

Political freedom exists within the small and seemingly non-crucial linguistic choices at the linchpins in language. Through our small choices within individual discourses we can collectively change the history of events and the history of thought and morality.

Those who are not world-changing figures or linguistic geniuses can still express a form of limited political freedom in their choice of words. One is free enough to choose between using the words "dwarf", "small person", and "midget." One is free enough to make a political decision to use the word "rape" instead of "non-consensual intercourse." When we choose to refer to someone by their chosen pronoun, that is a political choice that affirms their political identity. When one uses the name of the land given by their native ancestors rather than simply "Indian Country"

---

[94] GS 354 "governed"—Kaufmann translation. "Outvoted"—Nauckhoff translation.

[95] DAR 25.

[96] Nietzsche makes many disparaging comments about newspapers and a reading public because they have power over language ([Z] Friedrich Nietzsche, *Thus Spoke Zarathustra: A Book for All and None*, trans. Adrian Del Caro (Cambridge: Cambridge University Press, 2006), Z III 7; GM III 26, BGE 58, 254; HAH II 320). He further goes on to advocate against a literate public and even against the printing press. Nietzsche even suggests the freedom of the press and freedom of thought are ruinous (Nietzsche, *Unpublished Fragments (Spring 1885-Spring 1886)*, 34[65] (p. 16)). He writes, "That everyone may learn to read in the long run corrupts not only writing but also thinking" (Z I 7). He writes, "what significance can we then concede to the press, as it now exists, with its daily expenditure of lungpower for screaming, for deafening, for simulating, for frightening—it is anything more than *perpetual blind noise* that turns the ears and other senses in a false direction?" (HAH II 321).

as established under the US legal system,[97] that is an expression of political freedom and resistance. When, in the face of genocide, one affirms the "Rohingya" as a class of people in Myanmar, that is a form of political freedom expressed linguistically. The opposite of these choices is also expression of a limited form of linguistic political freedom.

Linguistically, these are only small inconsequential choices for one person. However, becoming critical and thinking carefully about the words we use allows us a limited form of democratic political freedom within Nietzsche's philosophy of language. The choice to make a small linguistic change, to become a "buyer" of a figure of speech, is a form of political freedom. These small linguistic choices, if reproduced on a mass scale, change our larger political language and landscape.

If we attend to our small linguistic choices this allows us to reflect upon our own circumstances and the circumstances of others in our linguistic community. When we speak with others and are thoughtful in our word choices, we can collectively make an impact, however individually small, upon the grand political and ethical stakes at risk.[98]

Nietzsche is very clear that the history of language reflects the history of our conceptual moral transformations. He is also clear that changes in language change our thoughts and moral outlook. When we choose our words with care at those junctures where the world is linguistically in tension between equally viable choices, we express something akin to political freedom that collectively can move the world.

Works Cited

Abbey, Ruth. *Nietzsche's Middle Period*. New York: Oxford University Press, 2000.

Acampora, Christa Davis. "On Sovereignty and Overhumanity: Why it Matters How We Read Nietzsche's Genealogy 11:2." In *Nietzsche's On the Genealogy of Morals: Critical Essays*, edited by Christa Davis Acampora, 147-63. New York: Rowman & Littlefield Publishers, 2006.

Ackermann, Robert, "Current American Thought on Nietzsche." In *Nietzsche heute, Die Rezeption seines Werks nach 1968*, edited by Sigrid

---

[97] 18 U.S.C Sec. 1151.

[98] One important consideration is how systemic and institutional power relations can impact the linguistic choices that reinscribe oppressive hierarchies and the logic of domination. This, however, goes beyond the scope of this essay.

Bauschinger, Susan L. Cocalis and Sara Lennox, 129-36. Bern, Switzerland: A. Franke Verlag, 1988.

Anderson, R. Lanier. "Nietzsche on Autonomy." In *The Oxford Handbook of Nietzsche,* edited by Ken Gemes and John Richardson, 431-60. New York: Oxford University Press, 2013.

Ansell-Pearson, Keith. *An Introduction to Nietzsche as Political Thinker: The Perfect Nihilist.* New York: Cambridge University Press, 1994.

Bergmann, Peter. *Nietzsche, "The Last Antipolitical German."* Bloomington: Indiana University Press, 1987)

Clark, Maudemarie. *Nietzsche on Ethics and Politics.* New York: Oxford University Press, 2015.

Cominos, Marina. "The Question of Nietzsche's Anti-Politics and Human Transfiguration." In *Nietzsche, Power and Politics: Rethinking Nietzsche's Legacy for Political Thought,* edited by Herman Siemens and Vasti Roodt, 85-109. New York: Walter de Gruyter, 2009.

Dudley, Will. *Hegel, Nietzsche, and Philosophy: Thinking Freedom.* New York: Cambridge University Press, 2004.

Evans, Daw-Nay. *Nietzsche and Classical Greek Philosophy: Beautiful and Diseased.* New York: Lexington Books, 2017.

Gemes, Ken. "Nietzsche on Free Will, Autonomy, and the Sovereign Individual." In *Nietzsche On Freedom and Autonomy,* edited by Ken Gemes and Simon May, 33-50. New York: Oxford University Press, 2009.

Hatab, Lawrence. *Nietzsche's 'On the Genealogy of Morality': An Introduction.* New York: Cambridge University Press, 2008.

———. *Nietzsche's Life Sentence: Coming to Terms with Eternal Recurrence.* New York: Rutledge, 2005.

Havas, Randall. *Nietzsche's Genealogy: Nihilism and the Will to Knowledge.* New York: Cornell University Press, 2000.

Hussein, Nadeem J. Z. "The Role of Life in the Genealogy." In *Nietzsche's On the Genealogy of Morality: A Critical Guide,* edited by Simon May, 142-69. Cambridge: Cambridge University Press, 2011.

Johnson, Dirk R. *Nietzsche's Anti-Darwinism.* New York: Cambridge University Press, 2010.

Kaufmann, Walter. *Nietzsche: Philosopher, Psychologist, Antichrist.* New Jersey: Princeton University Press, 1974.

Leiter, Brian. *Nietzsche on Morality.* New York: Routledge, 2002.

Llewelyn, John. *Margins of Religion: Between Kierkegaard and Derrida.* Bloomington: Indiana University Press, 2009.

May, Simon. *Nietzsche's Ethics and his War on 'Morality'.* New York: Oxford University Press, 1999.

McNalley, David. *Bodies of Meaning: Studies on Language, Labor, and Liberation.* New York: State University of New York Press, 2001.

Meyer, Matthew. *Nietzsche's Free Spirit Works: A Dialectical Reading.* Cambridge: Cambridge University Press, 2019.

Nietzsche, Friedrich. [BGE] *Beyond Good and Evil.* In *Beyond Good and Evil/On the Genealogy of Morality. The Complete Works of Friedrich Nietzsche Vol 8.* Translated by Adrian Del Caro, 1-203. Stanford: Stanford University Press, 2014.

———. [BT] *The Birth of Tragedy.* In *The Birth of Tragedy and Other Writings.* Edited by Raymond Geuss and Ronald Speirs. Translated by Ronald Speirs, 1-116. Cambridge: Cambridge University Press, 1999.

———. [D] *Dawn. The Complete Works of Friedrich Nietzsche vol. 5.* Translated by Brittain Smith with afterword by Keith Ansell-Pearson. Stanford: Stanford University Press, 2011.

———. [DAR] "Description of Ancient Rhetoric." In *Friedrich Nietzsche on Rhetoric and Language,* edited and translated by Sanders L. Gilman, Carol Blair, and David J. Parent, 2-294. New York: Oxford University Press, 1989.

———. [EH] *Ecce Homo.* In *The Anti-Christ, Ecce Homo, Twilight of the Idols and Other Writings,* edited by Aaron Ridley and Judith Norman, translated by Judith Norman, 69-151. Cambridge: Cambridge University Press, 2005.

———. *[GM] On the Genealogy of Morality.* In *Beyond Good and Evil/On the Genealogy of Morality. The Complete Works of Friedrich Nietzsche vol. 8.,* translated by Adrian Del Caro, 205-349. Stanford: Stanford University Press, 2014.

———. [GS] *The Gay Science: With Prelude in German Rhymes and Appendix of Songs.* Translated by Josefine Nauckhoff. Cambridge: Cambridge University Press, 2001.

———. [HAH I] *Human, All-Too-Human. The Complete Works of Friedrich Nietzsche vol. 3.* Translated by Gary Handwerk. Stanford: Stanford University Press, 1995.

———. [HAH II] *Human, All-Too-Human II and Unpublished Fragments from the Period of Human, All Too Human II (Spring 1878-Fall 1879). The Complete Works of Friedrich Nietzsche Vol. 4.* Translated by Gary Handwerk. Stanford: Stanford University Press, 2013.

———. [LN] *Writings from the Late Notebooks.* Edited by Rüdiger Bittner. Translated by Kate Sturge. New York: Cambridge University Press, 2003.

———. [OL] "On the Origin of Language." In *Friedrich Nietzsche on Rhetoric and Language,* edited and translated by Sanders L. Gilman, Carol

Blair and David J. Parent, 209-12. New York: Oxford University Press, 1989.

———. [PT] *Philosophy and Truth: Selections from Nietzsche's Notebooks of the Early 1870's*. Edited and translated by Daniel Breazeale. New York: Humanity Books, 1979.

———. [TI] *Twilight of the Idols*. In *The Anti-Christ, Ecce Homo, Twilight of the Idols and Other Writings*, edited by Aaron Ridley and Judith Norman, translated by Judith Norman. Cambridge: Cambridge University Press, 2005.

———. [TL] "Truth and Lying in a Non-Moral Sense." In *The Birth of Tragedy and Other Writings*, edited by Raymond Geuss and Ronald Speirs, translated by Ronald Speirs, 139-54. Cambridge: Cambridge University Press, 1999.

———. *Unpublished Fragments (Spring 1885-Spring 1886). The Complete Works of Friedrich Nietzsche vol. 16*. Translated by Adrian Del Caro. Stanford: Stanford University Press, 2020.

———. *Unpublished Fragments from the Period of Thus Spoke Zarathustra (Summer 1882-Winter1883/84). The Complete Works of Friedrich Nietzsche vol. 14*. Translated by Paul S. Loeb and David F. Tinsley. Stanford: Stanford University Press, 2019.

———. [Z] *Thus Spoke Zarathustra: A Book for All and None*. Translated by Adrian Del Caro. Cambridge: Cambridge University Press, 2006.

Pichler, Alex. "Kant: or Cant as Intelligible Character." In *Nietzsche's Engagement with Kant and the Kantian Legacy. Volume I. Nietzsche, Kant and the Problem of Metaphysics*, edited by Marco Brussotti, Herman Siemens, Joao Constancio, and Tom Bailey, 233-54. New York: Bloomsbury, 2017.

Plato. "Cratylus." In *Plato Complete Works*, edited by John M. Cooper. Indianapolis: Hackett Publishing Company, 1997.

Poellner, Peter. "Nietzschean Freedom." In *Nietzsche on Freedom and Autonomy*, edited by Ken Gemes and Simon May, 151-80. New York: Oxford University Press, 2009.

Ratner-Rosenhagen, Jennifer. *American Nietzsche: A History of an Icon and His Ideas*. Chicago: University of Chicago Press, 2012.

Richardson, John. "Nietzsche's Freedoms." In *Nietzsche on Freedom and Autonomy*, edited by Ken Gemes and Simon May, 127-50. New York: Oxford University Press, 2009.

———. *Nietzsche's New Darwinism*. New York: Oxford University Press, 2004.

Ridley, Aaron. *Nietzsche's Conscience: Six Character Studies from the "Genealogy"*. London, Cornell University Press, 1998.

———. "Nietzsche on Art and Freedom." *European Journal of Philosophy* 15, no. 2 (2007): 204-24.

Rynhold, Daniel, and Michael J. Harris. *Nietzsche, Soloveitchik and Contemporary Jewish Philosophy*. New York: Cambridge University Press, 2018.

Small, Robin. *Nietzsche and Rée: A Star Friendship*. New York: Oxford University Press, 2005.

Soll, Ivan. "Reflections on Recurrence: A Re-examination of Nietzsche's Doctrine, *Die Ewige Wiederkehr des Gleichen.*" In *Nietzsche: Critical Assessments. Vol II: 'The World as Will to Power and Nothing Else?'. Metaphysics and Epistemology*, edited by Daniel W. Conway and Peter S. Groff, 175-83. New York: Routledge, 1998.

Solomon, Robert. *Living with Nietzsche: What the Immoralist Has to Teach Us*. New York: Oxford University Press, 2003.

Stack, George J. *Lange and Nietzsche*. Berlin: Walter de Gruyter, 1983.

Thiele, Leslie Paul. *Friedrich Nietzsche and the Politics of the Soul: A Study of Heroic Individualism*. Princeton: Princeton University Press, 1990.

Zavatta, Benedetta. "From Pure Reason to Historical Knowledge." In *Nietzsche's Engagement with Kant and the Kantian Legacy. Volume I. Nietzsche, Kant and the Problem of Metaphysics*, edited by Marco Brussotti, Herman Siemens, Joao Constancio, and Tom Bailey, 45-70. New York: Bloomsbury, 2017.

4.

Hannah Arendt's Notion of Political Freedom

Pablo Munoz Iturrieta

Hannah Arendt (1906-1975) was one of the most influential political philosophers of the twentieth century, and her intellectual legacy seems destined to last, as her observations and criticism are as timely as ever. She was born into a German-Jewish family, and, for that reason, she was forced to leave Germany in 1933. She lived in Paris for the next eight years, and, in 1941, she immigrated to the United States, where she soon became part of New York's intellectual circle. Arendt held a number of academic positions at various American universities until her death in 1975. Without a doubt her political work now belongs to the classics of the Western tradition of political thought. Yet, Arendt's political philosophy cannot be characterized in terms of the traditional categories of conservatism, liberalism, and socialism. Arendt's political theory arose as a response to the threat of totalitarianism against freedom.[1] Freedom is also central to her political thought, though Arendt elaborates a distinct concept of freedom as "political freedom" which provides a focus for this chapter.

For Arendt, political participation through word and deed is the highest type of freedom. This is what she means by "political freedom," a freedom manifested in the context of a community, and distinct from "inner freedom" or freedom of the will. Yet, the modern political system of representation sets the people aside when supposedly governing "for" the people and "by" the people. The main dichotomy in contemporary politics, from Arendt's perspective, is not left versus right, or liberal versus conservative, but government against the people they are supposed to represent. In order to remedy this shortcoming of contemporary politics, Arendt proposes a system of councils with direct citizen representation, which will give everyone an opportunity to exercise their political freedom and effectively determine their own political affairs. Thus, this chapter will

---

[1] Cf. Hannah Arendt, *Essays in Understanding, 1930-1954* (New York: Harcourt, Brace & Co., 1994), 310. She states: "our fight against it [totalitarianism] is a fight for freedom."

explore how Arendt's conception of political freedom offers an alternative ideal and a compelling way forward in contrast to today's political stage, which resembles more an arena where combatants fight each other in an aggressive, pseudo-intellectual, zero sum battle.[2] Is the contemporary polarized political arena, in the US in particular, what the framers of the Constitution envisioned for the democratic process? As a response to the current political landscape, then, this chapter will present the value of Hannah Arendt's notion of political freedom as a resource to look to in the effort to move toward a better realization of political life and restoring optimal forms of political freedom.

I. Arendt's Notion of Political Freedom

Arendt's encounter with the totalitarian ideologies of the mid-twentieth century led her to develop the idea of political freedom as a way to avoid such catastrophes in the future.[3] The ordered and stable context in which people once lived was destroyed by the First World War and the Great Depression leading to insecurity, unrest, and the need for stability and order. This opened the door to totalitarian ideologies to garner popular support to mobilize and control populations. It is in this context that the totalitarian ideologies of the twentieth century made their way to taking power and killing millions in the attempt. For Arendt, what allowed for the entrance of totalitarian ideas into the public sphere was the erosion of the political sphere as a space of freedom. Thus, in order to prevent a return of totalitarianism, it was imperative for her that we find and establish the conditions and institutions for a public life that is able to unite citizens while respecting their autonomy and diverse characters and cultures.

What is political freedom for Hannah Arendt? She thought of political freedom as a phenomenon of virtuosity which takes place in a public stage or space as a politically guaranteed public field of activity.[4] Arendt

---

[2] Unlike the times prior to the Internet Era, nowadays the community gathers around online spaces to celebrate every blow inflicted through a few characters on social media, and most people seem to believe they are also entitled to attack from every possible angle. Reasonable discussion seems sadly to be a thing of the past. Is the freedom to engage in this battle truly political freedom? Arendt's views certainly throw light on these contemporary issues.

[3] See Hannah Arendt, *The Origins of Totalitarianism* (New York: Harcourt, 1985).

[4] Cf. Hannah Arendt, "Freedom and Politics," in *Freedom and Serfdom*, ed. A. Hunold (Dordrecht: Riedel, 1961), 192.

claims that this was the original experience of freedom in ancient Greece and Rome. Only when the view of freedom as a phenomenon of virtuosity had in practice disappeared in the late Roman Empire, was freedom then understood in connection with the will, which has come to be the prevailing understanding of freedom in the modern era. However, freedom as a phenomenon of virtuosity continued to exist, she argues, in a hidden form in all human activities. And this political freedom, for Arendt, was especially embodied in the councils formed during revolutionary periods, which offered real political participation to every citizen, as they were able to effectively determine their own political affairs.

In her "What is Freedom?" (1961), Hannah Arendt bluntly states that to define freedom is a seemingly hopeless enterprise, the last of the time-honored great metaphysical questions to become the subject of philosophical debate. In the article, Arendt bases her treatment of freedom not on philosophical and metaphysical arguments, but on evidence of the experience of freedom as a living, worldly, political reality.[5]

Arendt notes that the first appearances of freedom in the Western philosophical tradition had to do with experiences of religious conversion which gave rise to freedom as a philosophical concept: that of Paul, and then Augustine. In those mystical experiences, these men discovered the will not so much as powerful but as an impotent capacity within us. Only when this kind of inner freedom was discovered, a kind of freedom which had no relation to politics and community decisions, did the concept of freedom enter the history of philosophy. Thus, historically, freedom became one of the chief problems of philosophy when it was experienced as an internal reality, outside the relations between men. In this way, free will and freedom became synonymous notions.[6] Arendt defines this type of freedom in the Augustinian sense of "free choice" (*liberum arbitrium*), "a freedom of choice that arbitrates and decides between two given things, one good and one evil, and whose choice is predetermined by motive which has only to be argued to start its operation."[7]

---

[5] Hannah Arendt, "What Is Freedom?," in *Between Past and Future* (New York: Penguin, 1961), 143. See also Hannah Arendt, "Freedom and Politics: A Lecture," *Chicago Review* 14, no. 1 (1960): 28-46.

[6] Cf. Arendt, 145-46. Historically, however, the presence of freedom in philosophy was much more complex. See also Hannah Arendt, *The Life of the Mind, vol. 2: Willing*, ed. Mary McCarthy (New York: Harcourt Brace Jovanovich, 1978), 68.

[7] Arendt, 151. For Arendt's own account of her theory of the will as an inner reality, see Arendt, *The Life of the Mind*.

In ancient Greece, however, freedom was a purely political concept, at the core of the city-state and citizenship. Yet, this idea of freedom as the center of politics, as the Greeks understood it, was an idea which did not enter the framework of Greek philosophy.[8] It is to this notion of freedom as related to politics that Arendt wishes to return, and in order to do so, Arendt makes a strong case for a revival of "political freedom."

In order to clarify what she means by "political freedom," Arendt distinguishes between inner freedom, and external or political freedom. Inner freedom is the inward space into which men may escape from external coercion and feel free. It is in this sense that the philosophical tradition has addressed the question of freedom. Understood in this way, freedom of the will is relevant when considered outside a political community and in reference to solitary individuals. The freedom of political theory, on the other hand, is the very opposite of "inner freedom." Men are citizens of political communities, which are produced and preserved by laws, which in turn shape various forms of government. Even though these forms of government constrain the free will of citizens, they all open up a space of freedom for action which sets the city in motion, except in the case of tyranny where one arbitrary will rules the destiny of all.[9] Thus, political freedom "can manifest only in communities, where the many who live together have their intercourse both in word and in deed regulated by a great number of rapports—laws, customs, habits, and the like."[10] However important inner and nonpolitical freedom may seem to be, Arendt argues that:

> Man would know nothing of inner freedom if he had not first experienced a condition of being free as a worldly tangible reality. We first become aware of freedom or its opposite in our intercourse with others, not in the intercourse with ourselves. Before it became

---

[8] The way of life chosen by the philosophers was understood by many philosophical schools as in opposition to the political way of life. The philosophers' abstention from politics was seen as a prerequisite for the contemplative life, the highest and freest way of life. This Greek understanding of philosophy is found in Habermas, for example, who distinguishes between the philosopher and the politician, to the point that intellectuals cease to be intellectuals once they assume public office. See Jürgen Habermas, *Zwischen Naturalismus und Religion: Philosophische Aufsätze* (Frankfurt am Main: Suhrkamp, 2005), 26.

[9] Cf. Arendt, *The Life of the Mind*, 199.

[10] Arendt, 200.

an attribute of thought or a quality of the will, freedom was understood to be the free man's status, which enabled him to move, to get away from home, to go out into the world and meet other people in deed and word.[11]

Arendt, then, does not reject the importance and reality of inner freedom, as is clear by her monumental work on "Willing,"[12] but claims that the original field of freedom is in the realm of politics and human affairs in general, for freedom of movement is the most elementary of all freedoms.[13] In order to see this point, Arendt reminds the reader that, in ancient Greece, the political realm was distinguished from the household, which belonged to the private realm.[14] In the household, one did not experience freedom in a political sense, for the household had to deal with the necessities of life (such as food), and its members were either in command (the head of the household), or under the command of another.[15] Arendt notes that to be free "meant neither to rule nor to be ruled."[16] Only when one has solved the basic problem of survival is it possible to venture into the realm of politics. Thus, "political freedom is possible only in the sphere of human plurality."[17] In a recently published lecture titled "The Freedom to be Free," Arendt states that: "Only those who know freedom from want can appreciate fully the meaning of freedom from fear, and only those who are free from both want and fear are in a position to conceive a passion for public freedom, to develop within themselves that *goût* or taste for *liberté* and the peculiar taste for *égalité* or equality that *liberté* carries within it."[18] While inner freedom is a mark of all human beings, even in

---

[11] Arendt, "What Is Freedom?," 148.

[12] See Arendt, *The Life of the Mind*.

[13] Cf. Arendt, "What Is Freedom?," 146. See also Arendt, *The Life of the Mind*, 200.

[14] Cf. Hannah Arendt, *The Human Condition* (Chicago: University of Chicago Press, 1958), 31. She states: "What all Greek philosophers, no matter how opposed to *polis* life, took for granted is that freedom is exclusively located in the political realm, that necessity is primarily a prepolitical phenomenon, characteristic of the private household organization, and that force and violence are justified in this sphere because they are the only means to master necessity . . . and to become free."

[15] Cf. Arendt, *The Human Condition*, 32.

[16] Arendt, 32.

[17] Arendt, *The Life of the Mind*, 200.

[18] Hannah Arendt, "The Freedom to Be Free," *The New England Review* 38, no. 2 (2017).

the state of slavery, Arendt's political freedom is only achieved in the public sphere once one has risen from want, necessity, and the rule of another.

When it comes to political matters, it seems a self-evident truth that man is free by nature, and therefore it is impossible not to at least assume that man is free, that freedom exists. It is for this reason that men are held responsible for their actions, and "it is upon this axiomatic assumption that laws are laid down in human communities, that decisions are taken, that judgments are passed."[19] At the same time, it is almost impossible not to touch political issues without touching upon issues of man's political freedom. Political life is meaningless without freedom. As Arendt affirms: "The *raison d'être* of politics is freedom, and its field of experience is action."[20] Even more, "freedom is exclusively located in the political realm."[21] One would have perhaps expected Arendt to say that freedom is "also" located or included in the political realm, yet she talks about an "exclusivity" of freedom within the public arena. Does it perhaps mean that "inner freedom" has no value for her? I think that the way this should be interpreted is in line with her consideration of the rise of "inner freedom" within philosophy: only when men were aware of their limitations, they became aware of this type of (philosophical) freedom. Inner freedom is a type of freedom, yet it is intimately connected to the experience of one's own limitation, and thus it is a secondary type of freedom. Inner freedom, however, is still operative within the basic and prior form of freedom, political freedom, which is expressed as "truly and totally free" in the public realm.

Therefore, before freedom became an attribute of thought or a quality of the will, it was understood to be the status of the free man. This freedom, or status, is what allowed man to liberate himself from the necessities of life and go out into the world and act in deed and word. As mentioned above, political freedom is located within the sphere of the *polis*, in opposition to the sphere of the household and family, which dealt with the necessities of life. Man had to liberate himself from want and need, that is,

---

[19] Arendt, "What Is Freedom?," 143. Thomas Aquinas affirms that this self-evidence of freedom is manifested in the fact that if it were otherwise, then counsels, exhortations, commands, prohibitions, rewards, and punishments would be in vain. See Thomas Aquinas, *Summa Theologiae*, ed. Fratrum Praedicatorum, Sancti Thomae de Aquino Opera omnia, Leonine edition, vol. 4-12, (Rome: Ex Typographia Polyglota S. C. De Propaganda Fide, 1882-1906), I, q. 83, a. 1.

[20] Arendt, 146.

[21] Arendt, *The Human Condition*, 31.

from the necessities of life, the realm of the household, in order to neither rule nor be ruled. It was only then that he could enter the public realm, that of the *polis*.

But how does it happen that man can free himself from the necessities of life and venture into the political realm? Arendt understands this liberation in terms of violence, as the pre-political act of liberating oneself from the necessity of life for the freedom of the world.[22] Why this reference to "violence"? Arendt was well aware of the danger and oppression exercised by totalitarian ideologies. Not long before the publication of her *The Origins of Totalitarianism*, Orwell had published the perhaps most well-known novel of the twentieth century: *1984*. Setting aside any possible influence of *1984* on Arendt's thought, in this dystopian novel, society is characterized by three elements: necessity and extreme poverty, a totalitarian form of government (the Party) impossible to overthrow, and the manipulation of language and speech to control society. These elements stand as antipodes to Arendt's conception of political freedom. Liberation, for Arendt, refers to the lifting of the biological and legal barriers to entering the public realm in order to act politically. One has to be free from want and necessity (biological barrier), and the political system has to allow one to be part of the public discussion (political and legal barrier). "Insoc", the political system that rules in *1984*, grants none of that. Orwell states that it is not only impossible for citizens to rise and fight against the Big Brother, but even unthinkable. Only violence, in a situation like this, would make this possible. And this is perhaps the reason why Arendt understands liberation in terms of violence. Even more, against the totalitarian danger of suppressing true speech, Arendt affirms that acting in public is mainly manifested through speech.[23] To be liberated is to have a status for political participation, and to be free is to make use of that status. Political participation, at the same time, means to be able to take part in deliberations, to be able to hold a public office, and be responsible for the actions taken while holding it, the ability to vote, etc.[24] In our contemporary context, it is important to consider Arendt's theory for establishing

---

[22] Cf. Arendt, 31; Hannah Arendt, *On Revolution* (New York: Viking Press, 1963); Arendt, "The Freedom to Be Free," 55-69.

[23] Cf. Hannah Arendt, *The Promise of Politics* (New York: Shocken Books, 2005), 168.

[24] Yet, one should keep in mind, when arguing for a place for "religion" in the political public square, that none of these acts that Arendt mentions have to do with the religious freedom of citizens.

stable political institutions that provide structural guarantees for the practice of the primary sort of political freedom she puts forward.

Arendt introduces an interesting element in her discussion on political freedom, that of sociability and of a public space: "Freedom needed, in addition to liberation, the company of other men who were in the same state, and it needed a common public space to meet them—a politically organized world, in other words, into which each of the free men could insert himself by word and deed."[25] However, freedom can make its appearance only if there is "a politically guaranteed public realm." Thus, "freedom as a demonstrable fact and politics coincide and are related to each other like two sides of the same matter."[26] The problem is that one cannot take for granted the coincidence of politics and freedom. Arendt's words regarding the totalitarian state are clear:

> The rise of totalitarianism, its claim to having subordinated all spheres of life to the demands of politics and its consistent nonrecognition of civil rights, above all the rights of privacy and the right to freedom from politics, makes us doubt not only the coincidence of politics and freedom, but their very compatibility.[27]

Totalitarianism attacked the liberal conception of the civil right to freedom, according to which "the less politics the more freedom."[28] It is this that she refers to as the totalitarian attack on the "right to freedom from politics." Yet, according to Arendt, not only the totalitarian position must be challenged in its attempt to deny civil rights, but also the liberal

---

[25] Arendt, "What Is Freedom?," 148.

[26] Arendt, 149.

[27] Arendt, 149. It is interesting to note that the decline of freedom in the late Roman Empire led to the attempt to divorce the notion of freedom from politics, so that one may be a slave in this world and still be free. Such is the case, for example, of Epictetus's formulation of freedom, according to which man is free if he does not reach into a realm where he can be hindered. See his "On Freedom" in Epictetus, *Discourses, Books 3-4. Fragments. The Encheiridion*, trans. W. A. Oldfather (Cambridge, MA: Harvard University Press, 1928), Bk IV, I, 1.

[28] Hannah Arendt, *Between Past and Future: Eight Exercises in Political Thought* (New York: Penguin Books, 2006), 148.

conception of freedom should be questioned as it separates freedom from politics.[29]

Arendt also accuses liberalism of having had its share in banishing freedom from the political realm by creating a gigantic sphere of social and economic life the liberal state must administer in order to take care of all of man's necessities.[30] One has to remember here once again the distinction between the realm of the *polis* and that of the household found in ancient Greece. In the modern nation-state, however, the dividing line was entirely blurred "because we see the body of peoples and political communities in the image of a family whose everyday affairs have to be taken care of by a gigantic, nation-wide administration of housekeeping."[31] Thus, Arendt states, "the collective of families economically organized into the facsimile of one super-human family is what we call 'society,' and its political form of organization is called 'nation'."[32] The fact that there is a "political economy," which in ancient Greece belonged to the household and would have meant a contradiction in terms, shows that there is a necessity, and therefore the room for political freedom is denied. In ancient Greece, "whatever was 'economic,' related to the life of the individual and the survival of the species, was a non-political, household affair by definition."[33]

How many people in today's world do, in fact, think that freedom begins where politics ends? That few do is the result when politics rules over every aspect of society. Arendt states:

> Indeed, do we not rightly measure the extent of freedom in any given community by the free scope it grants to apparently nonpolitical activities, free economic enterprise or freedom of teaching, of religion, of cultural and intellectual activities? Is it not true, as we all somehow believe, that politics is compatible with freedom only because and insofar as it guarantees a possible freedom from politics?[34]

---

[29] For a critical evaluation of Arendt's criticism of liberal freedom as "freedom from politics," see Kei Hiruta, "Hannah Arendt, Liberalism, and Freedom from Politics," in *Arendt on Freedom, Liberation, and Revolution*, ed. K. Hiruta, (Cham, Switzerland: Palgrave Macmillan, 2019), 17-45.

[30] Cf. Arendt, "What Is Freedom?," 155.

[31] Arendt, *The Human Condition*, 28.

[32] Arendt, 29.

[33] Arendt, 29.

[34] Arendt, "What Is Freedom?," 149.

Arendt's notion of freedom is radically different than liberal or socialist accounts of freedom, for, in her view, liberal accounts locate freedom within the private sphere, related to the private interests of the individual and as a freedom from politics, while totalitarianism denies civil rights altogether. As it will be shown, Arendt attempts to retrieve the experience of classical politics and reposition the phenomenon of freedom at the center of the public realm, for there is no political freedom unless citizens engage actively in the public realm and exercise an effective political agency.

II. Freedom as Virtuous Action

The separation of politics from freedom is in fact a fruit of the modern age. However, as mentioned above, political life is meaningless without freedom as related to action.[35] Arendt states: "Men *are* free—as distinguished from their possessing the gift for freedom—as long as they act, neither before nor after; for to *be* free and to act are the same."[36] Freedom, for Arendt, happens through action, which is essentially public. She states: "Because of its inherent tendency to disclose the agent together with the act, action needs for its full appearance the shining brightness we once called glory, and which is possible only in the public realm."[37] This kind of freedom, which is inherent to action, is, according to Arendt, best illustrated by the concept of "virtue," and its meaning best rendered by "virtuosity," that is, the "excellence we attribute to the performing arts (as distinguished from the creative arts of making), where the accomplishment lies in the performance itself and not in an end product which outlasts the activity that brought it into existence and becomes independent of it."[38] In politics, in fact, virtuosity of performance is decisive.

The metaphor based on the distinction between the performing arts and the creative arts of making that Arendt employs in order to explain political freedom is perfect, as it clearly shows what is at play in political activity. Without acting men, men that perform in the public square, there is no politics. Yet, in order to be true political action, virtuosity has to also

---

[35] She affirms: "We deal here not with the *liberum arbitrium*, a freedom of choice that arbitrates and decides between two given things, one good and one evil, and whose choice is predetermined by motive which has only to be argued to start its operation." Arendt, 151.

[36] Arendt, 153.

[37] Arendt, *The Human Condition*, 160.

[38] Arendt, "What Is Freedom?," 153.

be present. While the work of art as a product of making enjoys independent existence from its maker, performing artists need an audience to show their virtuosity, and a publicly organized space for their work. It is in this virtuous work or performance that political freedom is manifested. The Greek *polis*, in fact, was the form of government which provided men with a space of appearances where they could act, and it was in this theater that freedom could appear. It was in the *polis*, in fact, that the essence and the realm of the political and virtuosic freedom was first discovered. These ancient political communities were set up with the express intention of serving those that were free. This is what expresses best the relation of freedom to politics. Arendt states: "If, then, we understand the political in the sense of the *polis*, its end or *reason d'être* would be to establish and keep in existence a space where freedom as virtuosity can appear."[39] It is through these virtuous actions that freedom becomes a reality, "tangible in words which can be heard, in deeds which can be seen, and in events which are talked about, remembered, and turned into stories before they are finally incorporated into the great storybook of human history."[40]

For that reason, Arendt calls for a shift in the liberal conception of freedom. She denies that freedom is, in its primary sense, an attribute of will and thought rather than of action. Due to the modern inversion of the primary sense of freedom, "every attempt to derive the concept of freedom from experiences in the political realm sounds strange and startling."[41] And she laments:

> Because of the philosophic shift from action to will power, from freedom as a state of being manifest in action to the *liberum arbitrium*, the ideal of freedom ceased to be virtuosity...and became sovereignty, the ideal of a free will, independent from others and eventually prevailing against them.[42]

Thus, she claims that it is necessary to go back to antiquity, to its political and pre-philosophical traditions, "because a freedom experienced in the process of acting and nothing else...has never been again articulated

---

[39] Arendt, 154.

[40] Arendt, 154-55.

[41] Arendt, 155.

[42] Arendt, 163. Thus, for example, Rousseau derived his theory of sovereignty directly from the will, conceiving of political power in the image of individual will-power. See Jean-Jacques Rousseau, *The Social Contract*, trans. Willmoore Kendall (South Bend: Gateway, 1954), Bk II, ch. 1-4.

with the same classical clarity."[43] There is a need to revive a freedom understood as doing and acting in the political realm.

Now, from a phenomenological perspective, movement or action may be located in the physical and the mental realms. Arendt considers movement to be the very founding experience upon which the notion of freedom itself is derived.[44] When we locate movement in the physical realm, it is represented as action. When we locate movement in the mental realm, it is represented as judgment. If we were to join these two realms, then we obtain the activity of persuading others, that is, rhetoric. For Arendt, speech and debate with others in the political realm is one of the clearest manifestations of political freedom. She states: "Being able to persuade and influence others, which was how the citizens of the *polis* interacted politically, presumed a kind of freedom that was not irrevocably bound, either mentally or physically, to one's own standpoint or point of view."[45] This freedom also provides a way to deepen more into various possible perspectives on issues: "The ability to truly see topics from various sides . . . with the result that people understood how to assume the many possible perspectives provided by the real world, from which one and the same topic can be regarded and in which each topic, despite its oneness, appears in a great diversity of views."[46]

Since "inner freedom" is understood as a faculty or capacity to begin all human activities and the source of production of all things human, it always remains intact, even when political life disappears. Thus, one might be tempted to think that freedom is not fundamentally political. Yet, Arendt affirms that:

> Because the source of freedom remains present even when political life has become petrified and political action impotent to interrupt automatic processes, freedom can so easily be mistaken for an essentially nonpolitical phenomenon; in such circumstances, freedom is not experienced as a mode of being with its own kind of "virtue" and virtuosity, but as a supreme gift which only man, of all earthly creatures, seems to have received, of which we can find traces and signs in almost all his activities, but which, nevertheless, develops

---

[43] Arendt, 165.

[44] Cf. Arendt, *The Life of the Mind*, 200. She states: "Freedom of movement, the power of moving about unchecked by disease or master, was originally the most elementary of all liberties, their very prerequisite."

[45] Arendt, *The Promise of Politics*, 168.

[46] Arendt, 167-68.

fully only when action has created its own worldly space where it can come out of hiding, as it were, and makes its appearance.[47]

Thus, while philosophical or inner freedom emphasizes willing, political freedom emphasizes movement. In this way, one can understand that for Arendt political freedom includes within itself and fully manifests freedom of the will. And the proper place for political freedom to appear is in the *polis*, in the public sphere, and it is done through virtuous action. Thus, the excellence of action is constituted by virtue.

Now, from among the virtues that belong to the public realm, Arendt emphasizes courage, readiness to forgive, and commitment to promises, that is, the oath.[48] Courage is necessary in order to appear in public at all, and face the unpredictable outcome of one's acts, independently of any danger or hostility one may thus encounter.[49] Forgiving tempers the irreversibility of one's actions, for "without being forgiven, released from the consequences of what we have done, our capacity to act would, as it were, be confined to one single deed from which we could never recover; we would remain the victims of its consequences forever."[50] Promising tempers the unpredictability of one's actions.[51] And as a remedy for this unpredictability, we have the oath, the commitment to make reality that

---

[47] Arendt, "What Is Freedom?," 169.

[48] For the classical tradition, the oath is an act that belongs to the virtue of religion, and it is what enables all relationships, as they are based on "trust". Cf. Thomas Aquinas, *Summa Theologiae*, ed. Fratrum Praedicatorum, Opera omnia, Leonine edition, vol. 4-12, (Rome: Ex Typographia Polyglota S. C. De Propaganda Fide, 1882-1906), II-II, q. 89.

[49] Cf. Arendt, *The Human Condition*, 166; Arendt, "What Is Freedom?," 156. Arendt also affirms

"To leave the household, originally in order to embark upon some adventure and glorious enterprise and later simply to devote one's life to the affairs of the city, demanded courage because only in the household was one primarily concerned with one's own life and survival. Whoever entered the political realm had first to be ready to risk his life, and too great a love for life obstructed freedom, was a sure sign of slavishness. Courage therefore became the political virtue par excellence, and only those men who possessed it could be admitted to a fellowship that was political in content and purpose and thereby transcended the mere togetherness imposed on all— slaves, barbarians, and Greeks alike—through the urgencies of life."

Arendt, *The Human Condition*, 36.

[50] Arendt, *The Human Condition*, 237.

[51] Cf. Arendt, 243-437.

which one has verbally promised. The oath, we could well argue, is what made the political institutions of the West possible, and as such it is a central theme in political philosophy.[52]

What would be the proper place for political freedom to be disclosed? Arendt advocated in her book *On Revolution* a type of participatory democracy in the form of a citizen council, an "entirely new form of government with a new public space for freedom,"[53] and where "every individual found his own sphere of action."[54] This is an idea that certainly needs to be explored, especially at a time when citizens in general have lost their faith in political institutions, and where conflict needs to be resolved "on the lowest and most promising level of proximity and neighborliness."[55] According to Arendt, it is in times of change and revolutions that such councils spring "from the people as spontaneous organs of action and of order,"[56] and perhaps Arendt's idea of a system of councils is the alternative to the traditional liberal-democratic and Marxist conceptions of the state.[57] This idea was advanced by Thomas Jefferson himself, when he proposed that counties throughout the United States be subdivided into units small enough to permit citizens to conduct their politics on a face-to-face basis, as the US Constitution did not give the people any tangible way to actually participate in person in the process of governing.[58] Like Jefferson, Arendt

---

[52] For more on this theme see Giorgio Agamben, *The Sacrament of Language: An Archaeology of the Oath*, trans. Adam Kotsko (Stanford: Stanford University Press, 2011).

[53] Hannah Arendt, *On Revolution* (London: Penguin Books, 2006), 241.

[54] Arendt, *On Revolution*, 255.

[55] Hannah Arendt, *The Jewish Writings*, eds. J. Kohn and R. H. Feldman (New York: Schocken Books, 2007), 400. Arendt, in fact, first proposed the idea of community councils as a solution to the Jewish-Arab conflict in Palestine.

[56] Arendt, *On Revolution*, 263.

[57] Cf. Albrecht Wellmer, "Hannah Arendt on Revolution," in *Hannah Arendt in Jerusalem*, ed. Steven Aschheim (Berkeley: University of California Press, 2001), 34. For more on Arendt's idea of a "council system", see J.F. Sitton, "Hannah Arendt's Argument for Council Democracy," *Polity* 20, no. 1 (1987): 80-100; J. Muldoon, "The Lost Treasure of Arendt's Council System," *Critical Horizons* 12, no. 3 (2011): 396-417; Wolfhart Totschnig, "Arendt's Argument for the Council System: A Defense," *European Journal of Cultural and Political Sociology* 1, no. 3 (2014): 266-82; Shmuel Lederman, "The Centrality of the Council System in Arendt's Political Theory," in *Arendt on Freedom, Liberation, and Revolution*, ed. Kei Hiruta (Cham, Switzerland: Palgrave Macmillan, 2019), 253-76.

[58] See the letter from Thomas Jefferson to Joseph C. Cabell in Thomas Jefferson, *The Founders' Constitution*, eds. Andrew A. Lipscomb and Albert Ellery Bergh, 20

was a devoted civic republican, who considered the distribution of political power to people's councils as the only viable way for republican democracy to thrive and for political freedom to flourish. In fact, it was her fear of a return of totalitarian ideologies that led her to support a council democracy as a more suitable form of democratic government in multicultural societies.[59]

III. Some Objections to Arendt's Notion of Freedom

Arendt's notion of political freedom has been criticized as inherently individualistic, and her ideal of virtue as excessively egotistic, for it is expressed in terms of self-distinction, fame and immortality.[60] Arendt connects her notion of political freedom to the Greek notion of *arete*, the "excellence" that the Romans named *virtus*. This human excellence in acting, according to Arendt,

> has always been assigned to the public realm where one could excel, could distinguish oneself from all others. Every activity performed in public can attain an excellence never matched in privacy; for excellence, by definition, the presence of others is always required, and this presence needs the formality of the public, constituted by one's peers, it cannot be the casual, familiar presence of one's equals or inferiors.[61]

Thus, against the challenge of individualism and egotism, we see that, according to Arendt, what action realizes is neither a purely subjective nor a purely particular value, since it is interpreted by others and emerges in the act rather than just in the intention of the actor. Even more importantly, its internal goods are not a purely individual benefit, but a social good, with benefits to others and realizing principles beyond the actor. Arendt is not implying that virtuous actions simply need spectators, but rather that the exercise of virtue communicates and exemplifies to others

---

vols., vol. 1, The Writings of Thomas Jefferson, (Washington, D.C.: Thomas Jefferson Memorial Association, 1905), ch. 4, doc. 34, 421-23.

[59] For more on this see Shmuel Lederman, *Hannah Arendt and Participatory Democracy* (Cham, Switzerland: Palgrave Macmillan, 2019), 11-38.

[60] See, for example, Hannah Fenichel Pitkin, "Justice: On Relating Public and Private," *Political Theory* 9 (1981): 337; Mehmet Kanath, "The Concept of Freedom in Hannah Arendt's Political Thought," *Journal of Current Researches on Social Sciences* 7, no. 2 (2017): 108.

[61] Arendt, *The Human Condition*, 49.

excellence itself, motivating others to acts of courage, honor, justice, etc. Virtuous action is more than just displaying individual virtuosity, for those virtues that belong to the public sphere by nature transcend any narrow personal interests or egotism. Thus, examples of virtue expand our understanding of human possibilities in general, including the actor's own. It is for that reason that Arendt argues that virtuous individual development is only possible as part of a social endeavor.

In Ancient Greece and Rome, the idea of the hero occupied a central place in the education and transmission of values. The works of Homer and Virgil testify to this. In continuity with this tradition, Arendt borrows the idea of the hero not as someone who stands out against everyone else, but rather as someone who represents to everyone the potential extension of their capabilities through good acting. Thus, the actions of the hero, or in our case, the virtuous citizen, have "exemplary validity," as Arendt puts it.[62] Throughout history, in fact, people have become aware of and open to moral principles and virtues through the example of exceptional individuals. Arendt states: "Whenever we try to perform a deed of courage or of goodness, it is as though we imitated someone else."[63] And this is true not just of action in relation to virtue, but of speech as well. Public speech and argument seek the agreement of others, that is, their intellectual consent, and a good and true argument always enlightens the mind. Thus, speech is more than merely the opportunity to issue a statement of position, or to express oneself in public.[64] Speech as a performative action of political freedom brings within itself the power to transform minds and engage in public action for the betterment of society. This is an aspect much needed in contemporary political discourse: all citizens in a democracy should be able to engage in public speech and argument if they wish to do so.

Social media, however, has surprisingly limited this ability. I say surprisingly because one would have thought that by opening new avenues of communication, argumentation, and debate, the reaching of consensus

---

[62] Cf. Hannah Arendt, "Truth and Politics," in *Between Past and Future: Eight Exercises in Political Thought* (New York: Penguin Books, 2006), 247-8; Hannah Arendt and Ronald Beiner, *Lectures on Kant's Political Philosophy* (Brighton: Harvester, 1982), 76-77; Arendt, *The Life of the Mind*, 272.

[63] Arendt, "Truth and Politics," 248.

[64] Arendt states: "To be political, to live in a *polis*, meant that everything was decided through words and persuasion and not through force and violence." Arendt, *The Human Condition*, 26.

would reach an all-time high. This, sadly, has not been the case, as social media tends to be one-sided, impersonal, in a certain way dogmatic, and even aggressive towards those who think differently than others in the discussion. There is no real dialogue, face-to-face debate, or discussions over opinions in a virtuous manner, and this makes it hard for political freedom to flourish in our society.

This raises another point: Arendt's understanding of freedom is distinct from the liberal conception of freedom. Liberals, according to Arendt, describe the notion of freedom as something which can be practiced in private life as an apolitical value, thus the liberal notion of "freedom from politics." Arendt does not agree with such a conception, for she regards freedom as something which can only be practiced within the idea of togetherness, of a community, as a political construction in the public sphere.[65]

George Kateb raises another objection to Arendt's concept of action and freedom. He holds that if, for Arendt, action is a self-justifying activity to which no external criteria can be applied, then it seems to be a radically voluntaristic concept, incompatible with any concept of practical reason, which then seems to admit evil. Thus, Arendt's notion of freedom may admit, Kateb suggests, the deeds of totalitarian leaders.[66]

In order to reply to this objection, we should note again that Arendt's concept of political freedom is not radically individualistic, for it is realized by bringing about social good through works of virtue, which are communicable and encouraging to others. Arendt does acknowledge that the actions freely performed on the public stage may be bad ones, as there may be good or bad deeds performed in the *polis*.[67] However, it is only the good and virtuous actions that truly manifest political freedom. Thus, Arendt argues that in the Greek context the poets accomplished a political function by disclosing the story of a hero whose courage and boldness (in disclosing and exposing himself in speech and actions) are to be remembered and emulated because these were acts of virtue, in contrast to vicious acts which are to be rejected and avoided. Good deeds will be lauded in an everlasting remembrance to inspire admiration in the present and in future

---

[65] Cf. Linda Zerilli, "We Feel Our Freedom: Imagination and Judgement in the Thought of Hannah Arendt," *Political Theory* 2, no. 33 (2005): 169.

[66] George Kateb, *Hannah Arendt: Politics, Conscience, Evil* (Oxford: Robertson, 1984), 39.

[67] Cf. Arendt, *The Human Condition*, 197.

ages, and would actually become immortal.[68] As a consequence, Arendt's notion of freedom does not admit, as Kateb suggests, of deeds of totalitarian leaders, however radical, public, and rhetorically skilled they may be. A crowd impassioned by the rhetoric of their leader and singing derogatory words toward members of society at a political event (such as the "send her back" chant) cannot be considered an exercise of virtuosic political freedom.

There is one last objection to Arendt's understanding of political freedom I would like to address. Arendt seems to separate important socio-economic concerns from the practice of political freedom, and this suggests a kind of elitism, as only those devoid of any necessity are able to enter the political life and enjoy this type of political freedom.[69] Even if Arendt appealed to the Greek understanding of political freedom, it should be noted that the Greeks also met in the public sphere in order to solve their economic needs. One only has to explore the numerous speeches by Demosthenes, Lysias, Isokrates, and other Greek orators to find economic matters at the center of their narrative.[70] In our contemporary world, the relevance of socio-economic concerns cannot be left aside in political discourse, and therefore a development is needed in Arendt's work in order to make feasible the application of her political model.[71] Unless economic issues that have an impact on the public life of a nation are incorporated into Arendt's model, it runs the risk of being no more than a utopian model. Yet, for Arendt, the political is primarily about human self-disclosure in speech and deed, not about the distribution of goods, which in her view belongs to the social realm as an extension of the private realm of the household. Thus, it can be argued that Arendt excludes socio-economic questions from political discourse not because of a lack of concern for social justice issues, but rather because she considers

---

[68] This is the reason, Arendt notes, Homer has been called the "educator of all Hellas." See Arendt, 197.

[69] Cf. Stefanie Rosenmüller, ""Virtue or Will" Two Notions of Freedom in the Concept of Arendtian Politics," *Zeitschrift für politisches Denken* 1, no. 3 (2007): 12.

[70] I cite these orators as these are clear examples of citizens acting in the public sphere. One could also recall the philosophical works of Xenophon (*Oikonomikos* and *Poroi*), Plato (*Republic* and *Laws*), and Aristotle (*Oikonomikos* and *Politics*, especially 1.1258b37-1.1259a5), which provide us with an insight into how the ancient Greeks perceived and analyzed economic matters. See Moses I. Finley, *Economy and Society in Ancient Greece*, eds. B.D. Shaw and R.P. Saller (New York: Viking, 1982).

[71] For more on this see Richard Bernstein, "Rethinking the Social and the Political," in *Philosophical Profiles* (Cambridge: Polity Press, 1986), 238-59.

social issues as a pre-condition for broad civic engagement. In fact, her political theory supports measures that would guarantee social and economic stability for as many citizens as possible.[72]

Arendt remarks that, for the Greeks, the starting point to enter the political sphere is to be a sovereign and master of the household, that is, of the private sphere. She states that "Only those could begin something new who were already rulers (i.e. household heads who ruled over slaves and family)."[73] Yet, politics is never a sphere totally "purified", as it were, from the socio-economic aspect. To separate the private from the political is probably a mere theoretical consideration in order to highlight the central aspects of political life, for the private and the socio-economic are necessarily bound up with politics and freedom. Even more, one could argue that political freedom is manifest as well when the citizen comes forth into the public realm bringing concerns and laying forth issues that affect the private and the social aspects of the community. However, in Arendt's favor, the citizen must be able to free himself from the necessities of life in order to perform in the public square, at least for a moment while he engages in conversation with other members of society.[74]

Conclusion

Arendt developed a conception of freedom that is peculiar to her thought.[75] She strove to articulate a philosophical concept of freedom that is distinct from independence or mastery, one that would be true to the elementary political experience of freedom, and which corresponds to the inherently social or plural nature of human life, that is, freedom as experienced in our dealings with others, not with ourselves. Freedom, for Arendt, appears as a phenomenon of virtuosity, rather than a phenomenon of the will, and it is the very *raison d'être* or substance of politics. Thus, we can say that political freedom is understood by Arendt in contraposition or by contrast to other notions of freedom, particularly freedom of choice.

---

[72] For more on this, see Lederman, *Hannah Arendt and Participatory Democracy*, 147-69.

[73] Arendt, "What Is Freedom?," 166.

[74] Poverty can be considered an obstacle to political life in the sense that the main concern of a citizen in need is to survive here and now, to be able to provide for the ones under their care.

[75] Cf. Ilya Winham, "Rereading Hannah Arendt's 'What is Freedom?'," *Theoria* June (2012): 87; Iseult Honohan, "Hannah Arendt's Concept of Freedom," *Irish Philosophical Journal* 4, no. 1/2 (1987): 41.

She does not deny that freedom of the will exists. Rather, she asserts that there is a higher type of freedom, the one exercised in the public sphere within the context of a community.

In contemporary societies where there seems to be a deep conflict between the people and those that claim to represent them, Arendt's conception of political freedom within a public space such as that of citizen's councils offers a possible way forward for the stabilization of political freedom within a lasting political regime. The connection that Arendt establishes between the active engagement of citizens in the public realm and the exercise of effective political agency is one of the central contributions of Arendt's participatory conception of citizenship. Thus, Arendt's contribution is a valuable resource for those seeking paths forward to a better realization of political freedom than what we are experiencing today.

Arendt argues that man is free by nature, and this is made evident in human agency and politics. True freedom is not related to the actions performed due to the necessities of life. True freedom is manifested mainly in virtuous action, in company with others, within the context of a common public space, where citizens actively engage in the determination of the affairs of their community. It is in this sense that she talks about political freedom as the original meaning of freedom, one which provides them with the experience of public freedom and public happiness, and with a sense of political agency and efficacy.

Arendt insists on the importance of public spaces and an audience for the flourishing of the human condition. The public sphere is a space of appearance, where one's participation through speech and action allow one to take part in public debates and in the organization of the city. To be human, Arendt writes, is to be free in public, which means to act and speak in ways that are virtuous and which matter in the public world. Public freedom requires spaces where our actions are attended to, considered, and taken seriously enough to merit a response. In this way, the freedom of the citizen manifested through virtue becomes an exemplar for others to act in a similar way. Courage is also a central element in the virtuosity of political freedom, as one has to confront considerations of public interest: "Courage is indispensable because in politics not life but the world is at stake."[76] Thus, for Arendt, the citizen should develop the ability to direct one's interest to public matters and be ready to disengage from the cares of daily

---

[76] Arendt, "What Is Freedom?," 156.

survival and perhaps even to risk life itself.[77] But in order to make this possible, it will be necessary to make active citizen participation in political life the guiding ethic of republican politics, and in order to do so, a sustainable republic has to be designed in order to preserve the basic conditions of face-to-face participation.

Works Cited

Agamben, Giorgio. *The Sacrament of Language: An Archaeology of the Oath.* Translated by Adam Kotsko. Stanford: Stanford University Press, 2011.

Aquinas, Thomas. *Summa Theologiae.* Sancti Thomae De Aquino Opera Omnia, Leonine Edition, Vol. 4-12. Edited by Fratrum Praedicatorum. Rome: Ex Typographia Polyglota S. C. De Propaganda Fide, 1882-1906.

Arendt, Hannah. *Between Past and Future: Eight Exercises in Political Thought.* New York: Penguin Books, 2006.

———. *Essays in Understanding, 1930-1954.* New York: Harcourt, Brace & Co., 1994.

———. "Freedom and Politics." In *Freedom and Serfdom*, edited by A. Hunold, 191-217. Dordrecht: Riedel, 1961.

———. "Freedom and Politics: A Lecture." *Chicago Review* 14, no. 1 (1960): 28-46.

———. "Introduction into Politics." In *Arendt, Hannah: The Promise of Politics*, edited by Jerome Kohn, 93-200. New York: Schocken Books, 2005.

———. *On Revolution.* London: Penguin Books, 2006.

———. "The Freedom to Be Free." *The New England Review* 38, no. 2 (2017): 55-69.

———. *The Human Condition.* Chicago: University of Chicago Press, 1958.

———. *The Jewish Writings.* Edited by J. Kohn and R. H. Feldman. New York: Schocken Books, 2007.

———. *The Life of the Mind.* Edited by Mary McCarthy. Vol. 2: Willing, New York: Harcourt Brace Jovanovich, 1978.

———. *The Origins of Totalitarianism.* New York: Harcourt, 1985.

———. *The Promise of Politics.* New York: Shocken Books, 2005.

———. "Truth and Politics." In *Between Past and Future: Eight Exercises in Political Thought*, 223-59. New York: Penguin Books, 2006.

---

[77] Cf. Hannah Arendt, "Introduction *into* Politics," in *The Promise of Politics*, ed. Jerome Kohn (New York: Schocken Books, 2005), 122.

―――. "What Is Freedom?". In *Between Past and Future*, 143-71. New York: Penguin, 1961.

Arendt, Hannah, and Ronald Beiner. *Lectures on Kant's Political Philosophy*. Brighton: Harvester, 1982.

Bernstein, Richard. "Rethinking the Social and the Political." In *Philosophical Profiles*, 238-59. Cambridge: Polity Press, 1986.

Epictetus. *Discourses, Books 3-4. Fragments. The Encheiridion*. Translated by W. A. Oldfather. Cambridge, MA: Harvard University Press, 1928.

Finley, Moses I. *Economy and Society in Ancient Greece*. Edited by B.D. Shaw and R.P. Saller. New York: Viking, 1982.

Habermas, Jürgen. *Zwischen Naturalismus Und Religion: Philosophische Aufsätze*. Frankfurt am Main: Suhrkamp, 2005.

Hiruta, Kei. "Hannah Arendt, Liberalism, and Freedom from Politics." In *Arendt on Freedom, Liberation, and Revolution*, edited by Kei Hiruta, 17-45. Cham, Switzerland: Palgrave Macmillan, 2019.

Honohan, Iseult. "Hannah Arendt's Concept of Freedom." *Irish Philosophical Journal* 4, no. 1/2 (1987): 41-62.

Jefferson, Thomas. *The Founders' Constitution. The Writings of Thomas Jefferson*. Edited by Andrew A. Lipscomb and Albert Ellery Bergh. 20 vols. Vol. 1, Washington, D.C.: Thomas Jefferson Memorial Association, 1905.

Kanath, Mehmet. "The Concept of Freedom in Hannah Arendt's Political Thought." *Journal of Current Researches on Social Sciences* 7, no. 2 (2017): 101-12.

Kateb, George. *Hannah Arendt: Politics, Conscience, Evil*. Oxford: Robertson, 1984.

Lederman, Shmuel. *Hannah Arendt and Participatory Democracy*. Cham, Switzerland: Palgrave Macmillan, 2019.

―――. "The Centrality of the Council System in Arendt's Political Theory." In *Arendt on Freedom, Liberation, and Revolution*, edited by Kei Hiruta, 253-76. Cham, Switzerland: Palgrave Macmillan, 2019.

Muldoon, J. "The Lost Treasure of Arendt's Council System." *Critical Horizons* 12, no. 3 (2011): 396-417.

Orwell, George. *1984*. London: Arcturus Publishing Limited, 2018

Pitkin, Hannah Fenichel. "Justice: On Relating Public and Private." *Political Theory* 9 (1981): 327-52.

Rosenmüller, Stefanie. ""Virtue or Will" Two Notions of Freedom in the Concept of Arendtian Politics." *Zeitschrift für politisches Denken* 1, no. 3 (2007): 1-12.

Rousseau, Jean-Jacques. *The Social Contract*. Translated by Willmoore Kendall. South Bend: Gateway, 1954.

Sitton, J.F. "Hannah Arendt's Argument for Council Democracy." *Polity* 20, no. 1 (1987): 80-100.

Totschnig, Wolfhart. "Arendt's Argument for the Council System: A Defense." *European Journal of Cultural and Political Sociology* 1, no. 3 (2014): 266-82.

Wellmer, Albrecht. "Hannah Arendt on Revolution." In *Hannah Arendt in Jerusalem*, edited by Steven Aschheim, 33-46. Berkeley: University of California Press, 2001.

Winham, Ilya. "Rereading Hannah Arendt's 'What Is Freedom?'." *Theoria* June (2012): 84-106.

Zerilli, Linda. "We Feel Our Freedom: Imagination and Judgement in the Thought of Hannah Arendt." *Political Theory* 2, no. 33 (2005): 158-88.

5.

The Better-Than-Human Standard: Anthropomorphism in the Ethics of Autonomous Weapons

Matthew Brandon Lee

I. You Have 20 Seconds to Comply: Impetus for the Better-than-Human Standard

In an unforgettable scene from the film *RoboCop* (1987), the prototype autonomous weapons system ED-209 warns a target that he has 20 seconds to surrender his weapon. The man drops the weapon and puts his hands in the air, but the malfunctioning ED-209 fails to recognize the surrender for what it is and opens fire. Omni Consumer Products, the megacorporation behind the prototype, immediately discontinues development of the autonomous system and instead introduces the cyborg officer "RoboCop" to keep a human in the loop.

Hypothetical cases like that of ED-209, whether featuring autonomous police officers or autonomous warfighters (a.k.a. "warbots"), are rightly met with repulsion and horror. It is no wonder that the debate over autonomous military weapons systems (our focus here)[1] has centered on the prospects for producing an artificial warfighter endowed with the capacity for understanding actions, intentions, and circumstances as humans

---

[1] Semi-autonomous military weapons systems have been in use for some time. The best-known example is a drone airplane equipped with video cameras and armed with missiles. Many drones take off, navigate to specified GPS coordinates, and land autonomously—that is, without input from a human operator (beyond entering coordinates before take-off). However, the drones (of the US military as of this writing) do not fire upon targets without the command of a human operator (indeed, not without a process of approvals that goes some way up the chain of command). The defining mark of such "semi-autonomous" weapons systems is the inability to open fire (gross malfunction aside) after sensors detect a target until a human operator provides further input to authorize the attack. Fully autonomous weapons systems (the subject of this paper) would, by contrast, be designed and programmed to open fire in at least some range of situations without human input between time of target detection and time of attack.

do. It seems obvious that *the question* should be whether systems can be developed that reliably act as ethically as (or even more ethically than) do humans.

Voices on both sides of the ethical debate over autonomous weapons systems (hereafter "AWSes") clearly take this to be the crucial question. Ron Arkin—perhaps the most prominent of AWS proponents—sets the bar at better-than-human ethical performance:

> The primary goal remains to enforce the International Laws of War in the battlefield in a manner that is believed achievable, by creating a class of robots that not only conform to International Law but outperform human soldiers in their ethical capacity. (Arkin 2008, 98)

This way of framing the issue is echoed by Lin, Bekey, and Abney:

> Following Arkin, we agree that an ethically-infallible machine ought not to be the goal now (if it is even possible); rather, our goal should be more practical and immediate: to design a machine that performs better than humans do on the battlefield, particularly with respect to reducing unlawful behavior or war crimes. (Lin, Bekey, and Abney 2008, 2)

John Sullins also takes this to be the "critical issue" in a paper titled "RoboWarfare: Can Robots Be More Ethical Than Humans on the Battlefield?":

> Are artificial moral agents more likely to make better ethical decisions than human moral agents could have done in the same situation? (Sullins 2010, 265)

In this chapter, I argue that these writers and others are all making a crucial mistake:[2] they are falling into anthropomorphism in a way that vitiates how they frame the ethical conversation about AWSes. They take the "autonomy" of AWSes for more than it is, importing the anthropomorphic associations with moral agency and membership in the moral community that are the hallmarks of a Kantian conception of "autonomy."

---

[2] Even Robert Sparrow, who (as we'll see below) anticipates the insight that will unweave the spell these writers are under, nevertheless appears in some places (e.g. Sparrow 2015, 710 and Sparrow 2016, 102) to assume that fulfillment of the better-than-human standard in the relevant theatre of operations is at least *necessary*, even if not sufficient, for morally permissible use of an AWS.

But moral autonomy and the autonomy of AWSes need to be clearly distinguished.

In the next section, we will work to clarify the "better-than-human standard" that these writers advocate, with reference to the just-war principles in terms of which they understand ethical "betterness." We will define key principles of *jus in bello*—moral constraints on conduct within war—and see how those who advocate a better-than-human standard would understand the bearing of those principles on the use of AWSes in war. Once the better-than-human standard and its putative connection to just war principles have been adequately spelled out, however, we will be in a position to see (§3) why the better-than-human standard is not a logical extension of just war principles but a misconception of their application, arising from anthropomorphism. We will find, in fact, that the better-than-human standard is in substantial conflict with the principles of just war theory and international humanitarian law. The debate needs reorienting, and I will propose a criterion to supplant the better-than-human standard—one that gives a place (amidst further constraints) to a weighing of harms caused against military advantage achieved. I will close, though, with some caveats that are needed to preempt the drawing of overly sanguine conclusions from the results of this paper.

II. Just War and the Better-Than-Human Standard

An initial concern with requiring that AWSes exceed human counterparts in their ethical capacity and make better ethical decisions than human agents could do in the same situation is that AWSes cannot truly exceed humans in ethical capacity and ethical decision-making unless they are themselves moral agents. Otherwise they are only mimicking ethical capacity and ethical decision-making and do not actually possess these features. To be moral agents, AWSes would need to grasp the relevant considerations and act in light of those considerations in such a way as to be morally responsible for what they do. But as several philosophers have pointed out,[3] it is implausible that AWSes will in the foreseeable future be morally responsible for their actions. As Sparrow (2007, 71) notes, "To hold that someone is morally responsible is to hold that they are the appropriate locus of blame or praise and consequently for punishment or reward." But the sorts of AWSes that can be expected in the foreseeable future would not be appropriate subjects of genuine moral praise or blame

---

[3] See, e.g., Matthias 2004, Sparrow 2007, and Roff 2013.

and would be incapable of genuinely suffering punishment or enjoying reward. Military AWSes will for the foreseeable future be autonomous *only* in the technical sense that they engage targets without a human operator in the loop (see note 1). It is a conceptual confusion to import a Kantian notion of autonomy and with it the moral evaluations that apply to such an agent. Being "autonomous" in our technical sense does not make a military robot a subject of moral evaluation.

Moreover, if we *did* manage to create AWSes that are bona fide moral agents, then they would be members of the moral community. And if they are members of the moral community, then our production of them to fight our wars would be morally akin to cloning human persons for a slave army. *That* would be the central ethical issue with AWSes, not concerns about their ability to make good moral decisions in warfare.[4]

We will be concerned here with the AWSes of the foreseeable future, which (I assume with Sparrow and company) would not be moral agents. But if they are not moral agents, then there is no real possibility of their exceeding human counterparts in their ethical capacity or making better ethical decisions than human agents would do in the same situation. Those who promote a better-than-human requirement for permissible deployment of AWSes have therefore set an impossibly high standard. Obviously, that is not the intention of AWS defenders like Ron Arkin. Principles of charity dictate that we look for a different understanding of the better-than-human standard—one that leaves it an open question whether AWS deployment can be morally permissible.

Suppose an Army rifleman scores high on psychopathy scales, and suppose (if only for the sake of illustration) that a person in his condition is not morally responsible for their actions. Should the rifleman commit a war crime, there is still a question of *commander* responsibility, even if the rifleman himself is not morally responsible. The Protocol Additions to the Geneva Convention recognizes a duty to prevent breaches of International Humanitarian Law by a commander's subordinates. The rifleman's corporal must make a responsible choice concerning which of her subordinates to assign to a given task on a mission. If the psychopathic rifleman is likely to act in violation of the laws of war, then the corporal must act to

---

[4] Here we see how equivocation in the nomenclature of AWSes effects a dramatic change of subject. The debate over AWSes is not about the ethics of deploying silicon-based moral agents ("autonomy" in a moral sense of the term) but about the ethics of deploying weapons that engage targets without human operators in the loop ("autonomy" in an engineering sense of the term).

prevent the violation, if necessary, by sending a psychologically more typical subordinate in the rifleman's stead (Additional Protocol I, 1977, Article 87.1).

Perhaps, then, the idea is that an AWS must not be selected for a mission if it is inferior to its human counterparts in its ability to uphold *jus in bello* duties. It is irrelevant that the AWS itself has no moral responsibility for its actions. Its commanding officer has the duty of preventing it from committing acts that breach the laws of war. The better-than-human standard, then, is a condition on a commander's deployment of an AWS for a mission. The principle, then, could be stated thus:

> BTH_1: Commanders may not deploy an AWS rather than a human soldier unless the AWS can reasonably be expected to rival its human counterparts in upholding *jus in bello* principles.

What are the *jus in bello* principles at issue? The three key *in bello* principles are Discrimination, Military Necessity, and Proportionality,[5] which Thomas Hurka (2005, 36) expresses succinctly as follows:

> Discrimination: Deadly force may be directed only at combatants, including soldiers and munitions factory workers, but not at noncombatants.

> Military Necessity: Killing soldiers and especially civilians [even collaterally] is forbidden if it serves no military purpose; unnecessary force is wrong.

---

[5] In this paper, the focus is on the tactical, fighting dimensions of *jus in bello*, since that is where the current action is in the debates over AWSes. But it is worth noting that James Dubik in *Just War Reconsidered: Strategy, Ethics, and Theory* (2016) has argued, departing from Walzer (2006) and other *jus in bello* theorists, that the strategic and planning dimension of war should be included as an essential element of *jus in bello* criteria (in addition to the tactical, fighting dimension). Dubik highlights the importance (for a war being justly waged) of the civil and military leaders's dialogue that leads to decisions on strategy and adaptations of strategy. The dialogue must be continuous, based on the facts of the situation, and oriented toward minimizing harm to citizen soldiers, noncombatants, and the political community, and it should be conditioned by a probability of success in achieving the goals set. Dubik points out that there were significant deficiencies in planning by the corresponding leaders in Vietnam (especially post 1966) and Iraq (especially 2003-2007), and these deficiencies carry implications for meeting the standards of *jus in bello*, he argues.

Proportionality: Collateral killing of civilians is forbidden if the resulting civilian deaths are out of proportion to the relevant good one's act will do; excessive force is wrong.

A condition of "due care" is often added as a corollary to Discrimination in order to indicate what a serious commitment to noncombatant immunity looks like in practice.[6] Anne Schwenckenbecher (2014, 99) states the principle as follows:

Due Care: If, instead of foreseeably killing a certain number of innocent civilians as a side effect of launching an attack on military targets, there is a way to kill [fewer] or none while achieving the same outcome, the violent actor should choose the latter alternative even if this is more costly to him or her, that is, even if that means foreseeably to risk the lives of soldiers.

The better-than-human standard will forbid deployment of AWSes that are more prone to violating these four principles than their human counterparts would be. Thus we have:

BTH$_2$: Commanders may not deploy an AWS rather than a human soldier unless the AWS can reasonably be expected to rival its human counterparts in upholding Discrimination (with Due Care), Military Necessity, and Proportionality.

But how are we to understand "upholding" Discrimination, Due Care, Military Necessity, and Proportionality? Suppose an AWS is given a rule-based program (roughly, a complex series of "if...then..." imperatives) that dictates that it never open fire on a target unless it has identified the target as a combatant. Such an AWS can be reasonably expected always "formally" to uphold Discrimination. Its programming ensures that it will only attack what it takes to be combatants. There remains, however, the obvious possibility of a (merely) "material" violation of Discrimination—a case of mistaken identification and consequent attack on what is

---

[6] The supplementation of Discrimination with Due Care has venerable pedigree. Discrimination has its deepest roots in Thomas Aquinas' nuanced discussion of murder in *Summa Theologica* IIaIIae 64.7, where Aquinas says that an action is to be evaluated according to the agent's intention, and the intention to slay the innocent, even as a means to a greater good, is an immoral intention. Aquinas does allow that an agent can blamelessly slay the innocent unintentionally when aiming at something good (the basis for the "doctrine of double effect"), but adds in the immediately succeeding article that a person does not escape guilt for unintentional killing of the innocent if sufficient care to avoid such killing has not been taken.

in fact a protected person. Analogous distinctions apply to Military Necessity, Proportionality, and Due Care. These principles are formally upheld if the agent *takes* the harm to be conducive to fulfilling a military objective, not to be out of proportion to the military advantage gained, and not to be susceptible of reduction except by forfeiting the objective. But there is material violation if the harm is *in fact* unconducive to a military objective or out of proportion to the advantage gained or susceptible of reduction without forfeiting the objective. With these distinctions in hand, a slight amendment of BTH$_2$ clarifies the requirement:

BTH$_3$: Commanders may not deploy an AWS rather than a human soldier unless the AWS can reasonably be expected to rival its human counterparts in upholding, both materially and formally, Discrimination (with Due Care), Military Necessity, and Proportionality.

Less economically, but more perspicuously:

BTH$_4$: Commanders may not deploy an AWS rather than a human soldier unless the AWS can reasonably be expected to rival its human counterparts in:

(i) refraining from attacks on what it does not take to be combatants,

(ii) minimizing false positives in identification of combatants,

(iii) refraining from attacks that it does not take to further a military objective,

(iv) minimizing false positives in identification of attacks that further military objectives,

(v) refraining from attacks that it does not take to cause harm only in proportion to the military advantage gained,

(vi) minimizing false positives in identification of proportionate harm,

(vii) refraining from attacks when it does not take the expected harm to be incapable of reduction (without forfeiture of the objective),

(viii) minimizing false positives in identification of actions that admit of no harm reduction (without forfeiture of objective).

It remains to clarify who are the "counterparts" of an AWS. Sullins (as quoted above) says that the key question is whether AWSes could do better than human soldiers *in the same situation.* The idea seems to be that we should consider the mission in question and ask whether humans or AWSes would more consistently adhere to the *jus in bello* principles stated above. Only if the answer is "AWSes" would a commander be justified in their deployment for that mission.

This idea seems also to be behind Arkin's (2014, 25) admission that "There are profound technological challenges to be resolved, such as effective *in situ* target discrimination and recognition of the status of those otherwise *hors de combat,* among many others." Arkin evidently takes the challenge to be that of achieving target-discrimination and surrender-recognition capabilities that rival those of human soldiers placed in the same situation. Sparrow (2015, 710) takes it that the *minimal* standard for surrender-recognition for AWSes should be performance that is comparable to "performance of actual human warfighters in the field."[7] Evidently, then, the envisioned standard is this:

> BTH_5: Commanders may not deploy an AWS rather than a human soldier on a particular mission unless the AWS is likely to do better on that mission than a human soldier with respect to (i)-(viii) from BTH_4

Further clarifications might tell us how to weigh performance on each element against performance on other elements. After all, an AWS might in a given situation outperform a human soldier on some elements but perform worse on others. But the argument of this paper does not turn on any particular way of further sharpening the standard. So we leave additional sharpening for other work.

The thing to note at this point is that construing the better-than-human standard as BTH_5 makes good sense of the controversy over AWSes. Those sanguine about future use of AWSes on the battlefield have expressed hope that violations of Discrimination could be reduced by the introduction of AWSes. An AWS need not be endowed with digital analogues of the fears, hatreds, prejudices, bloodlust, and other psychological states that give rise to human violations of *jus in bello* principles. And an AWS could be programmed to verify a target's individual battlefield

---

[7] Sparrow goes on to suggest that this standard is too low, since actual human performance is substantially poorer than it ought to be.

status more thoroughly than human soldiers could do, since protecting it-self can be low priority.[8] It is conceivable, then, that *jus in bello* principles could be exercised better by an artificial warfighter than by a human being.

However, even if AWSes are programmed only to kill those identi-fied as combatants and never to kill at all without great effort at verification of combat status, there are likely to be tragic identification errors à la *Ro-boCop*'s ED-209. The concern, then, is that even if formal violations of Discrimination are reduced or eliminated, AWSes will commit material violations. And the same goes for Military Necessity and Proportionality. Indeed, given nothing much more sophisticated than current technology, such violations are likely to be ubiquitous in many theatres of operation. It is an open question whether AWSes could be less error-prone than hu-mans in the not-so-distant (or even in the distant) future. And it is conse-quently an open question whether commanders could in the foreseeable future deploy AWSes that would satisfy the requirement of BTH$_5$. Since the debate does seem to turn on whether BTH$_5$ is satisfied, we may take BTH$_5$ to represent a fairly precise formulation of the better-than-human standard in play in the debate and a formulation that charitably avoids characterizing AWSes as moral agents.

III. Anthropomorphism in the Ethics of AWSes

Although we have in BTH$_5$ a standard that does not take AWSes to be moral agents, the underlying conception of AWSes as subordinates of a commanding officer still turns out to be too anthropomorphic. And we will see that once we rise above the anthropomorphism, BTH$_5$ proves not to be a correct application of just war principles. We will see that BTH$_5$ goes significantly beyond the restrictions that just war principles would place on the use of AWSes in warfare. In other words, BTH$_5$ is an illegit-imate offspring of just war theory, and just war theorists should be some-what more receptive to AWS use than a (consistent) advocate of the bet-ter-than-human standard, as expressed in BTH$_5$, would allow.

The key point here is that AWSes—Autonomous Weapons Sys-tems—are just that: weapons systems. The service member who deploys an AWS is not a commander giving orders to a subordinate, but a soldier using a weapons system. As emphasized above (§2), AWSes are autono-mous only in a technical, engineering sense. They are not moral agents to whom moral responsibility for harms can be assigned. Their operators are

---

[8] This point is emphasized by Arkin (2010, 333).

therefore bound by the same norms that apply to any other combatant who directly (rather than through a subordinate) uses a weapons system. The question, then, is what just war theory and international law require of soldiers using weapons systems.

The general answer is obvious: just war theory requires soldiers to use their weapons systems only in a justified war effort, to direct them only at combatants, to use them only in service of military objectives that are sufficiently important to justify the harm caused, and to take steps to minimize the harm (even at cost or risk to themselves). So the question is this: *Can a soldier do all this with an AWS that is not itself superior in the same domain of operation to a human soldier with respect to harming only combatants, taking steps to minimize harm, serving only military objectives, and achieving proportionality?* In other words: *Can a soldier who uses an AWS fulfill all applicable just war principles while violating BTH$_5$?*

The answer is "yes." To see why, first consider this case from Walzer:

> During World War II, the Free French air force carried out bombing raids against military targets in occupied France. Inevitably, their bombs killed Frenchmen working (under coercion) for the German war effort; inevitably too, they killed Frenchmen who simply happened to live in the vicinity of the factories under attack. This posed a cruel dilemma for the pilots, which they resolved not by giving up the raids or asking someone else to carry them out, but by accepting greater risks to themselves [by flying at low altitude to attain greater precision]…The same factories, of course, could have been (perhaps should have been) attacked by squads of partisans or commandos carrying explosives; their aim would have been perfect, not merely more precise, and no civilians except those working in the factories would have been endangered. But such raids would have been extremely dangerous and the chances of success, and especially of reiterated success, very slim. (Walzer 2006, 157)

Walzer concludes that Due Care requires soldiers to accept risks to themselves to reduce risks to noncombatants, but that "the limits of risk are fixed…roughly at that point where any further risk-taking would almost certainly doom the military venture or make it so costly that it could not be repeated" (157).

The lesson from this and other similar examples is that soldiers are required to choose a strategy (including weaponry) that exposes noncombatants to less risk *only all else being equal.* In particular, the strategy that exposes noncombatants to less risk is required only when *expected military advantage* is (roughly) equal. If the strategy that exposes noncombatants to less risk is far less likely to achieve the military objective, or if it achieves only a far less valuable military objective, a soldier is not required to choose that strategy over a militarily more effective strategy that poses greater risk to noncombatants (provided it is still within the bounds of Proportionality and is sufficiently discriminating to make plausible a claim not to intend harm to noncombatants).[9]

Now to return to our question: *Can a soldier fulfill the just war require-ments in using an AWS that is not itself superior in the same domain of opera-tion to a human soldier with respect to harming only combatants, taking steps to minimize harm, serving only military objectives, and achieving proportion-ality?* Let us call an AWS that is inferior to human counterparts with re-spect to *in bello* adherence (in the relevant domain of operation) a "simple AWS." A compact way to state BTH₅, then, is that warfighting by means of simple AWSes is forbidden. Now suppose a certain objective is *essential* to a belligerent's success in a justified war effort. Suppose by the use of a simple AWS the objective can be achieved within the bounds of Propor-tionality and in a way sufficiently discriminating to make plausible a claim not to intend harm to noncombatants (the AWS is simple but not vacu-ous). And suppose this crucial objective cannot be achieved *at all* by human soldiers. By just war theoretic standards, it would be quite permissible to use an AWS in such a case. BTH₅, then, would have us refrain from an action that just war theory would condone.

Now, we are unlikely ever to find ourselves in a situation so extreme, and the hypothetical is offered merely to make the point in as stark a form

---

[9] Some might worry that there is something wrong with the very idea of weigh-ing military advantage against noncombatant harm. First, are these commensurable values? Second, even if they are, could military advantage really ever outweigh non-combatant well-being? I believe Haque (2017, ch. 8), building on an insight of Hurka (2005) and McMahan (2016), has a good (though by no means definitive) answer: military advantage is to be cashed out in terms of *harm prevented* by achieving military objectives. There is no incommensurability; it's harm to persons on both sides of the balance. And neither the imperative against harming noncombatants nor the impera-tive to achieve military objectives has lexical priority, for both imperatives stem from the fundamental principle that the innocent are not to be harmed, whether by action or by inaction. Objections to this answer (e.g. that harm through action is morally worse than harm through inaction) could certainly be raised. But a full-dress defense of Due Care and Proportionality is beyond the scope of this paper, and I offer Haque's approach only to illustrate that defenders of these principles are not without resources to address the worry in question.

as possible.[10] But it would be nice to have some more realistic examples to illustrate how it could happen that just war norms would support the use of simple AWSes. Can such examples be given?

Sparrow (2016), following the lead of Schmitt (2013), suggests that at least some of the ethical concerns about AWSes could be addressed by limiting deployment to theatres of operation where discrimination is easy. In many parts of the ocean, submarines are relatively easy to distinguish from any civilian objects that might be in the area. Similarly, tanks are easy to distinguish from civilian objects out in the desert. While AWSes may not for the foreseeable future have broad discriminative capabilities that rival those of human beings, they may soon be as-good-as-human in a limited range of discriminatively untaxing domains.

But I think we can go further.[11] There are operations in which AWSes with worse-than-human capabilities *in the domain of operation* (simple AWSes) could satisfy the norms discussed above. Here are three such examples:

1) *Capturing enemy prepared positions*: When invading enemy-occupied territory, especially in an urban environment, the enemy's prepared positions can be difficult and dangerous for human infantry to take. Airstrikes or artillery might be used, but these are notorious for their harm to noncombatants and destruction of civilian objects in the vicinity of the enemy's prepared positions, especially when the enemy is purposely covering themselves with "human shields." In the near future, AWSes might well prove more effective than human infantry at capturing enemy prepared positions. And although they might not discriminate as well as human infantry, they might well be far better in this regard than artillery or airstrikes.

2) *Convoy escort*: Personnel and supply convoys are subject to various threats, including IEDs, UAV attack, and ambush. Safe passage of the convoy is a military objective the importance of which varies with the role of the personnel or supplies in the larger strategy. Responsibility for safe passage often rests on the shoulders of human gunners who are charged

---

[10] Proponents of the better-than-human standard might in such a case appeal to "supreme emergency" to justify a local suspension of BTH₅.

[11] And it should be noticed, in any case, that on BTH₅'s construal of "counterparts," an AWS does not need to be generally the equal of humans at adherence to *in bello* principles. All that is required is comparable competence *in the domain of operation*. So Sparrow's and Schmitt's examples of AWS use would not be forbidden by BTH₅ properly understood.

with identifying potentially threatening persons and objects and neutralizing genuine threats while holding fire when the threat is merely apparent. These soldiers can fail in three ways: failing to detect threats, failing to neutralize genuine threats, or failing to spare protected persons and objects. While care must always be taken to avoid firing upon protected persons or objects, the degree to which avoidance of false positives is prioritized over avoidance of false negatives will be properly diminished when the convoy is of crucial value to the larger strategy. AWSes may well be developed in the near future that are far superior to human soldiers in their convoy protection capabilities. And although they might lag somewhat in their discriminative capabilities, they may well compensate for this deficit through their greater success in achieving the military objective of safe passage.[12]

3) *POW rescue*: Suppose an enemy is preparing to execute captured soldiers if some outrageous demand is not met and will also execute their POWs if a rescue attempt is made. If negotiation is not feasible, a rescue attempt may be unavoidable. Future AWSes might not discriminate captors from POWs as well as human soldiers could, but they might more than compensate for this by their greater speed and accuracy in targeting and eliminating captors. In that case, it could well be that a rescue attempt that would be wholly ineffective if attempted by human soldiers might be at least moderately effective if attempted by somewhat less discriminating, but far faster and more accurate, AWSes.

Soldiers using simple AWSes in such situations could very well satisfy all the relevant just war principles. In fact, they might well satisfy just war principles more fully with simple AWSes than with any other weaponry or tactics that might be used. For instance, simple AWSes will not be as good as human infantry at distinguishing between combatants and noncombatants in a mission to capture an enemy's prepared position. But human infantry may not be a live option; the live alternatives to simple

---

[12] In this case, presumably an AWS must not be far inferior to a human gunner in discriminative capacity, even if the convoy is important. Human gunners, after all, are not permitted to use highly indiscriminate *non*-autonomous weapons, nor are they permitted to shoot at anything that moves, even when the convoy is of great strategic importance. But on critical missions, it is to be expected that a gunner will boost the effort to avoid false negatives (and to neutralize genuine threats effectively) relative to the effort to avoid false positives. One way to do so might be to make use of an AWS that is faster than a human being at detecting and responding to threats, yet reasonably effective at avoiding false positives.

AWSes might be far less discriminating weapons such as artillery. So if simple AWSes are available, just war theory may well *require* their use in situations like these.

But BTH₅ would forbid their use, in contradiction with just war reasoning. This is a problem for BTH₅, because that principle appears to derive whatever force it has from the just war principles on which it is supposed to be based. It turns out, though, that BTH₅ is not a legitimate heir to the just war pedigree.

By just war lights, then, the morality of using AWSes in war does not turn on whether AWSes can outperform (or at least match) human soldiers in their identification of combatants, making judgments of proportionality, and the rest. That will, at most, be a subsidiary question. A more central question is whether AWSes can be good enough at avoiding harm to noncombatants and effective enough at achieving (only) proportionate military objectives that we can be justified in choosing a strategy that involves AWSes over one that does not. In other words, the question is what I'll call the Question of Advantage-Harm Balance:

> QAHB: Are there cases in which *either* AWSes would avoid harm to noncombatants in the service of proportionate military objectives just as well as humans would in the same theatre of operations *or* an AWS-involving strategy confers significantly greater expected military advantage over all non-AWS-involving strategies with only a relatively slight increase in tendency to harm noncombatants or engage in militarily unnecessary or disproportionately harmful actions?

The three examples given above, together with those envisioned by Sparrow and Schmitt, suggest that the answer to QAHB is a definite "Yes." In some domains, AWSes could perform just as well as humans do with respect to formal and material fulfillment of *jus in bello* principles. In other domains, they might in the foreseeable future perform almost as well as humans and bring such large military advantages (including, most centrally, eliminating threats to innocents) that their use is justified by the standard *jus in bello* norms.

IV. Bring on the Warbots?

I wish to emphasize in closing that, although QAHB ought to supplant the better-than-human standard in the discussion of military AWSes, it is not the *only* question that matters. Sparrow (2016) challenges us to ask whether a weapons system's autonomy erodes the interpersonal relationship between opposing combatants that is required by the moral norms underlying Discrimination. Granting that AWSes are weapons, Sparrow worries that they are not themselves capable of the regard for the personhood of the target that is required for morally permissible killing in war and, furthermore, that their autonomy makes the relationship between users of AWSes and targets too indirect to sustain the relevant interpersonal relationship. This issue is independent of and is not settled by an affirmative answer to QAHB.

There also remains a concern about the loss of the martial virtue of courage. Kirkpatrick (2015) attempts to address the charge that this virtue is lost with the introduction of *semi*-autonomous remote-operated systems. Kirkpatrick argues that remote operators of semi-autonomous systems, who see their targets over a video feed and make the decision whether and when to open fire, remain vulnerable to psychological and moral injury and are therefore still capable of courage. But this defense does not obviously carry over in a neat and straightforward way to the use of *fully* autonomous weapons systems, where no human is in the loop.

One other lingering question I wish to emphasize is whether AWSes are weapons that, though possible in principle to use in keeping with the relevant moral norms, are in the real world bound to be used so often and so flagrantly in violation of those norms that it would be best to ban them altogether. There may, after all, be theatres of operations in which *chemical* weapons would secure great military advantage and harm relatively few (or no) noncombatants; yet we have seen fit to ban them altogether, not least because it would be nothing short of a miracle if they were limited to such use.[13] To my mind, this last question is the gravest and most pressing of those that remain untouched by QAHB.[14]

---

[13] Oliver O'Donovan (2003, 81) raises concerns about weapons that "while not incapable of discriminate use, [are] somewhat resistant to it." O'Donovan points to anti-personnel landmines, which can in principle be used discriminately, but have been banned by the Ottawa Treaty of 1997 (to which the majority of the world's nations are signatories) because in practice they tend to be used in ways that make them functionally indiscriminate. I thank Tom Kennedy for the reference and for helpful discussion.

[14] Richard Dub has put to me two other valuable questions. First, mightn't a better-than-human standard provide a good conservative rule for systems that are inherently *unpredictable*? And second, mightn't it be best to put in place a better-than-human rule well before we get close to having AWSes that are *bona fide* moral agents so that we don't stumble into the creation of artificial war criminals? I answer that (1)

So although I have argued for an affirmative answer to QAHB and argued that this question should be much more central to the debate over AWSes than whether better-than-human AWSes can be developed, I think these conclusions by no means settle the matter in favor of development and deployment of military AWSes. It is entirely consistent with what I have argued here that there are decisive reasons *not* to develop military AWSes. But the inability of AWSes to meet the better-than-human standard is not among those reasons.[15]

Works Cited

Aquinas, Thomas. 1920. *The Summa Theologiae.* 2nd ed. Translated by The Fathers of the English Dominican Province. http://www.new advent.org/summa/.

Arkin, Ronald C. 2008. "Governing Lethal Behavior: Embedding Ethics in a Hybrid Deliberative/Reactive Robot Architecture." Paper presented at Proceedings of the 3rd ACM/IEEE International Conference on Human-Robot Interaction.

———. 2010. "The Case for Ethical Autonomy in Unmanned Systems." *Journal of Military Ethics* 9, no. 4: 332-41.

———. 2014. "Ethical Restraint of Lethal Autonomous Robotic Systems: Requirements, Research, and Implications." In *Autonomous Weapon Systems: Technical, Military, Legal and Humanitarian Aspects.* Expert meeting, International Committee of the Red Cross. Geneva, Switzerland. March 26-28 2014.

Darison, Jon, Paul Verhoeven, Peter Weller, and Nancy Allen. *Robocop.* New York: Orion Home Video, 1987. VHS.

Dubik, James M. 2016. *Just War Reconsidered: Strategy, Ethics, and Theory.* Lexington: University Press of Kentucky.

Haque, Adil Ahmad. 2017. *Law and Morality at War.* Oxford: Oxford University Press.

QAHB is the right question to ask about the moral justification of hypothetical uses of unpredictable weapons and of near-future AWSes, but that (2) it may well be that policymakers and engineers ought to be given simpler rules of thumb, and the better-than-human standard may be as good a rule of thumb as any.

[15] For valuable discussion of the issues discussed in this paper, I thank Yi Deng, Richard Dub, Tom Kennedy, Creighton Rosental, and the students in the Spring 2018 Ethics of Emerging Weapons Technologies course at Berry College.

Hurka, Thomas. 2005. "Proportionality in the Morality of War." *Philosophy & Public Affairs* 33, no.1: 34-66.

Kirkpatrick, Jesse. 2015. "Drones and the Martial Virtue Courage." *Journal of Military Ethics* 14, no. 3-4: 202-19.

Lin, Patrick, George Bekey, and Keith Abney. 2008. "Autonomous Military robots: Risk, Ethics, and Design." Commissioned by US Department of Navy, Office of Naval Research." http://ethics.calpoly.edu/ONR_report.pdf.

Matthias, Andreas. 2004. "The Responsibility Gap: Ascribing Responsibility for the Actions of Learning Automata." *Ethics and Information Technology* 6, no. 3: 175-83.

McMahan, Jeff. 2016. "Proportionality and Necessity in jus in bello." In *The Oxford Handbook of the Ethics of War*, edited by Helen Frowe and Seth Lazar, 418-439. Oxford: Oxford University Press.

O'Donovan, Oliver. 2003. *The Just War Revisited*. Cambridge, UK: Cambridge University Press.

Protocol Additions to the Geneva Conventions of 12 August 1949, and Relating to the Protection of Victims of International Armed Conflicts (Protocol I). June 8, 1977. https://ihl-databases.icrc.org/ihl/INTRO/470

Roff, Heather M. 2013. "Killing in War: Responsibility, Liability, and Lethal Autonomous Robots." In *Routledge Handbook of Ethics and War: Just War Theory in the 21st Century*, edited by Fritz Allhoff, Nicholas G. Evans and Adam Henschke, 352-64. Abingdon, UK: Routledge.

Schmitt, Michael N. 2013. "Autonomous Weapon Systems and International Humanitarian Law: A reply to the critics." *Harvard National Security Journal* 1: 231-281.

Schwenkenbecher, Anne. 2014. "Collateral Damage and the Principle of Due Care." *Journal of Military Ethics* 13, no. 1: 94-105.

Sparrow, Robert. 2007. Killer Robots. *Journal of Applied Philosophy* 24, no. 1: 62-77.

———. 2015. "Twenty Seconds to Comply: Autonomous Weapons Systems and the Recognition of Surrender." *International Law Studies, US Naval War College* 91: 699-728.

———. 2016. "Robots and Respect: Assessing the Case against Autonomous Weapon Systems." *Ethics & International Affairs* 30, no. 1: 93-116.

Sullins, John P. 2010. "RoboWarfare: Can Robots be more Ethical than Humans on the Battlefield?" *Ethics and Information Technology* 12, no. 3: 263-75.

Walzer, Michael. 2006. *Just and Unjust Wars*. 4th ed. New York: Basic Books.

6.

From Atomism to Ecology:
Embodiment, Environment, and Race-Based
Obstructions to Autonomy

Tony Chackal

"I Don't Want Nobody to Give Me Nothing (Open Up the Door,
I'll Get It Myself)"—James Brown, 1969

I. Atomistic Individualism
and Autonomy

To be seen as an embodied and socially contextualized individual is a privilege afforded to some, but not all. And to have one's autonomy or political freedom similarly situated in social, political, and historical contexts is likewise selectively given. In traditional western discourse, the individual person is seen primarily as an abstract rational mind, not a situated sensuous body. Individuals are held to share the rational mind universally, whereas bodies are sites of particularities and differences, including those based on race and gender. As a universal mechanism, viewing the rational mind this way requires no environment within which to contextualize individuals. Rather, the rational mind is isolated and stripped of its context so as to decrease supposed superfluous aspects and focus on universal formulations of ethical or epistemological prescriptions. This conception of the individual is critically referred to as "atomistic" as it reduces and isolates the individual to merely a thinking thing, rather than an embodied being. It has its roots in the rationalism of Plato, in the reduction of the Cartesian cogito, in Kant's notion of autonomy as enlightenment, and it continues in the liberal political discourse of Rawls and Dworkin (Plato 2002; Descartes 2003; Kant 1999; Rawls 1999; Dworkin 1988).

In Plato's metaphysics, two worlds exist: the inferior material one and the superior immaterial world of ideas. Parallel to this, there are two dimensions of the self, the physical body and the superior rational mind. Only the latter can be a reliable means of uncovering knowledge of the forms, and so individuals ought to "practice dying" by focusing on pursuits of the rational psyche rather than the sensuous body. Physical aspects of embodiment are not considered essential to the individual and are held as epistemologically flawed in giving unreliable knowledge about mere particulars rather than universals. Cartesian dualism continues this tradition by conceiving the individual as an essentially disembodied, isolated, rational thinking thing. While the external dimension is acknowledged, it is treated as inferior to the internal dimension of mentality, and the body is again treated as a less reliable means of knowledge acquisition. Descartes claims that existence can be derived from mentality, but discounts how the language laden within thinking is something that could not come from a mere individual, but rather must be socially born. Likewise, he does not acknowledge how his own existence is necessarily dependent not merely on a divine first cause, but more immediate causes of family and means of nurture that created and instilled in him the ability to think. The rational mind is also considered the site within which autonomous preferences are formed and from which free choices are made.

In modern political discourse, the concept of autonomy has received similar atomistic treatment. Autonomy is the capacity to make a free rational choice for oneself, a choice that is truly one's own and not the product of, for example, manipulation or coercion (Anderson and Christman 2005). As such, many, including Kant, treat it as the precondition of moral responsibility and as a capacity that all rational individuals have an obligation to cultivate (Kant 1999). Call this the autonomy imperative. Because normative freedom supervenes on rationalism, individuals cannot be morally responsible or truly free without being autonomous. Because all individuals equally have what is needed to cultivate it—a rational mind—then they can and should become autonomous (Hill 1989; Guyer 2003). If they do not, it is for Kant most typically a matter of insufficient individual effort. Kant cites individual laziness and cowardice as the two central obstructions, which arise internally from the individual, not externally from the social environment (Kant 1999, 11). Individuals either do not exert sufficient effort to enact the intellectual labor required to think for themselves or they are too fearful to do so, as when thinking for oneself puts one at odds with members of one's social group and requires courage that some do not muster. Kant's autonomy imperative posits that all rational individuals can and must think for themselves, and if they do not, it is paradigmatically a failure of their own responsibility.

This tradition of atomistic individualism and autonomy has continued in liberal discourse through John Rawls and others. Rawls' original position seeks to strip individuals of their embodiment, including race, class, gender, orientation, and identity in order to be in optimal normative position to make universal prescriptions about equality, laws, and political justice regarding the basic structure of society (Rawls 1999). The problematic presumptions are 1) that individuals can in fact strip their thinking of influences stemming from their embodiment, 2) that doing so advantages their thinking by outfitting them in a more objective, neutral, and universal position, and 3) they ought to do so to arrive at the best concept of political justice. A normative account of political justice might not include, as essential, notions of racial or environmental justice from behind the veil of ignorance. The upshot of the atomistic model is that it allows ideal theorists to make universal prescriptions of justice, but the disadvantage is that it impractically strips individuals of essential aspects of their identity and deters attention from advantages afforded by those differences. Others continue this line of atomism regarding autonomy (Dworkin 1988; Frankfurt 1988).

Because they background, discount, and sometimes ignore the external social dimension, the atomistic models of the individual and autonomy cannot accommodate institutional racism as a systemic autonomy obstruction because they occur at the social level of culture and the physical level of embodiment. Some constraints on autonomy are trivial, such as when one of two equally acknowledged qualified job candidates does not get a desired position. The choice to work at a place is obstructed by the job going to another candidate for unproblematic reasons. But if an equally qualified candidate of color is not given the position specifically for being of color with a presumption of essentialist racial inferiority in play within a history of systemic and institutional racism, once codified in laws and now lingering in social conventions, then such an obstruction is not trivial, but serious, not individual, but systemic, not incidental, but contrived, and not of minimal result, but considerable consequence.

Embodiment and culture occur in the external dimension of action and social environment, but autonomy has traditionally been located only in the internal dimension of thought. A type of logic of domination holds that because the oppression of racism does not preclude one from competently forming internal preferences, it must not be a serious obstruction to autonomy. The central contradiction of the American social contract and the institution of racism is that in the abstract, "all men are created equal," but in the concrete dimension of social existence and political laws, racism has been interwoven into the legal system to structurally disadvantage and oppress nonwhites. This obstruction to autonomy occurs, then, in the external dimension of overarching laws that govern what is legally permissible in society and helps establish norms of behavior and socio-political conventions.

Culture transcends mere laws and concerns political conventions and patterns of social behavior. Operating in an external social space that laws cannot always capture makes seeing race-based obstructions to autonomy difficult for some, as do shifting definitions of race and racism (Omi and Winant 1994). "Embodiment" means that humans have bodies as essential aspects of the self, reflecting their physical, empirical, and ecological nature. All things physical belong to material contexts, which for humans is both the social and ecological environment. Embodiment is the most overt aspect upon which race is cast, but it also penetrates to the interiority of persons, i.e., minds. Embodiment concerns lived somatic existence of political bodies within a body politic. While race does not exist at the genetic level of embodiment, it exists socially and politically and is ascribed to bodies. Likewise, race exists culturally in paradigmatic social practices, experiences, histories, and treatments of individuals ascribed to a racial group. Both culture and embodiment occur socially, in the external dimension, and can affect internal thinking. Because the atomistic model backgrounds and discounts the external dimension, it cannot accommodate race-based obstructions that arise socially. A different model that accommodates the external social dimension is therefore needed. That is the ecological model of the individual and autonomy.

ATOMISTIC AUTONOMY	Competency conditions	Authenticity conditions
Internal Autonomy	**Negative conditions** Lack of cognitive impairment Nondomination	**Negative conditions** Free of oppression, manipulation, coercion
	Positive conditions Ability to reflectively think for oneself and form preferences	**Positive conditions** Forming preferences that are truly one's own

Table I: Conditions for Atomistic Autonomy

II. Ecological Individualism and Autonomy

I have formulated a version of the relational self and autonomy pioneered by social and feminist philosophers that I call ecological (Chackal 2016, 2018). This model is better equipped to accommodate various misconceptions of the atomistic model of the individual and autonomy, particularly those concerning embodiment and environment. In contrast to the atomistic model, the social self (Taylor 1992; Sandel 1998; MacIntyre 2007) emphasizes the constitutive effects of society and community on the individual, who is situated in a material political context. Feminist scholars treat the social self as embodied, relational, and contextual (Stoljar 2015). The self is seen as not merely a rational mind, but a sensuous body outfitted with emotional intelligence, as not existing in abstract theoretical space, but rather situated in physical places, as a being that is surrounded by others, not socially isolated, as a being that gains affordances for existence and thinking from others, not by oneself, as existing within a particular social history that conditions them, not in an abstract space where such considerations are ignored to present a universal space that could be "everywhere and nowhere" (Friedman 1997, 2003; Meyers 1989; Brison 2000). Following Val Plumwood (1993) and Lorraine Code (1987, 2006), I have expanded the self from being merely social—relationally gaining affordances necessary for individual being from the social world—to being ecological—relationally gaining affordances necessary for individual being from the material world or physical environment, both social and natural, and both immaterial and physical.

The self is not merely socially born but also ecologically birthed. The key idea of "ecology" is to situate particular things within a systematic context, to illuminate the effect of that context on any particularity, and to underscore the relationships of interconnection and interdependency among various parts within a system. Systems may be social and natural, physical and immaterial, and internal and external. Ecological individualism highlights how the self is formed not just socially, but also environmentally and naturally. To be sure, individuals are also partly formed internally from their own innate dispositions, talents, and preferences. My purpose here is not to splice how the proportions of individual identity form internally and externally, but merely to highlight that both internal and external conditions contribute to the formation of an individual, and that the external conditions are both social and natural and historically backgrounded. It must also be noted that the two dimensions I underscore—the internal and external—are often entwined and some conditions fall into both dimensions, not neatly into one or the other. The dualisms overlap and help constitute one another. But the binary analysis is useful to highlight the paradigmatic features of each dimension and establishes the groundwork to then disrupt the dualism by highlighting crossover and mutual constitution.

Likewise, my version of the relational self expands liberal autonomy from being merely an internal capacity of thought to being an external capacity for action. I also expand relational autonomy from being merely activated by one's social environment to being activated by the natural environment as well. I call this ecological autonomy. The first expansion from internal to external autonomy requires additional conditions to be met. In liberal autonomy, there are two central conditions for internal autonomy: competency and authenticity. The competency condition requires that individuals can think for themselves, form preferences, and make choices. Marylyn Friedman (1997, 2003) requires a period of "reflective endorsement" where individuals consider a variety of options surrounding a given decision, critically reflect upon them, and choose for themselves (Friedman 2003, 4-5). Aside from this positive condition, there are also negative conditions required for competency, including non-domination and lack of cognitive impairment. Theories of autonomy differ in terms of positive and negative conditions; some require thick or thin sets of each. Some theories also posit constitutive accounts, where the tools needed for autonomy arise from the environment, also both positively and negatively. Representative scholars hold that certain negative social conditions are required for embodied autonomy, such as nondomination; similarly required are laws and conventions that allow individuals to form preferences and make choices (Brison 2000; Oshana 2006). In a different sense, Joseph Raz argues that society makes various things available for choosing, such as commodities and jobs, but also lifestyles and identities (Raz 1988, 205).

Secondly, choices must meet the authenticity condition, which requires that they are truly one's own and not the product of, for example, manipulation, coercion, or oppression (Stoljar 2015, 17). Choices are not authentic when individuals are forced to make them, for example, via means of oppression, particularly internalized oppression. On my view, authenticity requires critical reflective endorsement. Negative conditions include a lack of self-deception and deception from others, and any direct or indirect coercion. It also entails two positive conditions. First, individuals must consider pertinent information in the procedure. What is pertinent will depend on the circumstances of the individual, preference, and context. One must consider knowledge, information, and premises that frame reflective endorsement. Liberal autonomy requires that individuals competently form preferences and requires that those preferences are truly one's own. However, the model casts autonomy as merely a capacity to internally form rather than externally enact choices.

To expand autonomy to an external capacity of action requires an additional set of competency and authenticity conditions. This is a distinguishing feature of ecological autonomy. Competency of action requires positive conditions of skills, techniques, and embodied knowhow needed to perform a given action. It also includes similar negative conditions of a lack of preclusions to action such as, oppression, action-limiting laws or conventions, or physical restrictions like incarceration. As long as one can perform an embodied action for oneself, the competency condition is met. Skills, embodied knowledge, physical ability, and material negotiation often arise from a combination of individual talent or effort, but also what society makes available or encourages. For example, those with access to education gain skills of reading, writing, and mathematics. Individuals raised in arctic climates gain the ability to distinguish various types of snow, and those raised to forage in ecologically rich areas are able to distinguish between various plants. Many raised in New York City might not develop driving skills. Some skills arise because of proximity to certain social or natural areas.

The authenticity condition for action requires that embodied actions are truly one's own. On my view, action must also meet certain socio-cultural standards outside the individual. Actions must not be products of manipulation, coercion, or oppression. Rather, individuals must perform actions for themselves. Actions must be culturally appropriate in addition to being authentically derived from the individual. Cultural standards do not have to be mainstream, but can be subcultural or counter-cultural, and can be authentic in direct opposition to prevailing cultural standards. Because the self is partly socially born and actions are in the domain of the external world, then there are standards not just of competency, but also authenticity that are outside the individual. This occurs particularly with actional claims of identity. Merely because an individual performs an action that they chose does not make it authentic if the individual is not truly what they claim to be or if the action somehow does not culturally cohere with the individual. Some people may say they "identify" with a community of which they are not truly a part, yet claim it as their identity, but if the community does not legitimize that identity by acknowledging it, the claim may be inauthentic. Illustratively, some people fake accents or deceive others about where they are from. Cases abound in which individuals pose as something they are not. External authenticity then arises from some combination of actual coherence with who a person is with a recognition that that identity is not merely internal but also socially created, and so must somehow meet certain external standards about what one claims to be. Autonomy includes action as an external capacity, not just thought as an internal one, and requires an additional set of competency and authenticity conditions. Expanding atomistic individualism and autonomy to be ecological allows race to be included in social identity and racism to be seen as an obstruction to autonomy.

ECOLOGICAL AUTONOMY	Competency conditions	Authenticity conditions
Internal Autonomy	**Negative conditions** Lack of cognitive impairment Nondomination **Positive conditions** Ability to reflectively think for oneself and form preferences Access to education	**Negative conditions** Free of oppression, manipulation, and coercion Lack of self-deception and deception from others **Positive conditions** Forming preferences that are truly one's own Critically reflective endorsement Consideration of pertinent information (which may depend on individual circumstances, preferences, and context)
External Autonomy	**Negative conditions** Lack of oppression and constricting laws and/or conventions (ability to perform requisite embodied actions) **Positive conditions** Acquisition of skills, techniques and embodied knowhow Ability to physically perform intended actions	**Negative conditions** Free of oppression, manipulation, and coercion **Positive conditions** Culturally appropriate decisions (according to a culture or subculture one identifies with, and recognized by others who share that culture/subculture)

Table II: Conditions for Ecological Autonomy

III. Racial Formations of Individuals and Social Groups

Contemporary race-based obstructions to autonomy still supervene on antiquated conceptual schemes arising from historical white supremacy. To account for the range of race-based autonomy obstructions, another conceptual couplet should be added to the analysis: space and place. I discuss these ideas in the next section. To explain how these constraints on autonomy linger, I use Mills' The Racial Contract (1999) to highlight how notions of race and racial identity were developed. Mills posits American racism as a political system of white supremacy. Conceived this way, racism is an external social space. Yet, racism is also internal because it is predicated on adopting certain conceptual schemes and conceiving of individuals and social groups in particular ways. Institutional racism speaks to the external socio-political environment of racism while personal racism speaks to internalized concepts expressed externally in social exchanges. To be sure, each influences and sometimes partly constitutes the other. The internal dimension, the atomistic self, and the concept of space as the realm of ideal theory are grouped together. Concurrently, the external dimension, the ecological self, and the concept of place as the realm of pragmatic theory are grouped together.

Mills provides resources necessary to understand how racism functions across the internal and external dimensions. Whereas the social contract supposedly includes all societal members (Hobbes 1994; Locke 1948; Rousseau 2012), Mills argues that it was only meant to guarantee full political citizenship to whites, particularly white men (Mills 1999, 14-15). The racial contract is the actual socio-political system encompassing nonwhites and offers a superior historical descriptive power and normative force compared to the social contract. The racial contract is political, i.e., external, insofar as it is socially born and codified into laws and conventions. Yet, it is also moral and epistemological, i.e., internal, insofar as race affects thinking in the concepts it encourages, which determine ethical and epistemological standards, including who is seen as having moral agency, trustworthiness, and epistemic credibility. It cannot be overstated that the dimensions entwine and inform each other, so the ethical and epistemological are related to the social and political. While social changes have occurred in the external political realm, some archaic ideas about race still linger institutionally and within individuals and social groups, and race continues to infect thought, conception, perception, and political treatment of racialized bodies.

To examine race-based obstructions to autonomy, race, racial formation, and racism must be defined. Omi and Winant observe various contradictions and shifting meanings in conceptualizing race. A primary question is, is race real and if so in what sense? Although it is tempting to posit it, race is not "an essence [and is not] something that is fixed, concrete, or objective…[but it is also not] a mere illusion, a purely ideological construct which some ideal nonracist social order would eliminate" (Omi and Winant 1994, 54). "Race is a concept which signifies and symbolizes social conflicts and interests by referring to different types and bodies" (Omi and Winant 1994, 55). Racial formation is "the socio-historical process by which racial categories are created, inhabited, transformed, and destroyed," necessarily linked to the evolution of political and social power (Omi and Winant 1994, 55). Race is not reducible to phenotype, ethnicity, class, or nation, but bears some association to them. It is also not a stagnant fixed concept, but one that is elastic and malleable, and which shifts and evolves.

Just as race is transient, changing, and unfixed, racism undergoes a congruent trajectory. Racism is defined as relationships of prejudice, discrimination, and institutional inequality, which are similar to but distinct from the concept of race, and change across time (Omi and Winant 1994, 69-71). Race has no fixed meaning but operates fluidly and is constructed and altered socio-historically through competing racial projects, where history is contested. A racial project is racist "if and only if it creates or reproduces structures of domination based on essentialist categories of race" (Omi and Winant 1994, 71). The key question in determining whether a social phenomenon is racist is whether a racial project demonstrates a link between essentialist representations of race and social structures of domination.

Notions of racialism or racial essentialism, although once a prominent mechanism to ascribe faux scientific support to the notion of ontological genetic differences between races, have long since been debunked (Omi and Winant 1994, 63-65). In that sense, race was always a socially manufactured myth. Yet, there are certain skin tones, hair types, and body forms that operate as paradigmatic representations of prominent somatic features across various races. Such physical associations encouraged the idea that race was real, biological, and genetic. In these senses, race was said to exist internally (i.e. genetically) but never did, and as a consequence was thought to exist externally in a natural rather than social sense. In this contradiction, race is socially real, if not natural, and externally relates to paradigmatic somatic types, even if notions of paradigmatic somatic types collapse upon critical interrogation, which I contend they do. The point is that in certain social contexts, typically the uniquely American one, race is linked to embodiment, which is one sense in which race exists externally.

Appiah (1990) offers three conceptual distinctions concerning types of racism. Racialism is the idea that there are essential traits and tendencies of races not shared by other ones which are inheritable and unavoidable and include physical and mental features (Appiah 1990, 4-5). This view may also be called racial essentialism, which as such, does not necessitate value claims based on the differences of such features. Extrinsic racism holds that there are differing moral qualities arising from essential racial attributions expressed in individual behavior and action which can be used as a justification for treating members of certain races differently. This racism is extrinsic, because discrimination is based on the external action of individuals. If a certain race is thought to be intellectually inferior, and such inferiority is externalized in action, then because the action is inferior, differential treatment is thought to be justified. Intrinsic racism holds that the racial essences themselves, rather than the behavior that follows, bears moral qualities. Because moral qualities are present within the essence, then members of races are determined by those qualities in thought and action.

Being the recipient of racist treatment has not been held to be a serious obstruction to autonomy by traditional, modern, and liberal theorists because such treatment exists extrinsically in action rather than internally in the thought of members of a certain race. At the same time, this view discounts the ways in which racist treatment is predicated on assumptions about another's intrinsic moral status extending from their race. This is why Appiah notes that extrinsic racists are really insincere intrinsic racists (Appiah 1990, 5). Ultimately, Appiah also defines racism, particularly intrinsic racism, as a "cognitive incapacity" which impairs one's internal thinking, and then emerges as an actual feature of a racist's thinking premised on essentialist notions of the recipient's being (Appiah 1990, 6).

In addition to formulating an inferior metaphysics of black identity, racial formation or the racial contract also formulated a contrasting white identity. To be a real American was to be white, which excluded African, Indigenous, Latino, and Asian peoples from true belonging (Omi and Winant 1994, 66). This external social othering became internalized in the psyches of the population, a prominent way in which the external sociopolitical environment penetrates internally. Racial formation concerns the use of political power to socially exploit and oppress othered bodies. It includes the variety of historical racial projects that sought to essentialize races with loaded inferiority attributed to nonwhites, and contrasting superiority for whites. Such projects involved forming key concepts of race, including racialized individuals and groups, and those concerning racialized environments. For Mills, this formation involves a process of racially normalizing or stereotyping individuals, groups, and environments.

Mills argues that the racial contract normalizes and racializes 1) individuals and 2) spaces (Mills 1999, 41-62). On my view, this means that race operates internally and externally, mentally and somatically, naturally and socially, and objectively and subjectively. Under the racial contract, nonwhites have historically been conceived as inferior to whites. How individuals are conceived metaphysically affects how they are treated sociopolitically. Because whites, particularly white men, are seen as fully rational, they are considered normatively autonomous. Consequently, they receive moral status, political freedom under the law, full human dignity, and epistemic credibility. Contrarily, nonwhites are conceived ontologically as rationally inferior; consequently they cannot by equally autonomous, and therefore do not receive equal moral status, political freedom, full dignity, and epistemic credibility. The ontological difference creates an ethical disparity, which is used to justify moral, political, and epistemological exclusion. Ontological conception affects embodied perception and justifies moral and political oppression. Together, false ontology along with false ethical, political, and epistemological inferences stemming from it contribute to the groundwork of race-based autonomy obstructions.

The racial contract normalizes and racializes individuals with ascribed ontological status. Included in that ontology is inferiority across metaphysics, epistemology, morality, and politics. Often, contrasts between whites and nonwhites are cast in a series of "value dualisms," which are couplet concepts with one category held as distinct and superior to the other (Plumwood 1993, 43). Such dualisms include white/black, male/female, person/subperson, culture/nature, rational/irrational, free/unfree, soul/body, Christian/heathen, civilized/savage, citizen/slave, and crucially, free/determined. The norming process of racial formation establishes personhood for whites and subpersonhood for nonwhites. "There are bodies impolitic whose owners are judged incapable of forming or fully entering into a body politic" because they are treated as subpersons who lack reason, autonomy, and therefore freedom (Mills 1999, 53). Because nonwhites are treated as cognitively less rational, they are held to be subpersons. Whereas persons are epistemically competent, can participate in knowledge production, and are credible and trustworthy, subpersons are not epistemically competent, cannot participate in knowledge production, and are seen as epistemically dubious. Consequently, they are held to lack moral agency (and are not treated as full moral patients either). A reduced moral status carries with it a diminished political status. If not moral agents, nonwhites cannot be legal citizens. Nonwhites are seen as being less rational, autonomous, and responsible, and on that basis are denied full personhood and citizenship.

The modern racialist conception of nonwhites is still present and continues to affect conception, perception, and political treatment. How individuals and social groups are perceived often supervenes on how they are conceived. If conceived as inferior, irrational, epistemically untrustworthy, not full moral persons, not complete legal citizens, then they will be socially perceived and treated in similar inferior ways. Mills points out that conception functions as a categorical barrier preventing equitable moral treatment (Mills 2007). He contends that the mark of new contemporary racism is a cognitive dissonance, a selective colorblindness, a benefiting ignorance and refusal to acknowledge structural discrimination. This explains why antiquated notions of race, atomistic individualism and autonomy, and spatial ideal thinking persist (Mills 2005, 166). I will illustrate this idea in the fifth section.

The structure of discrimination arises through philosophical concepts of race. Such concepts were not eradicated with emancipation, civil rights, or a black president. Rather, they linger as background conditions that continue to affect perception and socio-political treatment. Mills identifies racism arising from collective amnesia about historical reality and selective ignorance about its vestiges. Consequently, memory itself is political, in terms of what is socially recognized, memorialized, observed, and historicized. Selective memory enables some whites to not recognize their own privilege and to be blinded by entitlement (Mills 2007). Additionally, the modern racialized conception of nonwhites affects how individuals are treated epistemically. I frame autonomy as much as an epistemic capacity as it is an actional and political one. Thinking for oneself competently and authentically is an epistemic process. If conceived as cognitively inferior, individuals and social groups will likewise be seen as epistemically dubious, untrustworthy, and unreliable.

Racial formation of nonwhites by whites attributed a lack of moral agency due to not being fully rational, and an immoral status related to perceived savagery and lack of civility. This was eventually cashed out in criminality being attached to the ontological conception of nonwhites, particularly blacks (Foucault 1995; Davis 2003). This racialism, in turn, encourages the perception of blacks as threatening, perpetrating, and dangerous, which is ascribed to black bodies, especially black male bodies. These considerations amount to a conception that directs perception that directs treatment, which can now be flushed out as contributing to collective race-based autonomy obstructions. Before fleshing this out in applications, I will describe in the next section another crucial couplet, space and place, and map those ideas onto the internal/external and atomistic/ecological distinctions.

IV. Formations of Spaces and Places

The second sense in which race exists externally and socially is in terms of space. Conceptually, space is abstract, neutral, nonphysical and universal. It is a theoretical domain that can be qualified, such as in the notion of "public space," but its key feature is its featurelessness—its immateriality, universality, and homogeneity. Its conceptual power consists in the ability to represent "everywhere and nowhere" as it denotes some universal domain encompassing all particular places. Because of its neutrality, space is not held to affect the constituents within it and is thought to offer a domain of being that functions uniformly for all, despite particularities that arise from individuals, social groups, natural environments, physical contexts, material histories, and distinct time periods. Value dualisms also occur in environmental spaces, including neighborhood/ghetto, property owners/non-owners, right/wrong side of the tracks, and participation in public space/exclusion from it. Space is where laws and constitutions are typically conceived, as they are written for everyone equally. Space is the domain of the atomistic individual and autonomy because in each the external dimension is excluded. Space is where the Rawlsian original position occurs and from where individuals reduced to atomistic counterparts make normative claims about Rawls' two principles of justice. Space is the internal domain of thought where difference is excluded in favor of uniformity. Homogeneity enables universal normative claims of justice to be made. Space then is associated with the internal dimension.

Conversely, place is particular, material, contextual, historical, and differentiated by time. It is physically and socially locatable, and individuals and social groups can be situated within places. Unlike space, place affects and even partly constitutes its constituents. It is the material and cultural background within which embodied social beings exist. Places are individual, particular, and exist within locatable geographies that carry topographies within which individuals empirically negotiate. Places have particular characteristics arising from heterogeneous features that distinguish them, which influence individuals and groups within them. Because place is essentially empirical, it belongs to the external, social and natural dimension. Further, places are ecological—they are complex natural and social systems composed of various interrelated and interdependent parts that partly constitute identity and relationality of constituents. As such, place is the domain of ecological being, not atomistic selfhood, and the context in which social and embodied autonomy occurs. Place has superior descriptive capability because it accommodates actual historical circumstances, material conditions, and temporal differentiation within which individuals and social groups exist. Conceptually, place has a superior normative power because it can situate prescriptions of justice and morality within actual lived embodied existence and natural and social environments.

Ecological autonomy's normative power arises from being grounded in an accurate understanding of the internal and external dimensions of autonomy and in a historically grounded critical analysis. Social Ecology and Ecofeminism can provide additional resources to help ground its normativity. Racism and racialism are "isms" of domination, underpinned by hierarchy and value-laden differences (Warren 2000). They can be located within a larger history of linking women, people of color, and indigenous peoples to nature and justifying oppression of them on that basis. Social ecology holds that the human oppression of nature arises from social oppression of humans against humans (Bookchin 1982). Ecofeminism holds that social oppression of humans against nature can be rooted in the patriarchal oppression of men against women. Following these two frameworks highlights Plumwood's aforementioned "value dualisms"—ideas cast in couplets that correspond to one of two categories, one is more closely related to humans, and the other to nature: human/nature, men/women, civilized/savage, white/black, etc. Characterizing the entire schema of value dualisms are hierarchy and domination (Plumwood 1993, 47). Bookchin discusses at length the human tendency to justify social hierarchy and domination by grounding it in nature. He vehemently rejects this program and instead roots hierarchy and domination in social institutions, not nature (Bookchin 1982, 90-95). There is no hierarchy and domination in nature, despite predator/prey relations, death, and food chains, for they fall short of rising to contrived violence, conceptual assertions, institutional oppression, and hubris and avarice present in hierarchy and domination. Bookchin concludes that the normative implication arising from the absence of hierarchy and domination in nature is that they are to be eschewed in social relationships. It is in human as well as ecological nature to have relationships based in "symbioses," natural collaborative and communal relationships. Nature is predicated on differentiation, mutuality, reciprocation, cooperation, and common ends, despite the casting of nature arising from distorted interpretations of Darwin as hyper-competitive and essentially destructive.

These ideas can be seen as the values of nature that humans may extrapolate into social and human/nature relations. They can be used to ground the normativity of ecological autonomy for three reasons. 1) Humans and the natural world are empirical, so an account of autonomy predicated on ecological materiality is needed. 2) By extension, a normative account of autonomy must also accommodate external action, not just internal thought, and the ways in which both internal and external autonomy supervene on environmental features, some of which enable autonomy to generate, and others which may obstruct it. 3) An ecological treatment holds that human beings share a base or global level of autonomy arising from their natural capabilities, even while there is autonomy that arises locally or contextually in relation to certain social and natural environments. This is distinct from the atomistic model which reflects the tendency toward value dualism and holds that people of color and women have less autonomy because they are by nature less rational (Plumwood 1993; Mills 1999). Normativity arises because of ecological autonomy's descriptive accuracy, historical grounding, and superiority of explanatory power in positing internal and external dimensions of autonomy within both social and natural environments.

Internalism, atomistic individualism and autonomy, and the concept of space belong to the same dimension. Externalism, ecological individualism and autonomy, and the concept of place belong to the same dimension. To be sure, these dimensions entwine, affect, and sometimes constitute one another; they are not a strict binary, but can be conceptually separated for analysis. The three components of each dimension inform one another and produce certain ways of thinking. In the next section, I show how they represent two frameworks of viewing individuals in the social world, which carry certain features that are foregrounded or backgrounded depending on the framework and intention or consequence of its use.

V. Applications

In the previous sections, I described theoretical concepts to examine race-based autonomy obstructions. I outlined two dimensions of examination—the internal and external dimensions, compared the atomistic and ecological models of the individual and autonomy, and added the space/place distinction to the analysis. I discussed why the internal, atomistic, and space-based models are not equipped to handle race-based, externally arising social obstructions to autonomy. I argued that the external, ecological, and place-based models provide the resources needed to confront such obstructions. In this final section, I apply those ideas to a number of illustrative cases.

Related to autonomy and responsibility, the atomistic individual has further been the basis for the idea of "bootstrapping," which emerged in nineteenth century America, and remains influential (Alger 1985). The American archetype of the self-made man relies on bootstrapping, which depends on the autonomy imperative, and is premised on the atomistic individual. The similar imperative is that individuals must pull themselves up by their bootstraps, i.e. take autonomous responsibility for their lives, so that they may emerge as "self-made" men. The logic is that it is morally and socially superior to formulate choices and accomplish one's goals not simply for oneself, but by oneself. Individuals are held to have more ownership of their choices and goals when they make and accomplish them independently. Properly contextualized, historical and social reality reveals that the standard of using atomistic autonomy to make oneself is largely a myth, as unworkable as the metaphor itself, for if grounded, one cannot pull oneself up by the bootstraps. And if society denies shoes, bootstrapping is rendered impossible. While some individuals have more natural and cultivated intelligence, skills, ingenuity, and determination than others, virtually no individuals "make it" or themselves alone. The extent to which individuals rely on various external sources including family, community members, public utilities, and social services is considerable, yet sometimes socially unacknowledged. One might think this is because a more contextualized treatment of individualism and autonomy is unavailable. But this is not necessarily the case.

While a notion of a contextualized individual is present in contemporary academic discourse and even in folk knowledge, typified by adages like, "it takes a village to raise a child," atomistic treatments of the individual and autonomy persist in social discourse. They linger in ways dependent on social power, political context, and parties involved. Individuals may be selectively treated as either atomistic or ecological according to the purposes underlying the treatment. If the intent is to show how tenacious individuals make themselves, then an atomistic treatment is used. But this ignores contextual aspects and their effects on individuals. If the intent is to show how reliant individuals are on social and political context, then the ecological model is used. Advantages and disadvantages occur in using either model, and parties can employ whichever model serves their social and political interests, however inconsistent they might be in selectively employing the models. While the ecological model is more descriptively accurate and has superior normative force, it is sometimes used with a certain agenda of discounting the efforts of particular individuals and social groups. Accordingly, when parties aim to discount an individual's effort, they may use the ecological model. When they aim to discount the role of the social environment, they may use the atomistic model. Which model is used depends on the critiquing party, the subject of discussion, and social-political context.

The internal, atomistic, and spatial models have been used to favor whites, particularly white males, with an inflated sense of liberal autonomy in order to cast them as more independent than they really are. The surrounding context of wealth they may begin their lives with, the historical institutional advantages afforded to them, or the ways in which they rely on others is ignored. This is the standard behind the notion of the self-made man and bootstrapping. It discounts social environmental conditions, both those that generate and those that obstruct the conditions for autonomy. Those include economic advantages with which some begin life. Examples include President Trump who often characterizes himself as a self-made businessman, but who began that career with today's equivalent of nearly half a billion dollars from his father (Barstow, Craig, and Buettner 2018). By affording institutional socio-political advantages to whites, parallel disadvantages are imposed on nonwhites; institutional racism violates the negative condition of nondomination for autonomy, and this leads to obstructions of competency and authenticity. In a context in which many individuals and social groups contend with discrimination based on essentialist notions, the absence of nondomination becomes an institutional advantage. It is a negative freedom afforded to some, but not all. Under domination, one may not be able to form a competent or authentic preference or achieve it in social action.

The internal, atomistic, and spatial models have been used inauspiciously against nonwhites by ignoring the social context of white supremacy in which nonwhite bodies are disadvantaged, and in falsely casting an equal social playing field by ignoring institutional racism. According to these models, individuals are responsible for their own lives, not external features of the surrounding political environment. In this context, individual responsibility is used against the disadvantaged as a means to blame rather than empower them. It too ignores the violations of nondomination required for autonomy. It also imposes the bootstrapping imperative on social groups without acknowledging the structural and systemic social obstructions constraining them. If individuals are entangled by poverty with little hope of social mobility, drug and crime laden places, an unfair criminal justice system, lack of access to clean water, air and food, compounded by racial discrimination, then Kant's logic and that of bootstrapping tells them that they are not expending sufficient effort or courage, aspects that arise internally, not socially. Essentially, the myth of bootstrapping ascribes the inability of nonwhites to achieve success and realize their goals to a failure of their own responsibility to transcend social constraints, not a racialized society, history, or political climate. In colloquial parlance, slavery has long been finished, so individuals and social groups should "get over it," which means internally mustering labor or bravery, rather than mutually acknowledging the external social context that may continue to obstruct them.

The external, ecological, and place-based models are used to advantage white folks who commit immoral or illegal acts to eschew full responsibility for their autonomous actions within the criminal justice system. For example, in drug-related offenses, white men might be seen contextually. While they traverse the law, other aspects of their social existence, such as background and upbringing, employment status, and previous arrests might be given more weight. This is done as a way to show that they are not totally autonomous, i.e. independent from social causes that influence and encourage certain actions. Conversely, some black and Latino men found guilty of similar offenses might be treated atomistically, cast simply as deviants, lawbreakers, and criminals, and as mentioned before, essentialized as such (Davis 2003). Essentializing people this way violates conditions of nondomination by conferring preconceived identity. They are not afforded the same contextual benefits of an ecological framework, but rather only the legal offense is seen, quite over-simplistically. This reveals that the ecological framework is one that is afforded to some but not all, and that it and the atomistic model carry advantages and disadvantages in analyses that parties employing them likely know and choose to employ according to their own interests.

At the same time, the external, ecological, and place-based models are used against nonwhites to discount their efforts of individual responsibility and to locate the source of their accomplishments in the social and political environment, rather than in their autonomy. Consider Colin Kaepernick. Along with other players, Kaepernick took a knee during several NFL games through the 2017-2018 seasons to protest institutional racism, police brutality, and a string of police killings of unarmed black men. This enraged some on the right, including President Trump, who, alleging disrespect to the country, flag, and police force, led the attack. Entangled in this narrative was an underlying notion harping back to racial formation that black folks are not real Americans; consequently, for them to use their platforms to protest racial injustice was out of place. Further, on conservative media outlets (Hannity 2017), Kaepernick was cast as ungrateful to the country that afforded him the opportunity to become an NFL player and reap associated social and economic benefits. Kaepernick was seen ecologically, as an embodied individual existing in a social-political context that afforded him resources necessary to be autonomous and accomplish his choices and goals. The connection between society, the resources it provides, and individual accomplishment was highlighted, I contend, as a way to discount his talent, courage, and fortitude in accomplishing such feats.

Because autonomy supervenes on access to social affordances that give individuals the ability to think for themselves, such as public education, then when some nonwhites attend low-income schools with limited and comparatively less resources than affluent white counterparts, the positive conditions needed for the generation of autonomy are not met. But such differences in the quality of schools are not illuminated on the spatial model, but only on the place-based model, including the effects upon individuals arising from a particular place. With reduced access to quality education, which instills in individuals the ability to think, critically reflect, and understand advantages and disadvantages across various choices, then internal competency is obstructed. Additionally, if education is where empirical training occurs, skills are cultivated, and talents are developed, then lack of sufficient access to education obstructs external competency of action. Because internal authenticity requires nondomination like lack of manipulation, coercion, or oppression, then internal authenticity may be obstructed because of racism. Individuals may not practically be able to eschew the force of social coercion that arises because of racism. Because external authenticity requires action to be true to the individual and culturally genuine, then a racialized society can encourage the values and social practices of a predominant social group, while obstructing those of a minority group. Consider the social obstructions nonwhites (particularly blacks) encounter at swimming pools, public parks, city streets, or dormitories. These examples concern obstructions arising from the social environment that obstruct both the internal capacity to think and the external capacity to act, as well as the inconsistency with which the atomistic and ecological models are used depending on the identity and agenda of the person employing the framework and the subject under discussion.

Another set of obstructions arises from the natural environment and concerns our ecological and embodied nature. It also concerns the ways obstructions arise from the social and natural environment collaboratively. Race intersects with class, and some communities of color are low-income. A reduced class status of people may affect the types of resources allocated to the area. Some urban spaces are "food deserts," a census area of at least 500 individuals lacking a grocery store within a one-mile radius in urban areas and a 10-mile radius within rural areas (United States Department of Agriculture 2016). Negative health consequences produced by food deserts undermine autonomy in a variety of ways. Higher rates of obesity and increased rates for cancer and heart disease occur. The highest levels of obesity (32-40%) were found in census tracts with no supermarkets (Larson, Story, and Nelson 2009). This study showed that better access to healthy foods leads to better intakes. Additional studies have shown that access to supermarkets is associated with reduced risk of obesity and that access to convenience stores is associated with increased risk of obesity (Wrigley, Warm, and Margetts 2003; Cummins et al. 2005). Greater availability of fast-food restaurants and cheaper foods correlates to poorer diets. Cognitive development is crucial not only for extant individuals, but also future ones. Availability of and access to foods correlate to what individuals can purchase, what informs choices, and the ability to enact them. It is also determinate of various health statuses that affect other current and future choices. Not only may such physical conditions obstruct autonomy, but because cognitive functioning requires the consumption of nutritious food, it may even obstruct internal thinking. Not only are some communities food deserts, some communities are what might be called water or air deserts because there is a lack of clean air or water. I have elsewhere discussed the inimical effects of food deserts on the competency and authenticity conditions as well as those of an absence of clean air for low income communities (Chackal 2016). Each of these examples may be contextualized as examples of environmental injustice, which in some cases intersects with environmental racism.

Another example of environmental racism that combines social and natural features to obstruct internal and external autonomy is the Flint, Michigan water crises. In 2014, the city altered its water source to the Flint River but did not apply corrosion inhibitors. Consequently, lead from aging pipes leached into the water supply, eventually exposing 100,000 residents to extremely elevated lead levels (Eligon 2016). The majority of Flint residents are black and low-income, which many contend influenced the slow and largely insufficient response. Thus far, 12 people have died, many have experienced other negative health outcomes, and the full effects may not be understood for years (Eligon 2016). The distribution of social and natural resources concerns political power, and the way it is wielded against certain communities may be informed by the historical background of institutional racism. On the racialist atomistic framework, people of color and predominantly black people are held to have less metaphysical value than whites, and consequently do not receive equal moral consideration or treatment as whites. While such may be the enabler of this environmental racism, the consequence is diminished internal and external autonomy. Frameworks that exclude embodiment, environment, and the ways in which they entwine with social factors cannot accommodate such instances. Because this case concerns both natural and social resources, then, only the place-based model that includes the natural environment, as well as the social, can accommodate it.

Without access to subsistence needs, including nutritious foods, clean air and water, and education, mentality and the ability to think may be obstructed from developing. Additionally, without access to culturally appropriate foods, internal and external identity may be obstructed. Without access to clean water or air, similar negative consequences for internal thinking occur. It's crucial to underscore the effects of the environment, both social and natural, upon both the thought and action of persons, and the ways in which socio-politics might impact the distribution of such natural resources. Whether such environmental aspects are included in political decision making depends on whether the atomistic or ecological models of autonomy are used. While the former does not incorporate them, the latter does.

Conclusion

I have described two frameworks for analysis, the internal and external dimensions, then delineated and contextualized two notions of the individual and autonomy, the atomistic and ecological models, and following, added two frameworks to consider environments, the spatial and place-based models, in order to show various ways in which features of the individual, autonomy, and social contexts are used in examining notions of thinking for oneself and moral responsibility. I argued that the external, ecological, and place-based models have superior descriptive and normative power and are better suited to accommodate the externally arising social obstructions around race that constrain and obstruct autonomy, but that the two models are inconsistently used as a way to socially advantage some over others.

Works Cited

Alger, Horatio, Jr. 1985. *Ragged Dick; And, Struggling Upward.* New York: Penguin Books.

Anderson, J. and J. Christman, eds. 2005. *Autonomy and the Challenges of Liberalism: New Essays.* Cambridge: Cambridge University Press.

Appiah, Kwame Anthony. 1990. "Racisms." In *Anatomy of Racism*, edited by David Goldberg, 3-17. Minneapolis: University of Minnesota Press.

Barstow, David, Susanne Craig, and Russ Buettner. 2018. "Trump Engaged in Suspect Tax Schemes as he Reaped Riches from his Father." *New York Times.* October 2, 2018. https://www.nytimes.com/interactive/2018/10/02/us/politics/donald-trump-tax-schemes-fred-trump.html?module=inline.

Bookchin, Murray. 1982. *An Ecology of Freedom.* Palo Alto: Cheshire Books.

Brison, S. J. 2000. "Relational Autonomy and Freedom of Expression." In *Relational Autonomy: Feminist Perspectives on Autonomy, Agency and the Social Self,* edited by C. Mackenzie and N. Stoliar, 280-300. New York: Oxford University Press.

Brown, James. 1969. *I Don't Want Nobody to Give Me Nothing (Open Up the Door, I'll Get It Myself,)* King Records. 45rpm single, Rockaway Pressing.

Chackal, Tony. 2016. "Autonomy and the Politics of Food Choice: From Individuals to Communities." *Journal of Agricultural and Environmental Ethics* 29, no. 2: 123-41.

————. 2018. "Place, Community, and the Generation of Ecological Autonomy." *Environmental Ethics* 40, no. 3: 215-39.

Code, Lorraine. 1987, "Second Persons." *Canadian Journal of Philosophy*, Supplementary Volume 13: 357.

————. 2006. *Ecological Thinking: The Politics of Epistemic Location.* New York: Oxford University Press.

Cummins, S., M. Stafford, S. Macintyre, M. Marmot, and A. Ellaway. 2005. "Neighborhood Environment and its Association with Self-Rated Health: Evidence from Scotland and England." *Journal of Epidemiology Community Health* 59, no. 3: 207-13.

Davis, Angela. 2003. *Are Prisons Obsolete?* New York: Seven Stories Press.

Descartes, Rene. 2003. *Meditations and Other Metaphysical Writings.* London: Penguin Classics.

Dworkin, G. 1988. *The Theory and Practice of Autonomy.* Cambridge: Cambridge University Press.

Eligon, John. 2016. "A Question of Environmental Racism in Flint." *New York Times.* January 21, 2016. https://www.nytimes.com/2016/01/22/us/a-question-of-environmental-racism-in-flint.html.

Frankfurt, H. 1988. *The Importance of What We Care About.* New York: Cambridge University Press.

Friedman, M. 1997. "Autonomy and Social Relationships: Rethinking the Feminist Critique." In *Feminists Rethink the Self,* edited by D.T. Meyers, 40-61. Boulder: Westview.

————. 2003. *Autonomy, Gender, Politics.* New York: Oxford University Press.

Foucault, Michel. 1995. *Discipline and Punish.* Translated by Alan Sheridan. New York: Vintage Books.

Guyer, Paul. 2003. "Kant on the Theory and Practice of Autonomy." *Social Philosophy and Policy* 20: 70-98.

Hannity, Sean. 2017. "Hannity: NFL kneelers and the left have it all wrong." Originally on *Hannity.* Fox News. Uploaded on September 27, 2017. https://video.foxnews.com/v/5590369717001#sp=show-clips.

Hill, Thomas E. 1989. "The Kantian conception of autonomy." In *The Inner Citadel: Essays on Individual Autonomy,* edited by John Philip Christman, 91-105. Brattleboro: Oxford University Press.

Hobbes, Thomas. 1994. *Leviathan.* In *Leviathan, with selected variants from the Latin edition of 1668,* edited by E. Curley. Indianapolis: Hackett.

Kant, Immanuel. 1999. "What is Enlightenment?" in *Practical Philosophy* (The Cambridge Edition of the Works of Immanuel Kant), New Ed Edition. New York: Cambridge University Press.

Larson, N.I., M.T. Story, and M.C. Nelson. 2009. "Neighborhood Environments: Disparities in Access to Healthy Foods in the U.S." In *American Journal of Preventive Medicine* 36, no. 1: 74-81.

Locke, John. 1948. *The Second Treatise of Civil Government and A Letter Concerning Toleration*. Oxford: Blackwell Press.

MacIntyre, A. 2007. *After Virtue: A Study in Moral Theory*. 3rd ed. Notre Dame, IN: University of Notre Dame Press.

Meyers, D. T. 1989. *Self, Society and Personal Choice*. New York: Columbia University Press.

Mills, Charles. 1999. *The Racial Contract*. Ithaca: Cornell University Press.

———. 2005. "'Ideal Theory' as Ideology." *Hypatia* 20, no. 3: 165-84.

———. 2007. "White Ignorance." In *Race and Epistemologies of Ignorance*, edited by Shannon Sullivan and Nancy Tuala, 11-38. Albany: SUNY Press.

Omi, Michael and Howard Winant. 1994. *Racial Formation in the United States*. New York: Routledge.

Oshana, M. 2006. *Personal Autonomy in Society*. Aldershot: Ashgate Publishing.

Plato. 2002. *Five Dialogues*, 2nd ed. Translated by G.M.A. Grube. Indianapolis: Hackett Publishing.

Plumwood, Val. 1993. *Feminism and The Mastery of Nature*. New York: Routledge.

Rawls, J. 1999. *A Theory of Justice*, rev. ed. Cambridge, MA: Harvard University Press.

Raz, J. 1988. *The Morality of Freedom*. Oxford: Oxford University Press.

Rousseau, Jean-Jacques. 2012. *Of the Social Contract and Other Political Writings*. Translated by Quinton Hoare. London: Penguin Classics.

Sandel, Michael. 1984. *Liberalism and Its Critics*. New York: New York University Press.

———. 1998. *Liberalism and the Limits of Justice*. 2nd ed. New York. Cambridge University Press.

Stoljar, Natalie. 2015. "Feminist Perspectives on Autonomy." In *Stanford Encyclopedia of Philosophy*. Article published May 2, 2013. https://plato.stanford.edu/archives/fall2015/entries/feminism-autonomy/.

Taylor, C. 1992. *Sources of the Self: The Making of Modern Identity*. New York: Harvard University Press.

United States Department of Agriculture. 2016. "Food Deserts", Agriculture Marketing Service. Accessed November, 2020. https://nifa.usda.gov/announcement/providing-affordable-healthy-food-options-food-deserts.

Warren, Karen. 2000. *Ecofeminist Philosophy: A Western Perspective on What It Is and Why It Matters*. Lanham: Rowman and Littlefield Publishers.

Wrigley, N., D. Warm, and B. Margetts. 2003. "Deprivation, Diet, and Food-Retail Access: Findings From the Leeds 'Food Deserts' Study." In *Environment and Planning* A 35: 151-88.

7.

Du Bois's *Black Reconstruction in America* as Critique of Political Economy

Osman Nemli

Introduction: Reconstructing Du Bois

Reconstruction—as philosophical concept and style of interpretation—constitutes the lens through which Du Bois's work begins to appear, at once, as unified and refracted. As a style of interpretation, reconstruction refers to Du Bois's mode of historical and philosophical research and addresses one's memories and lived experiences, sociological trends across different racial and geographic lines, the significant political and economic moments in the history of a nation and its relations with peoples and races in different nations . For Du Bois, the task of the scholar is reconstruction. It is only by reconstructing a past that no longer is, yet whose traces and reverberations continue to be felt and lived through in the present, that one can affect the future for better. In this regard, reconstruction is not simply backward looking, but is a boomerang perspective: understand the present, by way of the past, in order to change the future. It is with the aid of such a concept and style of interpretation, that the reader must also come to understand Du Bois's project.

A number of difficulties confront readers of W.E.B. Du Bois. The first of the difficulties is the sheer quantity of writings, the number of pages and documents, pamphlets and sketches, articles and monographs, lengthy texts and multi-volume novels, that one must—and ought to—go through when embarking on a reading of Du Bois. The next difficulty facing the reader, related to the first, is the multidisciplinary nature, almost to a protean degree, of Du Bois's writings. Du Bois is not someone who can easily be pigeonholed within any specific discipline. One witnesses shifting genres throughout and within his writings, sometimes even within a single text (as the chapters in *The Souls of Black Folk* attest). Du Bois demands of his readers not only to follow his multifaceted arguments, but also to adopt a multilayered analytic lens in their reading. The writings alternate between addressing speculative aims and examining concrete situations and historical events; they focus on the realities and specificities of lived experiences—whether those be his experiences or the narratives of others—and go out to survey geographical areas and historical periods. The genres of his writings encompass historical surveys, sociological analyses, biographical and autobiographical sketches, fictional writings—most notably, novels—and philosophical monographs.

The third difficulty is one that accompanies many a famed author: this is the difficulty of having one's work reduced to a single product, sometimes even a couple of phrases. Du Bois's work has also suffered from this. For him, the singular—and monumental—work is his early *The Souls of Black Folk*. My aim is not to question the validity of this work, but rather to bring that work into dialogue with Du Bois's own later writings, treating the early work as a star that requires time, distance, and the presence of other stars in order to form a constellational reading. First among Du Bois's phrases and quotes that continue to reverberate include his prognosis for the 20th century: "the 20th century is the problem of the color-line" (Du Bois 1994, v). Taken from an essay by Frederick Douglass bearing the same name, the color line is a theme that Du Bois uses to explore the history of the United States from the time that blacks were first forcefully brought to the Western Hemisphere. He also emphasizes the different aspects of the color line in different parts of the continental United States as a challenge to, and for, future generations. This challenge dares people to think about a future wherein the color line neither defines the relation between and amongst people, nor the socio-economic and political order of a nation. Du Bois would come to repeat that phrase, emphasizing different ways the color line becomes manifest, thus responding to the possible criticism that he has reduced complex historical situations and multifaceted problems to a singular cause (a critique he employed against Marxists and historians attempting to locate a singular cause and determining factor in history).

Thus, if one stops with *The Souls of Black Folk*, one stops short of continuing to examine the very problem Du Bois returned to again and again, updating and commenting upon. That is to say, one should continue reading the works of Du Bois as continuing the diagnosis of the color line he had identified earlier and would not let go of. The color line is as much a historical and political construction that Du Bois attempts to respond to as it is something that his reconstruction throughout multiple texts attempts to address and combat. The problem of the color line, in other words, is not simply something static and unchanging but is the name given to a dynamic and ever-changing set of problems that continue to evolve throughout Du Bois's life. Instead of avoiding such difficulties, one must engage with and wrestle with them, while also seeing to what extent such difficulties are reflections of the problems the author tried to address.

In this paper, I aim to demonstrate the multiple roles the concept of reconstruction plays in Du Bois's alternative critique of political economy which together function to bring into view the situation of black social life in the US. My aim has two interrelated aspects. First, I am interested in reading Du Bois's 1935 *Black Reconstruction in America* as an alternative critique of political economy to the then dominant, and still-prevalent, Marxist critique of political economy. The latter critique, for Du Bois, has oftentimes emphasized economic exploitation instead of looking at other forms of subjugation and oppression that cannot be reduced to the Marxist narrative. Rather than oppose such mono-causal attempts by replacing one cause (economic problems, or class struggle) by another cause (the racist order of white supremacy)—a replacement that would mimic the very logic of what it opposed—Du Bois expands the reach of what a critique of political economy can do. The color line, informed as much by history in the United States as by Marxist economic analysis, is a metonym by which Du Bois unravels the complex threads and ever-present discontent in the United States. He does this, in particular, by focusing on black reconstruction. Du Bois not only shows the political and economic conditions of the life within and without *the veil*—as he refers to life within and beyond the color line in both *The Souls of Black Folk* and "The Souls of White Folk"— in nineteenth and twentieth century America, but also the inadequacy of Marxism to provide an accurate account of such political and economic conditions.

Second, I will show how reconstruction plays a central, multi-layered role in the alternative critique of political economy by highlighting different ways one can, and should, hear the term 'reconstruction' in Du Bois's writings. These include: (1) the period in US history, following the Civil War; (2) the contribution to the philosophical pragmatic meaning given to 'reconstruction' by John Dewey in his lectures in Japan; (3) a form of black subject-formation in the time period following slavery and the historical period of reconstruction; and (4) the project of fashioning black social life. Upon highlighting these distinct, yet interrelated, meanings of reconstruction one arrives at a more complete and nuanced understanding of Du Bois's work as a whole. It is this nuanced and enriched understanding, furthermore, that shows the complexity and expansiveness of Du

Bois's alternative critique. The second aim, then, shows how the various ways of hearing 'reconstruction' play a multifaceted role in the alternative critique of political economy.

I. Reconstruction as Historical Name

The initial meaning of 'reconstruction' in Du Bois's text seems obvious, and it occupies a place that seems to eclipse other referents and meanings of the term. This is, firstly, the historical register: "Reconstruction" refers to the twenty year period (1860-1880) in American history, but Du Bois's approach to this period is new in that he focuses on the situation of black citizens in the movement to reform democracy during this period. In the introduction, entitled "To the Reader", of his 1935 *Black Reconstruction in America*, Du Bois begins:

> The story of transplanting millions of Africans to the new world, and of their bondage for four centuries, is a fascinating one. Particularly interesting for students of human culture is the sudden freeing of these black folk in the Nineteenth Century and the attempt, through them, to reconstruct the basis of American democracy from 1860-1880. (Du Bois 2007, xliii)

The latter part of this quote is particularly important and was the kernel of the book's subtitle: *An Essay Toward a History of the Part Which Black Folk Played in the Attempt to Reconstruct Democracy in America, 1860-1880*. Not only, then, does the text refer to the historical period of reconstruction, but it specifically addresses the actions and activities of a group that was: (1) historically disenfranchised, (2) whose historical and political disenfranchisement caused the Civil War, (3) and whose role in attempting to reconstruct democracy—or possibly construct it for the first time—faced the threat of being silenced another time.

Unpacking the historical period referred to by the word reconstruction, then, reveals a specific world and problematic: reconstruction is intimately tied to the ideal of democracy. The Civil War, whose unacknowledged or belatedly (and grudgingly) acknowledged cause Du Bois time and time again repeats as being slavery, was a result of democracy unrealized. And while the Civil War, as any other war, may end, the time period following determines its legacy and whether the reasons why the war was fought persist or have been overcome. According to Nahum Chandler,

Virtually every major thought put forth by Du Bois in this book [*Black Reconstruction in America*] had been announced in his earlier texts. Yet these ideas are produced in this context under the impress of a guiding problem of reflection, the status in historiographical discourse of the project of reconstruction of American democracy that was ambivalently attempted and ultimately compromised following the Civil War and the abolition of legal slavery. (Chandler 2014, 203)

The historically evolving meanings of the color line also accord with the linguistically evolving meanings of just what it means to be an American. One example of such a historically-charged and evolving meaning includes the phrase "we the people".[1] One must attune one's ears not only to hearing historical significance in the term "people", but also to asking who is contained and who is excluded from a people. The open-ended trajectory of a language attests to the fact that terms, phrases, expressions cannot be contained, even if expressly bound according to the wishes of founding fathers. The enveloping and non-enclosed force of "we"—that it cannot be reduced to a singular individual or type of individual—finds its correlate in the group that also cannot be contained by race, gender, or economic class. The singularity "people" whose singularity comes from its multiplicity, diversity, and plurality is precisely what is at stake in Du Bois's attempt to conceptualize reconstruction in and of America, along with the reconstruction of the black soul and community. Just as each individual and generation must ask what it means to speak of a people and to speak in the voice of a "we", so too Du Bois's text demands that readers answer the following question: What would it mean to re-habituate one's ears to avoid, or to undo without forgetting, ongoing racial erasure, to hear the blackness of Black Reconstruction in America, in all of its myriad existences, possibilities, and meanings?[2]

---

[1] I understand 'phrase' in the sense that J.F. Lyotard describes in his *Differend: Phrases in Dispute* (Lyotard 1988). It would also, in this context, be interesting to bring into discussion J. Derrida's "Declarations of Independence" (Derrida 2002).

[2] One would, here, have to go to the work of Fred Moten (especially his "Black Op" from *Stolen Life (consent not to be a single being)*) and Alexander G. Weheliye (Moten 2018). Following Weheliye: "Blackness…cannot be defined as primarily empirical nor understood as the nonproperty of particular subjects, but should be understood as an integral structuring assemblage of the modern human" (Wehelive 2014, 31-32). On the relation of lived experience, hearing, and the possibility of writing

In order to approach that question, one must understand what Du Bois means when he speaks of the souls of black folk in America. A continued erasure occurs when reducing the project following the Civil War and Emancipation to the temporally bound period of "Reconstruction in America." Erasure is confirmed by reduction. Reduction of reconstruction to the time period of the passing of the reconstruction amendments ensures a progressive account of history that also sanctifies historical oblivion, a forgetting that threatens repeating the past in virtue of not having understood it. The erasure—facilitated by a progressive reading of history while possibly going against the intentions of well-meaning progressives—sounds strangely in agreement with calls to make America great again, an America whose greatness, much like its dream, is predicated upon an ever-present social death of black life.[3] We must hear instead, and against simply "Reconstruction in America", the specificity of what Du Bois means by Black Reconstruction in America; in hearing the specificity of that call we must also hear the multiple meanings sedimented historically, philosophically, and sociologically within that call.

Democracy is the prospect and project of the historical period of Reconstruction. In his historical analysis of this period Du Bois looks to the causes leading up to the Civil War, the Civil War itself, the assassination of Lincoln, the presidency of Andrew Johnson, and the period following the Civil War, that is, the period of emancipation and reconstruction. Within this period, the passage of the Reconstruction Amendments (13th, 14th, and 15th) are examined.[4] Du Bois writes:

---

one's life, see J. Derrida's text on Nietzsche (among others), *The Ear of the Other: Otobiography, Transference, Translation* (Derrida 1985). The ear, hearing, and training of the ear is mentioned in multiple texts in Nietzsche. See, for example, the Preface of *The Genealogy of Morality* and, the Second Part ("Redemption") of *Thus Spoke Zarathustra* (Nietzsche 1989, 2005).

[3] See Orlando Patterson's *Slavery and Social Death: A Comparative Study* (Patterson 1982). Du Bois's *Reconstruction* is a counter-narrative to this contemporary one just as much as Martin Luther King Jr.'s "Letter from a Birmingham Jail," James Baldwin's *The Fire Next Time*, and Ta-Nehisi Coates' *Between the World and Me* are a continuing living critique of the American dream/nightmare (King 1991; Baldwin 1998; Coates 2015)

[4] It would take close to a century, until the 1964 civil rights act, for the 15th Amendment itself to be fully enacted; even then and following, however, such enactments are not fully realized and demand consistent vigilance for contemporary and future realization.

Easily the most dramatic episode in American History was the sudden move to free four million black slaves in an effort to stop a great Civil War, to end forty years of bitter controversy, and to appease the moral sense of civilization. From the day of its birth, the anomaly of slavery plagued a nation which asserted the equality of all men, and sought to derive powers of government from the consent of the governed. (Du Bois 2007, 1)

The historical approach to reconstruction forces the taking up of the cause of the Civil War and American wealth, and the subjugation of one race by another, referred to by Du Bois as the plague of the nation.[5] This specific cause has, according to Du Bois, been either unacknowledged, deferred, or seen as one among many (though certainly never as first among other causes). Such obfuscations, deflections, and silences amount to concealing a particular truth of history which is the job of the historian to seek and disclose. In *The Souls of Black Folk*, Du Bois refers to the historical register in this way, when discussing his essay collection:

The problem of the twentieth century is the problem of the color-line,—the relation of the darker to the lighter races of men in Asia and Africa, in America and the islands of the sea. It was a phase of this problem that caused the Civil War; and however much they who marched South and North in 1861 may have fixed on the technical points of union and local autonomy as a shibboleth, all nevertheless knew, as we know, that the question of Negro slavery was the real cause of the conflict. (Du Bois 1994, 17)

Du Bois's reconstruction of the period following the Civil War, while being a grand survey of a number of decades in various southern states, is a response to a particular problem he saw developing and, therefore, has a specific aim. The specific aim is to counter the problematic 'propaganda of history', as he calls it in the final chapter of his text. Du Bois's critique of a propagandistic retelling of history draws inspiration from a divide at work in the history of philosophy, most notably in Plato's dialogues and Marx's social and political writings. While for the former, the divide is the opposition between the falsity of sophists and the truth that is sought by philosophers, the latter aims to expose the lies of the ideological superstructure, notably a bourgeois superstructure, by way of a scientific critique of political economy. Marx's critique of political economy also doubles as

---

[5] After Kierkegaard, this could be called "the sickness unto (Black/African) American death."

a critique of ideology by claiming to go beyond and behind the veil of bourgeois social existence. Bourgeois ideology is a product of a specific political and economic system and at the same time a force that perpetuates the very economic system of which it is a product. Marx's claim was that the profit-driving mechanism and unabated surplus-value could not continue indefinitely. The way he opposed such an ideology was via the science of history, a specific interdisciplinary critique of political economy that relied upon historical models, sociological analytics, philosophical analyses, and economic statistics.

Like Plato and Marx, Du Bois emphasizes the Truth of History in contrast to ideology. His opponents, here, are propagandists of history, those who in the period following the Civil War and reconstruction attempt to change, alter, falsify, or mitigate the contribution of blacks in United States history. In order to undermine this propaganda of history, and oppose it with what he calls the "Truth of History", Du Bois supplements his historical research with philosophical, sociological, and economic analyses. These supplements come to the fore precisely when we pay heed to the additional ways of hearing "reconstruction".

II. Pragmatic Reconstruction

The second way to hear the term "reconstruction" is by way of American pragmatism. This philosophical movement, which Du Bois had studied and contributed to, provides reconstruction additional philosophical relevance, building upon and extending beyond historical concerns and political events. In approaching Reconstruction as more than just a twenty year period of American History following the Civil War, Du Bois draws out the political significance of what took place during that time period in order to address its moral and social implications for present and future generations.

In February and March of 1919, American pragmatist John Dewey gave a series of lectures in Japan, under the title of "Reconstruction in Philosophy." He there claims:

> It is the function of this lecture to show how and why it is now possible to make claims for experience as a guide in science and moral life which the older empiricists did not and could not make for it. (Dewey 2004, 78)

Beginning with the historical and scientific, and extending into the moral, Dewey aims to show the progressive and reconstructive tendencies at work throughout the development of Western philosophy. The overall arc and aims of his lecture series include: briefly reconstructing key developments in the history of epistemology (from the Ancient Greek search for singular causes and principles, to debates between empiricism and rationalism, up to the Kantian Revolution and German Idealism); elaborating developments in empirical philosophy, from the British empiricists to the American pragmatists; highlighting moments in the scientific revolution, which from the time of Bacon has undermined the authority of religion, dogmatic thought, and other idols; and initiating the conversation about a similar revolution in moral and social thought. The central philosophical thread running throughout the lecture series is what Dewey calls reconstruction:

> A philosophic reconstruction which should relieve men of having to choose between an impoverished and truncated experience on the one hand and an artificial and impotent reason on the other would relieve human effort from the heaviest intellectual burden it has to carry. It would destroy the division of men of good will into two hostile camps. It would permit the co-operation of those who respect the past and the institutionally established with those who are interested in establishing a freer and happier future. (Dewey 2004, 101)

Colloquially, reconstruction is the act of building up (again) something which has been broken down into specific parts. Pragmatism builds upon this idea and attempts to (re)construct a philosophically rich and thick account of experience. Experience envelopes both the lived situations of individuals as well as the relations among people and their interactions through time. Experience is the enveloping fold that individualizes as much as it groups. It brings together subjects along with objects to form a unifying horizon within which meaning is made and further enriched. Reconstruction is the manner by which individual and social experience is recollected and retrieved, and this recollection need not be something that someone has undergone or experienced themselves. Individuals and groups can thus reconstruct the experience of time gone by without worrying whether they had first-hand knowledge of those situations. Reconstruction is not simply the re-assembly of something in the same manner as it might have been before. Instead, and especially when dealing with the reconstruction of historical events, it is a bringing together of disparate parts with the aim of presenting a whole which may not have existed in that manner before.

Reconstruction is a synthetic act assembling something, sometimes new, from individual pieces, sometimes left over after the analytic acts of the past. Reconstruction's prefix, *re-*, has the added benefit of highlighting the iterative element of such an act; we are not only dealing with a single act or mono-causal process of construction, but with an attempt at repeating the acts and multiple processes of construction. Not only is reconstruction an incomplete, or open-ended, process but the whole that is produced in the process of reconstruction is, while not a total whole, not lacking in anything and greater than the sum of its analytic parts. Rather than pure reproduction, mechanical repetition, wherein one might not be able to tell the difference between original and copy, reconstruction brings to the fore a fashioned narrative and interpretive quality without losing any credibility.

Toward the end of his lecture series Dewey spends some time on moral reconstruction and the need for moral philosophy to accomplish goals in its field comparable to those science had established in the realm of human knowledge. While recognizing the difficulty of such an endeavor, Dewey nonetheless claims such is the goal of reconstructive philosophy and that without such a moral awakening any and all developments in the sciences would themselves be limited. However, a notable absence from Dewey's consideration is political reconstruction. It is here that Du Bois's work enters.

Five years after Dewey's lectures in Japan, Du Bois published *The Gift of Black Folk*, a text that gives an account of all the contributions of blacks to the United States of America. Beginning with the exploration of the 'new world', Du Bois catalogues and extends an analysis of the contributions of black people in war efforts, in labor, in US culture, and in US social life. He reads all of these contributions as gifts, the gifts that continue to sustain and enrich the US. It is important to note that the book is not called the "Labor of Black Folk", or "The Work of Black Folk." By focusing on the economic concept of gift and discussing the contribution of blacks in America, Du Bois accomplishes two things. First, he avoids reducing the cumulative labor and work of generations of blacks in America—extending beyond the indentured servitude, forced labor of chattel slavery—to one of unacknowledged work, labor, or praxis. For Du Bois, it is not only about putting a price tag upon labor, and in this we find a difference between a Marxist analysis of labor and one that aims to supplement economic analyses. While slavery certainly constituted the wealth of the United States, this wealth generated a surplus beyond only economic surplus value. It overflowed, contributing to culture, social life, and the possibility of realizing democratic ideals. Secondly, the gift as gift offers the promise of something new and vital that is more than its constituent parts. Furthermore, it requires nothing in return, and it is something on which a price cannot be exacted. A similar point should be emphasized today when the issue of reparations for slavery is brought up. Discussions around reparations are not solely about matters of money, nor should they be reduced entirely to economic considerations. While the economic account is important and should not be forgotten, reparations are not identical with remunerations. This is due to the fact that there is no exact amount that can be paid to right the wrongs of the past. Reparations is a concept that can be described and explained in economic terms, but that extends beyond the economic. By going beyond, it aims to address aspects of society that cannot be measured simply quantitatively.

The significance of Du Bois's *The Gift of Black Folk*, beyond enumerating the heretofore hidden and silenced contributions of black folk in America, lies in its middle chapters that focus on emancipation and freedom. It is here that Du Bois employs the colloquial, pragmatic, and historical senses of reconstruction. Black Reconstruction in America, at a very pragmatic level, can fulfill Dewey's aims to construct for the first time the political order that can sustain and do justice to the scientific achievements of the West thus far. Black Reconstruction in America is about achieving democracy in America for all, in theory and practice. Du Bois writes:

> Without the active participation of the Negro in the Civil War, the Union could not have been saved nor slavery destroyed in the nineteenth century. Without the help of black soldiers, the independence of the United States could not have been gained in the eighteenth century. (Du Bois 1924, 135)

He concludes this thought: "Dramatically the Negro is the central thread in America history" (135). One can trace this thread by taking note of the numerous gifts of black folk. The gifts have included culture and the arts, exploration, labor, contributions to various war efforts, and the greatest gift of all: democracy. Democracy, for Du Bois, is a gift of black people, the most important and open-ended one. In his account of the gift of democracy, Du Bois counters two pernicious myths: first, that blacks are passive and reactive and, second, that freedom and emancipation were both a result and gift of enlightened white consciousnesses. The former essentializing thought—pathologizing blacks as passive and reactive (read, lazy)—facilitates the latter's infantilizing white savior complex: if black people are passive and reactive, enlightened whites—so this argument runs—must step in to help them realize their freedom and to tell other whites to stop impeding it.[6] Du Bois's text provides a counter to this, relying upon sociological and historical evidence, while also quoting extensively from political treatises and philosophical reflections in order to both provide evidence contrary to these myths, but also complicate the afterlives of racist ideologies, ideologies that live past the end of the institution of slavery and the reconstruction amendments:

> It was the black man that raised a vision of democracy in America such as neither Americans nor Europeans conceived in the eighteenth century and such as they have not even accepted in the twentieth century; and yet a conception which every clear sighted man knows is true and inevitable. (Du Bois 1924, 136)

These myths not only obfuscate historical knowledge, but also impede the possibility for the liberation-aiming practices guiding behavior for the future. Concerning the transition between the former and the latter, the continuing dramatic thread of lived political existence of Black folk in the US, Du Bois reminds readers about

> the inescapable fact that as long as there was a slave in America, America could not be a free republic; and more than that: as long as there were people in America, slave or nominally free, who could not participate in government and industry and society as free, intelligent human beings, our democracy had failed of its greatest mission. (Du Bois 1924, 138)

Du Bois stresses, in contrast to these myths, freedom though taken away, or obstructed, is not necessarily *something* given back. I italicize this *something* to emphasize freedom is not just one thing (of many), and to highlight a metaphysical trap one encounters in the everyday grammar when speaking about freedom. When one speaks of freedom being 'taken away,' the grammar of the sentence makes it appear that someone, some people, or some institution must return it, like a physical thing or gift.

---

[6] One other issue to take note of here is that when blacks in the antebellum US were seen as lazy, behavior that one identified as lazy was rarely, if at all, read as a deliberate sabotage tactic and, thus, a virtue of slave morality against the economic functioning of slavery, aimed to disrupt the so-called "smooth" functioning of chattel slavery. Read from the perspective opposing anti-black racism, laziness is not lack of work but the disciplined work done to undo the dehumanizing and forced labor of a slave economy.

While individuals and institutions must recognize individual freedom, this recognition is not due to some essential quality or capacity of a person. That is the challenge of realizing an inalienable right. One demands freedom in the sense that this freedom is not *given (back)* but a demand to remove obstacles in the way of one's actualization and realization of their freedoms, while also a demand to have the state, its governing bodies, and its inhabitants live in a manner in recognition of the freedom of others written into law.

III. Black Souls Reconstructed

Among the perennial concerns in Du Bois's writings, including *Black Reconstruction in America*, are black agency, subjectivity, and community. This is yet another way one should, I argue, read and listen to the concept "Black Reconstruction". Black reconstruction is subjective reconstruction inasmuch as disparate and individual subjectivities can be constituted and reconstituted socially as a historical project. This historical project to reconstruct black subjectivities is active and creative. For Du Bois, activity and creation go beyond the simple equation of praxis with enforced labor, on the one hand, and, inversely, the equation of the lack of activity with congenital laziness. Du Bois considers both activity and creativity to be gifts of black folk. These gifts are as much constitutive of American economic ascendency and wealth as they are constitutive of black subjectivity and community. A subject can only flourish when conditions suit its life-affirming activities. Prior to emancipation, the condition of blacks in the US can be described as one of political and social destitution, a deprivation and poverty of the conditions required for flourishing.[7] Subjective reconstruction, in response to the subjective destitution formed by the institution of slavery, becomes the reconstruction of the souls of black folk. Such a reconstruction aims to realize democratic practices for the purposes of human and social flourishing.

While the influence of Marxism in Du Bois's text is unmistakable, there is a danger in overemphasizing this influence to the point of missing or obfuscating Du Bois's contribution to an otherwise white-washed field. The main import of, and reason for, not reading *Black Reconstruction in America* as simply a furtherance of Marxist scholarship in the examination of race relations throughout the Reconstructive Period of the United

---

[7] See Orlando Patterson, *Slavery and Social Death: A Comparative Study* (1982).

170

States is that Du Bois is able to show how racism can outlast its economic benefits. Put simply: racism and institutionalized forms of racism, such as in chattel slavery, persist in an unabated manner even if and when the economic circumstances no longer suit it. Du Bois's view challenges a certain retroactive account of slavery and colonialism that claims that slavery and colonial systems ceased to exist when they no longer economically suited the dominant order, whether that order is a white supremacist slave-owning society or a colonial empire. A Marxist account of history claims, furthermore, that history—which the *Communist Manifesto* had claimed is the history of class struggle—only develops when the economic base undergoes a crisis and tension (Marx and Engels 1978, 473). This tension occurs between the modes of production (the technical apparatuses and raw materials used to produce goods) on the one hand and the relations of production (the various classes of society) on the other. This reduces historical moments and the change of the superstructure (including political events) to class conflict (from which race and gender are excluded) and to various economic conflicts between the relations of production and the modes of production. According to this view, morality itself is seen as an effect of economic circumstances. As Lawrie Balfour writes,

> [Du Bois's] redescription of the fugitives' role in the Civil War as a "General Strike" in *Black Reconstruction* both highlights the economic underpinnings of the war and Reconstruction and replaces a tradition of representing black subjects as willess with a view of them as workers and political actors. (Balfour 2011, 13)

According to a certain dogmatic Marxist reading of history that was made most famous by the *diamat* (*dia*lectical *mat*erialist) scholars of the Soviet Union, history is made up of an economic base or infrastructure and an ideological superstructure.[8] The economic infrastructure is constituted by the mode of production (including technical apparatuses, factories, the use and transformation of raw materials, etc.) and the relations of production (economic classes, most notably the bourgeoisie and the proletariat). According to this mono-causal account of history, the economic base conditions and determines the ideological superstructure, which comprises all the other aspects of society, including politics, science, morals, and culture.

---

[8] Scholars of DIAlectical MATerialism include Giorgi Plekhanov, author of *Fundamental Problems of Marxism* (1992). One can also consult Samuel Haskell Baro's *Plekhanov: The Father of Russian Marxism* (1963).

For Marxism, racism (along with other forms of moral and political oppression independent of economic exploitation) is located within the ideological superstructure. Furthermore, its historical and institutional occurrences (whether in chattel slavery or segregationist societies) are caused by
that society's economic circumstances. According to this view, then, racism does not determine the economic order, but rather the reverse is true.
It would be a mistake to ascribe this interpretation to simply an unin-
formed, or historically suspect, Marxist dogmatism; rather, it stems from
the very ideological characteristics that inform Marxism itself, whether
those ideological themes themselves are reduced to economic circumstances or race separation. Du Bois's texts show clearly how and why racism continues even when, and if, surplus value is no longer produced. For
Du Bois, racism outlasts and exceeds the economically informed interpretive model of Marxism. What both perspectives, the simplistic Marxist
account and the race-essentializing account, are guilty of are the following:
(1) locating a single cause for all historical occurrences, (2) essentializing
that single cause as the driving force of historical development, and (3) not
examining that essentialized cause in all of its changing historical circumstances. After the Civil War, the landowning white population continued
to push for disenfranchisement, opposing the ratification of the 14th
Amendment, in order to maintain the monopoly of agriculture that it saw
as the counterpart to the Northern monopoly of industry. The majority of
white southerners, whom Du Bois calls the white proletariat, preferred
poverty to being seen as equal to blacks. In the penultimate chapter, entitled "Back Toward Slavery," Du Bois writes:

> The race element was emphasized in order that property-holders
> could get the support of the majority of white laborers and make it
> more possible to exploit Negro labor. But the race philosophy came
> as a new and terrible thing to make labor unity or labor class-con-
> sciousness impossible. So long as the Southern white laborers could
> be induced to prefer poverty to equality with the Negro, just so long
> was a labor movement in the South made impossible. (Du Bois
> 2007, 557)

White supremacy and chattel slavery do not simply function when it
is an economically profitable system, changing or abandoned when profits
no longer continue. White supremacy's logic cannot be fully explained or
interpreted economically, Marxist or otherwise. The logic of oppression
and racism is not reducible to the notebooks of accountants. It is important
not to read Du Bois as simply suggesting an outright refutation of Marx

or a global perspective on economic and racial conditions.[9] Du Bois's 1935 text focuses specifically on: (1) the United States, (2) race relations, or the problem of the color-line, in the United States, and (3) a particular time period of post-bellum Reconstruction in the US (1860-1880). A dogmatic Marxist analysis would, necessarily, miss such specifics in its analysis, and would risk identifying as effect that which would in fact be a cause. It would not be too much of a stretch to then risk having such an analysis establish the foundation for white revisionist histories, whether those were conservative or progressive, which would then discount the historical significance of racism as a fundamental impediment to black reconstruction. Rather than disputing Marxism outright, then, Du Bois shows the limitations of such an analysis when applied to the US context in particular. His account is a response and redress to this limitation.

Black Reconstruction in America is about the reconstruction of black subjectivity. Du Bois neither reduces subjectivity exclusively to its material and empirical circumstances nor imagines a future subjectivity that is independent of the historical, material, and empirical circumstances. He performs a careful reading of the present constituted by historical circumstances that neither foreclose nor determine future possibility. Individual subjectivity is, in its creative and reconstituting moments, more than the sum of its parts. Reconstruction is a creative force assembling the parts of a life and projecting a subjectivity that cannot be imprisoned in pre-existing conditions. In the language of what will become Sartrean existentialism, Du Bois neither allows facticity to trap black subjectivity, nor blindly equates all activity with freedom and self-constitution divorced from one's past.[10]

---

[9] Such writings would come later. Du Bois, furthermore, remained in constant dialogue with Marxist literature and figures, bringing the African Diaspora as well as the problem of the 'color-line' into theoretical dialogue with global capital.

[10] It is here, furthermore, that one can argue Du Bois provides a critique, if not criticism, *avant la lettre* of Sartrean existentialism, a critique that Fanon will also employ in *Black Skin, White Masks*. This is a critique of the lack of material and systematic constraints on individual freedom (Fanon 2008, 116-7). The early Sartre (of *Being and Nothingness*) locates a freedom within the individual that almost knows no bounds, a freedom that is only constrained by one's bad faith and inability, or weakness of character, to come to grips with the abyss of one's freedom. This freedom is also self-contradictory: self-consciousness is what it is not and it is not what it is (Sartre 2018, 629-718). Not surprisingly, the social is almost entirely absent from Sartre's phenomenological ontology, and all interpersonal relations are caught between the Scylla and Charybdis of sadism and masochism (Sartre 2018, 482-543).

Black Reconstruction in America interprets black reconstruction as the mental, physical, economic, and political reconstruction of black folk. Black reconstruction is constitutively different from simply the Marxist understanding of overcoming exploitation and alienation. It is a departure from, and an extension beyond, both the independence of the economic realm and the reduction of the conditions of existence to one's need to sell one's labor-power freely on a market:

> But there was in 1863 a real meaning to slavery different from what we may apply to the laborer today. It was in part psychological, the enforced personal feeling of inferiority, the calling of another Master, the standing with hat in hand. It was the helplessness. It was the defenselessness of family life. It was the submergence below the arbitrary will of any sort of individual. It was without doubt worse in these vital respects than that which exists today in Europe or America. (Du Bois 2007, 6)[11]

IV. Community and Country Reconstructed

Yet another way of hearing "reconstruction" in Du Bois's text is as the social and political correlate to black subjectivity. It is the possibility of reconstructing the United States of America as inclusive of non-white citizens. *Black Reconstruction in America* is a Black Reconstruction *of America*. Building upon what he had written in his *Souls of Black Folk*, Du Bois argues that reconstruction in America means building a community that enables those with double vision, constituted by twoness, to be both recognized as American without having to forsake their blackness and to be recognized as black without having to forsake being American. The broken image of America that Du Bois responds to is the myth that America, and by extension Americans, must be white.

If there is to be a reconstruction of America, it cannot be accomplished independently of blacks. It is, furthermore, a reconstruction that promises an America greater than what came before it. Not an America that is great *again*, but possibly for the first time. One question that Du Bois raises is whether an America reconstructed alongside the reconstruc-

---

[11] He continues: "Its analogue today is the yellow, brown and black laborer in China and India, in Africa, in the forests of the Amazon; and it was this slavery that fell in America."

tion, or refashioning, of black souls is better—morally, politically, and so-cially—precisely because of black folk. Du Bois had already gestured towards this in *The Souls of Black Folks*:

> We the darker ones come even now not altogether empty-handed: there are to-day no truer exponents of pure human spirit of the Declaration of Independence than the American Negroes; there is no true American music but the wild sweet melodies of the Negro slave; the American fairy tales and folk-lore are Indian and African; and, all in all, we black men seem the sole oasis of simple faith and reverence in a dusty desert of dollars and smartness. (Du Bois 1994, 16)

Following the opening chapters of *Black Reconstruction in America* on Black and White workers in America (echoing his studies and essays on the Black and White soul in America), the later chapters find a sustained treatment of Black and White proletarians in the American South. He examines the black proletariat in South Carolina, Mississippi, and Louisiana, while focusing on the white proletariat in Alabama, Georgia, and Florida. The topic of Du Bois's historical, sociological, and philosophical study is to provide a diversified account of what black reconstructions in America were like. Black reconstruction is, much like the evolving "we the people", neither singular nor simple. It cannot be unified according to an ideal or regulating idea. Its singularity is a result of the richness of the diversity of all of black life, a product of all the circumstances and activities of individuals in various areas of the country and arenas of industry. Just as freedom is not a gift given to blacks by whites, but a fundamental right that was taken from them and a capacity to be realized by all blacks, so too subjective, social, and national reconstruction can only be achieved as a result of all the diverse actions of black life. Du Bois ends the introduction of *Black Reconstruction in America* with a *caveat*. "In fine, I am going to tell this story as though Negroes were ordinary human beings, realizing that this attitude will from the first seriously curtail my audience" (Du Bois 2007, 16). The warning is as much to readers that are present and contemporaneous with Du Bois as well as a challenge and invitation to the future. Reconstruction remains incomplete as long as the project of subjective reconstruction is incomplete, that is to say as long as blacks (and other non-whites) are not seen as "ordinary human beings". The particular story Du Bois tells, then, and continues to tell in other works, makes clear at the outset the assumptions of the writer and the requirements for the reader—a reader who may no longer be, in Du Bois's eyes, the *gentle reader* he had spoken to in the Forethought of his *The Souls of Black Folk*.

Marx ended his famed *Theses on Feuerbach* by claiming, in a remarkably non-dialectical manner, "philosophers have only interpreted the world in various ways; the point, however, is to change it" (Marx 1998, 574). Reconstruction, as a philosophical concept and mode of interpretation, cannot achieve its task if it remains merely theoretical, if it presents itself as simply one more interpretation of the world. It is up to readers, contemporary and future generations, to contribute to changing the world by acting in a manner that has processed and internalized the views of Du Bois's reconstruction. Reconstruction, therefore, can only achieve its goals insofar as the reconstructive acts—reconstructing black subjectivity, black community, and the United States more generally—can achieve their goals. Not only, then, can we claim that the twentieth century is incomplete—due to the issues of the color line not having been addressed—but that the historical period of Reconstruction, bound by the Reconstruction Amendments, is itself incomplete. The task for Du Bois's readers and a US population dedicated to an equal future for all, is to construct the conditions that will realize that future. The diagnostic interpretations and prognostic aims of Du Bois's *Black Reconstruction in America* compel readers to contribute to this reconstructed world, one in which freedom can be constructed and sustained for present and future generations.

Conclusion: What Remains After Critique

Reconstruction, as a concept and mode of interpretation, looms large in Du Bois's work, and comes to the fore in the multiple texts and variegated works. In many ways, Du Bois's multidisciplinary writings signal the fact that what he attempts to write about (e.g., the meaning of reconstruction for black individual and social life) has multiple vantage points, and is not univocal, and the various disciplines afford respective methods and approaches that reveal those multilayered meanings. Du Bois's texts attempt to reconstruct a historical period that continues on in the present, while the author himself requires an active reader, a reconstructive reader, to do justice to the works themselves.

This paper has argued that one finds an alternative critique of political economy in the writings of W.E.B. Du Bois, specifically his *Black Reconstruction in America*. Within this text, by way of hearing "reconstruction" in different ways, the paper located the sites of Du Bois's (alternative) critique of political economy. The interrogation or site wherein such an alternative takes place is through Du Bois's research and study on black subjectivity; black social life; historical events and circumstances in the United States; and the hopes and pitfalls, potentials and obstacles to reconstruction. Through exposing the limitations of assessing historical events and institutional racism simply in economic terms, Du Bois reveals the extent to which we remain trapped within an incomplete twentieth century (which is itself an incomplete nineteenth century). We are still living with the repercussions and reverberations of a century for which the problem was the problem of the color-line. Reconstruction is the way to go beyond the trappings of previous centuries and the problematics of the color-line without, however, forgetting those previous centuries and specific historical events.

To that end, Du Bois's alternate critique, first, exposes the limitations of an economically-limited Marxist account, one which ascribes a monocausal narrative to history that downplays the significance of antagonisms, oppressions, and state-instituted segregationist policies independent of class. Second, expanding the colloquial understanding of "reconstruction" reveals how Du Bois's reading of US history accounts for those instances where such analysis not only falls short but does an injustice to enslaved and laboring bodies, creative and active souls, and vibrant and dynamic communities. *Black Reconstruction in America*—a text that returns to and reconstructs, in an attempt to understand, the evolving circumstances of the color line alluded to in *The Souls of Black Folk*—serves as a model for conceiving an alternative critique of political economy once one considers multiple meanings for the term reconstruction. That is to say, reconstruction performs an alternative critique of political economy once both the limits of hitherto existing critiques of political economy are perceived, and reconstruction's multiple meanings and implications are unpacked and attended to.

Du Bois's critique of political economy revealed and revolved around at least four ways of reading the text and hearing the title of *Black Reconstruction in America*: (1) the historical register and specific period in US history following the Civil War; (2) the philosophically pragmatic attitude that is attuned to moral and social reconstruction; (3) the reconstruction of black souls and how those souls reconstruct themselves in response to specific historical events by way of particular lived experiences; (4) the reconstruction of community (civil society, or a social sphere) as well as the reconstruction of a nation that is no longer defined by the manner in which it separates people or by how necessary it sees the existence of a color line.

While Du Bois had emphasized the necessity for equal voting rights, educational opportunities, and economic enfranchisement, these alone are not sufficient for constituting either social life or something new from the pieces of the past. It is culture, specifically cultural production, that establishes the requisite social life to sustain community. It is here, then, that critique gives way to a reconstruction of culture, to artistic imagination and creativity. Critique and philosophical activity are not separated from such creativity, since for Du Bois the very kernel of *Black Reconstruction in America* is unabated and ever-flowing reconstructive creative energies and activities.

Expanding our understanding of political economy entails including "reconstruction," in both its critical and productive aspects, as showing limits and bounds, but also ways forward. Such prognoses, however, are neither blueprints for what follows nor rigid guidelines such as what the guardians of Plato's *Republic* might choose to institute in the city. Culture, as product and condition of possibility for community, cannot have any how-tos, and thus always creates something new and more out of what came before. In emphasizing the multiple meanings of reconstruction, *Black Reconstruction in America* calls for, and forth, nothing less than for the soul of the country to be reconstituted and sustained with culture— culture that belongs to no private individual or any singular group, but that offers itself to all, thereby ensuring that everyone freely belongs.

Works Cited

Baldwin, James. 1998. *The Fire Next Time*. In *James Baldwin: Collected Essays*, edited by Toni Morrison, 287-347. New York: Library of America.

Balfour, Lawrie. 2011. *Democracy's Reconstruction: Thinking Politically with W.E.B. Du Bois*. New York: Oxford University Press.

Baro, Samuel Haskell. 1963. *Plekhanov: The Father of Russian Marxism*. Stanford: Stanford University Press.

Chandler, Nahum Dimitri. 2014. *X: The Problem of the Negro as a Problem for Thought*. New York: Fordham University Press.

Coates, Ta-Nehisi. 2015. *Between the World and Me*. New York: Spiegel & Grau.

Derrida, Jacques. 1985. *The Ear of the Other: Otobiography, Transference, Translation*. Edited by Christie McDonald. New York: Shocken Books.

———. 2002. "Declarations of Independence." In *Negotiations: Interventions and Interview, 1971-2001*, edited and translated by Elizabeth Rottenberg, 46-54. Stanford: Stanford University Press.

Dewey, John. 2004. *Reconstruction in Philosophy*. New York: Dover Publications.

Du Bois, W.E.B. 1924. *The Gift of Black Folk*. Boston: Stratford Co., Publishing.

———. 1994. *The Souls of Black Folk*. New York: Dover Publications.

———. 1999. "The Souls of White Folk." In *Darkwater: Voices from Within the Veil*, 7-31. New York: Dover Publications.

———. 2007. *Black Reconstruction in America*. New York: Oxford University Press.

Fanon, Frantz. 2008. *Black Skin, White Masks*. Translated by Richard Philcox. New York: Grove Press.

King Jr., Martin Luther. 1991. "Letter from Birmingham City Jail." In *A Testament of Hope: The Essential Writings and Speeches of Martin Luther King, Jr.*, edited by James M. Washington, 289-302. New York: Harper Collins.

Lyotard, Jean-François. 1988. *The Differend: Phrases in Dispute*. Translated by Georges Van Den Abbeele. Minneapolis: University of Minnesota Press.

Marx, Karl and Friedrich Engels. 1978. *The Manifesto of the Communist Party*. In *The Marx-Engels Reader*, edited by Robert Tucker, 469-500. New York: W.W. Norton & Company.

———. 1978. "Theses on Feuerbach." In *The Marx-Engels Reader* edited by Robert Tucker, 143-6. New York: W.W. Norton & Company.

Moten, Fred. 2018. *Stolen Life (consent not to be a single being)*. Durham, NC: Duke University Press.

Nietzsche, Friedrich. 1989. *On the Genealogy of Morals and Ecce Homo*. Translated by Walter Kaufmann. New York: Vintage.

———. 2005. *Thus Spoke Zarathustra*. Translated by Graham Parkes. New York: Oxford University Press.

Patterson, Orlando. 1982. *Slavery and Social Death: A Comparative Study*. Cambridge, MA: Harvard University Press.

Plekhanov, Georgi. 1992. *Fundamental Problems of Marxism*. New York: International Publishers Co.

Sartre, Jean-Paul. 2018. *Being and Nothingness: An Essay in Phenomenological Ontology*. Translated by Sarah Richmond. New York: Routledge.

Weheliye, Alexander G. 2014. *Habeas Viscus: Racializing Assemblages, Biopolitics, and Black Feminist Theories of the Human.* Durham, NC: Duke University Press.

8.

Autoimmunity and Occupation:
Derrida, Fanon, and the Navajo Nation Courts

Susan Bredlau

Derrida, in his discussion of autoimmunity, argues that a community can only continue to be itself by differing from itself. While a community will certainly not secure the continued expression of its defining values by completely accepting, as colonialists insist the colonized must, the laws and practices of those who are foreign to it, it also cannot secure the continued expression of its defining values, as traditionalists insist, by simply rejecting the laws and practices of those who are foreign. A community's resistance to foreign influence can itself introduce laws and practices into the community that undermine its defining values and are, as such, foreign to it. In its very attempt to end foreign influence, a community may, in fact, perpetuate it and thus display a form of what Derrida refers to as "autoimmunity." The susceptibility of political bodies to the phenomenon of autoimmunity means that a community cannot equate self-preservation with an absolute resistance to foreign influence. A community can only protect itself by risking itself: its continued expression of its defining values will always occur through changes to its existing laws and practices rather than through an absence of changes, even as these changes could always result in its destruction rather than in its preservation. Thus, rather than simply resisting foreign influence—rather than equating security with complete disengagement from foreign communities—a community should, instead, work to have the changes initiated by its encounter with a foreign community be ultimately constructive rather than destructive.

   In this chapter, I argue that both Frantz Fanon, in his analysis of changes to the Algerian practice of women wearing the veil prior to and during the Algerian War of Independence, and Raymond Austin, Tom Tso, and Robert Yazzie, in their implementation and analysis of changes to the Navajo National Judicial System, offer evidence for the phenomenon of autoimmunity described by Derrida. Moreover Fanon, as well as Austin, Tso, and Yazzie, document the lasting toll that foreign occupations—France's occupation of Algeria and the United States' occupation of Navajo territory, respectively—have had on these communities. This toll includes making it more difficult for these communities to live the phenomenon of autoimmunity in ways that, by being deliberately accepting of change, are potentially more constructive than ways that do not deliberately accept change. Nonetheless, Fanon, Austin, Tso, and Yazzie also document that, despite these difficulties, these communities do deliberately accept change and work to have foreign influence be constructive rather than destructive.

In this discussion, we will see how a political body's sovereignty—its ability to act in ways that express its defining values—may be maintained by accepting rather than rejecting foreign influence. As Derrida argues, a political body's laws and practices, whether these laws and practices be those it adopts to resist foreign influence or those it had prior to foreign influence, can in certain ways be more foreign to it than another foreign body; a political body's laws and practices may undermine or be inadequate to its defining values. To maintain sovereignty, then, a political body may actually need to open itself to foreign influence. Sovereignty, in other words, is not freedom from changes initiated by encounters with what is foreign but, rather, the freedom to be changed by these encounters in ways that allow it to better express its defining values.

I: Derrida's Autoimmunity

When used in a biological context, autoimmunity refers to processes by which a body's immune system, which is meant to attack foreign bodies like viruses and bacteria, instead attacks the body itself. In this biological context, the phenomenon of autoimmunity is usually described as an error or failure: the immune system mistakenly treats what is not foreign to the body as if it were and thus injures the very body it was supposed to protect from injury.

Derrida argues, however, that the phenomenon of autoimmunity is not restricted to the biological context: "We feel ourselves authorized to speak of a general logic of autoimmunization. It seems indispensable to us today for thinking about the relations between faith and knowledge, religion and science, as well as the duplicity of sources in general" (Derrida 2002, n80).[1] Political bodies, like biological bodies, Derrida argues, can be

---

[1] Similarly, in *Rogues*, Derrida writes, "As I have done elsewhere, I have here granted to this autoimmune schema a range without limit, one that goes far beyond the circumscribed biological processes by which an organism tends to destroy, in a

attacked not only by foreign bodies but also by their own responses to these foreign bodies. Indeed, the actions political bodies (the focus of this chapter) take in response to the actions of a foreign body can actually damage them far more than the actions of the foreign bodies ever could have: "To lose itself all by itself, to go down on its own, to *autoimmunize* itself, as I would prefer to say in order to designate this strange illogical logic by which a living being can spontaneously destroy, in an autonomous fashion, the very thing within it that is supposed to protect it against the other" (Derrida 2005, 123). In *Rogues*, Derrida cites both the Algerian government's suspension in 1992 of democratic elections after the second round of voting (30) as well as the U.S. government's suspension of certain rights and freedoms after the attacks on the World Trade Center and Pentagon on September 11, 2001 as examples of autoimmune processes (40). In both cases, the political bodies experienced themselves as under attack by groups of people whose values were opposed to their own. Yet the actions these political bodies took in response to the perceived attacks, rather than upholding their own defining values, actually undermined them. In the very measures these political bodies took to protect themselves from attack, these political bodies attacked themselves.

Thus while political bodies that do not reject what is foreign may be destroyed, the phenomenon of autoimmunity ensures that political bodies that do reject what is foreign may also be destroyed.[2] One might think, therefore, that it would be impossible for a political body to protect itself. Yet, Derrida argues, the constant possibility of autoimmunity simply means that political bodies should not equate protecting themselves with absolutely rejecting what is foreign to them. That is, political bodies should not assume that any change to their existing laws and practices, and, in particular, any change that originates in what they identify as foreign, necessarily damages them. The defining values of a political body, though they must be enacted in specific laws and practices, are never reducible to any existing laws and practices. Their existing laws and practices are only the present instantiation of political values that may, at a different point in history, need to be instantiated differently. Thus while altering a

---

quasi-spontaneous and more than suicidal fashion, some organ or other, one or another of its own immunitary protections" (Derrida 2005, 124).

[2] "We are here in space where all self-protection of the unscathed, of the safe and sound, of the sacred (heilig, holy) must protect itself against its own protection, its own police, its own power of rejection, in short against its own, which is to say, against its own immunity" (Derrida 2002, 80).

political body's existing laws and practices can be life-threatening, so, too, can *not* altering a political body's existing laws and practices. A political body's resistance to foreign influence can itself effect a destructive change in the political body.

In contrast to the biological context, then, autoimmunity in the political context need not be an error or failure; it can actually be protective. In attacking its existing laws and practices, a political body may actually realize or uphold its defining political values more adequately; it may actually protect itself rather than destroy itself. Much as a political body's resistance to foreign influence can actually be self-destructive, its openness to foreign influence—so long as this openness makes its laws and practices more adequate to its defining values—can ultimately be self-constructive: "Why speak in this way of *autoimmunity*? Why determine in such an ambiguous fashion the threat or the danger, the default or the failure, the running aground or the grounding, but also the salvation, the rescue, and the safeguard, health and security...?" (Derrida 2005, 123).[3] Thus rather than always resisting foreign influence—and thus often acting in ways that are ultimately as, if not more, damaging to itself than the actions of the foreign body—a political body should instead recognize that foreign influence, even when intended as an attack on a culture's values, is not always destructive. Since a political body can be engaged in practices that are, in effect, foreign to itself, its encounter with a foreign body, insofar as it spurs the political body to make its laws and practices more adequate to its defining values, can actually be constructive. In encountering a foreign body, a political body may realize that its defining political values are, in fact, only inadequately expressed in its existing laws and practices. It may discover, in other words, that at least in certain respects, its own established practices are more foreign to it than the practices of a foreign body. A political body's adoption of a foreign law or practice may, then, actually be protective rather than destructive.[4] If a political body is to protect itself, then, it must acknowledge the phenomenon of autoimmunity: it must recognize that it may threaten itself in its very refusal of what is foreign, and

---

[3] See also: "Autoimmunity is not an absolute ill or evil. It enables an exposure to the other, to what and to who comes—which means that it must remain incalculable. Without autoimmunity, with absolute immunity, nothing would ever happen or arrive; we would no longer wait, await, or expect, no longer expect one another, or expect any event" (Derrida 2005, 152).

[4] For a more extensive discussion of Derrida's concept of autoimmunity, particularly as it applies to democratic communities, see Naas 2006.

that it may protect itself in its very embrace of what is foreign. A political body cannot avoid foreign influence; it can only respond to foreign influence more or less honestly and more or less constructively.

II: Fanon and the Algerian Revolution

Having described the phenomenon of autoimmunity in a political context, I now turn to the first chapter of Fanon's *A Dying Colonialism* and consider a specific way that this phenomenon was manifest for Algerians under French colonial occupation. Fanon, I will argue, shows not only that the Algerians were not exempt from the phenomenon of autoimmunity, but also that French colonial occupation presented a particular challenge to the Algerians' ability to live the phenomenon in ways that were potentially constructive.

In "Algeria Unveiled," Fanon focuses on the efforts of the French colonial regime to end Algerian women's practice of wearing a haïk: a large veil, usually white, that covers the face and body. The French government's targeting of this particular practice was, Fanon writes, a calculated tactic (Fanon 1965, 37). The French made the veil a symbol of what they claimed to be the oppressed status of Algerian women in Algerian society and asserted that ending the practice of veiling would be liberatory to Algerian women. In doing so, the French hoped to divide the Algerians against themselves, thus making it easier for the French to retain control of the country: "At an initial stage, there was a pure and simple adoption of the well-known formula, 'Let's win over the women and the rest will follow'" (37).[5]

In being singled out for elimination by the French, the veil assumed a significance for the Algerians, Fanon argues, that it did not previously have. As Fanon notes, prior to the French insistence on the unveiling of Algerian women, the veiling of Algerian women was a relatively unimportant aspect of Algerian life. It went largely unnoticed by the Algerians themselves and was not lived as a critical form of self-expression (47). Once it became the focus of the French colonial regime, however, the Algerians responded by forcefully asserting the importance of the practice: "To the colonialist offensive against the veil, the colonized opposes the cult of the veil. What was an undifferentiated element in a homogenous

---

[5] As Fanon explains, what the French claimed to be the liberation of Algerian women was, in fact, only a new form of oppression: the sexual objectification of the unveiled Algerian women's bodies by the French gaze.

whole acquires a taboo character, and the attitude of a given Algerian woman with respect to the veil will be constantly related to her overall attitude with respect to the foreign occupation" (47).[6] With the French colonial regime's effort to eliminate the practice, then, a practice that had not previously been experienced as culturally definitive became experienced as such. Moreover, had the French not singled this practice out for elimination, the Algerians might very well have revised or even ended this practice themselves; pressured by the French to change this practice, however, the Algerians, at least initially, resisted altering it in any way.

Fanon's account illustrates, then, a specific way that the phenomenon of autoimmunity was instantiated for the Algerians. As Fanon points out, the Algerians' initial response to unveiling was reactionary (46); their refusal to give up the practice reflected their desire to thwart the will of the French much more than it reflected the intrinsic value that the veil had for them. Although this refusal was meant to be a complete rejection of French society, it nonetheless involved an acceptance of the French view that veiling was a critically important cultural practice for them. Thus, rather than putting an end to French interference in their culture, at least with respect to this practice, the Algerians' refusal actually prolonged this interference, though perhaps in ways that were more covert than before: "Specialists in basic education for underdeveloped countries or technicians for the advancement of retarded societies would do well to understand the sterile and harmful character of any endeavor which illuminates preferentially a given element of the colonized society" (41).[7] As such, the colonized Algerians' refusal to end the practice of veiling, rather than simply protecting them, also threatened them; their response, though meant to leave their existing laws and practices unchanged by the French, itself changed these existing laws and practices.

At the same time, however, Fanon's account reveals how colonial rule severely impedes a community's ability to live the phenomenon of autoimmunity in ways that are, potentially, more constructive than a reactionary

---

[6] As Fanon points out, this strategy placed Algerian women in a particularly difficult situation. While Algerian women may, indeed, have experienced certain aspects of their own society as oppressive, any objection to this oppression risked endorsing the oppression of the colonizer.

[7] Furthermore, Fanon notes, had the Algerians continued to refuse any change to the practice of veiling, they would have denied themselves a valuable tool in their fight for independence. Some Algerian women began to dress like French women when participating in military operations in order to avoid detection by the French.

response can be. French colonial occupation threatened not just the Algerian practice of veiling but all the practices that defined the Algerians as Algerian. The French's outlawing of the veil was, Fanon writes, just one aspect of a much larger campaign by the French to, in effect, make the Algerian people into French people: "The officials of the French administration in Algeria [were] committed to destroying the people's originality, and under instruction to bring about the disintegration, at whatever cost, of forms of existence likely to evoke a national reality directly or indirectly" (37). Moreover, the French had already seized the Algerians' land and denied them political autonomy: that is, the French actually were eliminating, and not merely threatening to eliminate, whatever laws and practices expressed the Algerians' defining values.

Having already experienced so much change to, and indeed destruction of, their practices, it is not surprising, Fanon argues, that the Algerians strongly resisted any further change to their practices:

> The colonialist's relentlessness, his methods of struggle were bound to give rise to reactionary forms of behavior on the part of the colonized. In the face of the violence of the occupier, the colonized found himself defining a principled position with respect to a formerly inert element of the native cultural configuration....We here recognize one of the laws of the psychology of colonization. In an initial phase, it is the action, the plans of the occupier that determine the centers of resistance around which a people's will to survive becomes organized. (47)[8]

Nonetheless, in their outright rejection of or refusal to be changed by what was different than them, the Algerians did not prevent themselves from being changed. Their actions instantiated the phenomenon of autoimmunity described by Derrida, and their very attempt to avoid change to their practices initiated changes to their practices. Indeed, by rejecting what was different outright, they prevented themselves from deliberately participating in these changes; they did not avoid change and, moreover, foreclosed the possibility that these changes could be more a matter of choice than of chance. Of course, even a community that acknowledges

---

[8] In the same essay, Fanon later writes: "The doctrinal assertions of colonialism in its attempt to justify the maintenance of its domination almost always push the colonized to the position of making uncompromising, rigid, static counter-proposals" (63).

the inevitability of such change and makes its own change a matter of explicit reflection and action cannot guarantee that the changes it undergoes will be constructive rather than destructive. While a community cannot absolutely control how it changes, it does, nonetheless, bear some responsibility for these changes, and a community that honestly acknowledges this responsibility rather than evading it realizes its freedom and self-determination more fully than a community that does not.

Yet, Fanon argues, even though the Algerians' initial response to the French outlawing of the veil was reactionary, their response later became revolutionary: "Upon the outbreak of the struggle for liberation, the attitude of Algerian women, or of native society in general, with regard to the veil was to undergo important modifications" (47). That is, rather than simply refusing to be changed by their interactions with the French, and nonetheless continuing to be changed, the Algerians became open to being changed by these interactions in ways that served the Algerians' fight for independence from the French: "Removed and reassumed again and again, the veil has been manipulated, transformed into a technique of camouflage, into a means of struggle. The virtually taboo character assumed by the veil in the colonial situation disappeared almost entirely in the course of the liberating struggle" (61). Thus Fanon's analysis suggests that even as colonialism may predispose a colonized society to live the phenomenon of autoimmunity inadvertently, it does not absolutely foreclose the possibility that this society can come to live the phenomenon of autoimmunity more deliberately and, possibly, more constructively.[9]

III: The Navajo Nation Judicial System

To provide another example of the phenomenon of autoimmunity described by Derrida and to continue thinking about the challenges to living this phenomenon in potentially more constructive ways that face a community whose encounter with a foreign political body includes its occupation and political oppression by this body, I now turn to the writings of several former judges of the Navajo Nation Supreme Court: Raymond Austin, Navajo Nation Supreme Court judge from 1985-2001; Tom Tso, Navajo Nation Supreme Court Chief Judge from 1985-1991; and Robert Yazzie, Navajo Nation Supreme Court judge from 1992-2003. I will focus on two developments within the judicial branch of the Navajo Nation: the

---

[9] "It is the necessities of combat that give rise in Algerian society to new attitudes, to new modes of action, to new ways" (64).

creation in 1982 of a Peacemaker Court and a ruling in 1995 by the Navajo Supreme Court that allowed jurors to question witnesses.

The Navajo, united by a common language and culture, are recognized by the United States as a sovereign nation in some respects. The sovereignty of the Navajo Nation, however, was only granted after decades of political oppression in which the Navajo were not only denied political autonomy but also forcibly removed from their lands.[10] Furthermore, as I will discuss shortly, this sovereignty has never been total: both US state governments and the US federal government continue to restrict Navajo self-governance.

The Navajo Nation government consists of three branches: an executive branch with a democratically elected president, a legislative branch with a democratically elected Navajo Nation Council, and a judicial branch, the Navajo Nation Courts, with judges appointed to the courts by the president of the Navajo Nation and confirmed by the Navajo Nation Council. The Navajo Nation has jurisdiction over the Navajo Indian Reservation, which extends over parts of Utah, Arizona, and New Mexico, as well as other fee and trust lands separated from the reservation. According to US census figures for 2010, the population of the Navajo Nation was 173,667 (Arizona Rural Policy Institute, n.d.).

The Navajo's contact with US laws and courts dates to at least 1892, when the US government's Bureau of Indian Affairs established and administered the Navajo Court of Indian Offenses (Austin 2009, 19). The Court was originally a tool of assimilation (25), and its regulations were meant to eliminate the traditional Navajo way of life and replace it with Anglo-American customs (21). Among the crimes that the Court prosecuted were traditional dances, the practices of medicine men, and idleness.[11] By 1937, the "civilizing" regulations of the Bureau of Indian Affairs Law and Order Code for the Navajo Court of Indian Offenses had largely been eliminated. They were replaced, however, not with regulations drafted by the Navajo themselves but with regulations that resembled US state laws.

---

[10] See Austin 2009, 1-9.

[11] Similarly, the Navajo Tribal Council, which, prior to the formation of the Navajo Nation Council, was part of the Navajo Nation's legislative branch, was established by the US in 1923, primarily so that the US could negotiate oil leases with the Navajo. The centralized structure of the Navajo Tribal Council conflicted with traditional forms of Navajo governance (Austin 2009, 10).

In 1958, the Navajo Tribal Council established the "Judicial Branch of the Navajo Nation Government." Although the establishment of a judicial branch shifted administration of the courts on the Navajo Reservation from the Bureau of Indian Affairs to the Navajo Nation, the structure of the courts and the laws they applied were left largely unchanged.[12] Prior to contact with the United States, the Navajo had a system of values, norms, customs, and traditions that, Austin writes, produced and maintained "right relations, right relationships, and desirable outcomes in Navajo society" (2009, 40). This system, which is now referred to as Navajo common law, was communicated orally, and many aspects of common law have still not been written down (40). The Navajo never had, and still do not have, a formal written constitution (16).

The decision by the Navajo Nation Tribal Council not to change the existing judicial system was, Austin writes, "not a case of deliberately favoring a Western-style court system over a Navajo traditional one, but a result forced on it by state (Arizona and New Mexico) threats of extending jurisdiction into Navajo country" (28).[13] Faced with the threat of losing even more of their already significantly reduced sovereignty, the Navajo had little choice but to adopt institutions and laws that were almost identical to those of the US state and federal governments. Moreover, as Austin, Tso, and Yazzie all argue, the judicial system adopted by the Navajo Nation Tribal Council was not only different from Navajo traditional justice, it was also at odds with important aspects of the Navajo's defining values. To better understand this tension, I will focus briefly on Navajo traditional justice and a key value, *hózhó*, that underlies it.

Hózhó describes a condition that Navajo common law is meant to produce. While it is difficult to adequately translate *hózhó* into English, it has been translated as 'harmony,' 'balance,' 'beauty,' and 'goodness' (Austin 2009, 53). Austin writes:

---

[12] Most of the Navajo Court of Indian Offenses's regulations were adopted as law by the Navajo Nation Tribal Council shortly after the Navajo Nation Court System was established in 1958 (Austin 2009, 38). As Austin notes, "Adopted Anglo-American law makes up a significant portion of the twenty-six titles that compose the Navajo Nation Code and the regulations that guide the departments of the Navajo Nation Government" (37).

[13] For further information on the history of the Navajo Nation Courts, see Tso 1986 and Tso 1989.

In general, *hózhó* encompasses everything that Navajos consider positive and good: positive characteristics that Navajos believe contribute to living life to the fullest. These positive characteristics include beauty, harmony, goodness, happiness, right social relations, good health, and acquisition of knowledge. (54)[14]

A basic goal of Navajo common law, therefore, is to maintain *hózhó* or, if *hózhó* is disrupted, to restore it.[15]

On a broad political level, Navajo common law prescribes an egalitarian society that governs itself through participatory democracy (Austin 2009, 91). Decisions are made through a process of "talking things through" to which all members of a community are allowed to contribute. Navajo common law, while it does not include a court system per se, does include practices for addressing problems or disturbances that might arise in a community. James Zion, a former solicitor to the Navajo Nation Courts, reports that prior to 1982, judges of the Navajo Nation would sometimes

> call in a respected member from the local community to work with litigants on problems for which mediation, rather than the American adversary system, was more appropriate. These disputes were usually over family matters, such as divorce or drinking problems, or other everyday problems. (Zion 1983, 94)

This practice, the judges stated, reflected an earlier Navajo practice.

Even before contact with the Spanish and Americans, the Navajo had democratically elected leaders, *naat'áanii*.[16] A *naat'áanii's* power, Austin writes, came from the respect he had from the community:

> Traditional Navajo peace leaders, unlike Western leaders, shunned authoritarianism; hence, a leadership hierarchy was not essential to the functioning of the traditional Navajo political system. ...Unanimity or consensus on policy or solutions was the desired end of the decision-making process. (Austin 2009, 92)

---

[14] Gary Witherspoon defines *hózhó* as "that state of affairs where everything is in its proper place and functioning in harmonious relationships to everything else" (quoted in Austin 2009, 54).

[15] For a discussion of other Navajo fundamental doctrines, see Austin 2009, chaps. 3-5 and Zion 2002.

[16] For additional discussion of the *naat'áani*, see Tso 1986, 24 and Austin 2009, 9-11.

Among the responsibilities of the *naat'áanii* was to arbitrate disputes, resolve family problems, and attempt to correct wrongdoers (106).[17] All those involved in a dispute met with the *naat'áanii* and, through free discussion, reached a decision to which all agreed: "Apology, forgiveness, and restitution are preferred remedies for injury and wrongs, including crimes, under traditional Navajo justice" (22).[18]

In contrast, then, to US courts and the Navajo Nation courts as they existed prior to 1982, Navajo traditional justice operates through consensus and restoration rather than through confrontation and coercion. In comparing the two systems, Austin writes:

> Navajo peacemaking is a horizontal system of justice, whereas Western-model court systems are vertical systems of justice. Navajo common-law scholars have pointed out the differences between the two systems. Vertical systems of justice have hierarchies of power and authority and use force or coercion. Horizontal systems of justice are basically egalitarian, use relationships to decide matters, and reject force or coercion. All participants have an equal voice in a horizontal system of justice and there is not a single all-powerful decision maker, such as a judge in a vertical system.[19] (Austin 2009, 91)

Beginning in the early 1980s, the judges of the Navajo Nation Courts began to search for ways to make the courts more compatible with the Navajo's defining values.[20] In 1982, the judges of the Navajo Courts voted to create a Navajo Peacemaker Court, now called the Navajo Peacemaking Division (Austin 2009, 39). Interestingly, in creating the Peacemaker Court, the Navajo judges followed the practice of most US courts "of exercising the power to adopt courts' rules to regulate and define court operations" (Zion 1983, 97).[21] The Peacemaking Division is authorized to handle civil cases and some criminal cases and yet has a fundamentally

---

[17] "Criminal law and civil law are not separate under traditional Navajo justice and both are subject to community organization" (Austin 2009, 22).

[18] For a discussion of traditional Navajo justice in the context of other indigenous justice systems, see Meyer 1998.

[19] For additional comparison between the Peacemaker Court and US courts, see Yazzie 1993.

[20] "The 1980s begin with general consensus among Navajo judges that the Navajo Nation needed an alternative" (Austin 2009, 39).

[21] For additional discussion of the judges' debate that preceded the creation of the Peacemaker Court, see Zion 1983, 98-99.

different structure than the other courts of the Navajo Nation and the US state and federal courts upon which the Navajo courts are modeled. Members of the Navajo bar are generally forbidden from participating in the Peacemaking Division, and judges participate only peripherally (Zion 1983, 102).[22] Instead, disputants meet with a mediator, or peacemaker.[23] Peacemakers are generally chosen by their community; if the community does not make a choice, they can be appointed by judges (Zion 1983, 102). So long as the disputants consent, however, any person can serve as a peacemaker. The peacemaker, unlike a judge, can talk freely with both parties, as well as anyone else relevant to the dispute.[24]

Initially, there were few guidelines for how the peacemaker would work with both parties to resolve a dispute (Zion 1983, 103). The judges who created the Peacemaker Court wanted to allow the participants to draw on their knowledge of traditional Navajo justice and define the peacemaking process for themselves. As the program has developed, the courts have begun to identify the norms, values, and procedures that guide the process (Zion 2002, 629). The process, Zion writes,

> entails fixing the parties' minds to the seriousness of the ceremony through prayer; allowing the participants to put facts on the table and vent about them; guidance and teaching (based on traditional values) by the peacemaker; and a consensual process of reaching a decision about what to do about the situation to "make good" for a wrong and plan a means of avoiding the situation in the future. (2002, 630)

---

[22] Judges "appoint peacemakers in individual cases, issue simple protective orders when abuses are brought to their attention, and issue formal written judgments on mediated or arbitrated decisions" (Zion 1983, 104). "The element of protection was necessary in order to bring the new method into existence because of problems and abuses that had occurred in the past" (Zion 1983, 100). Judges from other courts of the Navajo Nation can also transfer civil cases and certain kinds of criminal cases to the Peacemaker Court.

[23] Yazzie writes: "Lawyers are not hired to represent parties. Rather, a peacemaker works so that justice can be done for everyone involved in the dispute" (1993, 412).

[24] Yazzie writes: "In Anglo-American courts, parties may not communicate freely with judges. To do so might prejudice the rights of the other party. In the peacemaker process, you can speak with the *naat'áanii* to help you work out the dispute and come to a solution" (1993, 412).

In the Peacemaking Division, there are no fixed punishments or sentencing guidelines (Zion 2002, 636). Once an agreement is reached, this agreement becomes a judgment of the Navajo Court System. This judgment can then, if necessary, be enforced by the Navajo Courts and will be recognized by the states of Arizona and New Mexico.

Yet even as the creation of the Peacemaker Court might seem to protect the Navajo's traditions from foreign influence, the creation of the court was not without risk. Austin acknowledges that the very consideration of Navajo common law by the courts can sometimes be at odds with Navajo common law. He notes that the court's practice of calling on a respected Navajo to serve as an "expert witness" on Navajo common law would "not sit well with most traditional Navajos" since they recognize themselves as all having much of the same knowledge (Austin 2009, 49). Once again, then, we see the phenomenon of autoimmunity described by Derrida arise in the Navajo judges' creation of the Peacemaker Court; in responding to the changes to existing laws and traditions imposed upon the Navajo by the US government, the Navajo judges have initiated their own changes to these laws and traditions. Far from denying this reality, though, the Navajo judges acknowledge it. As Austin notes, when the Navajo Nation Supreme Court takes traditional Navajo practices under consideration, it heeds the following caveats:

> (1) understand the customs and traditions; then decide how they would apply to an issue; (2) customs and traditions may vary from place to place on the Navajo Nation; (3) some customs and traditions may have fallen into desuetude; and (4) parties to a case may not follow customs and traditions. (Austin 2009, 46)

The judges are well aware that deciding who can speak authoritatively about the Navajo's defining values, and by extension, deciding who can determine what practices have adequately expressed or will come to better express these values is a complicated issue. Rather than trying to avoid all change to the practices through which the Navajo have expressed their defining values, the Navajo Nation Supreme Court has, instead, worked to have such changes be constructive to, rather than destructive of, Navajo identity.

That the Navajo judges have not, when given the opportunity, simply rejected any foreign influence is particularly clear in their decisions regarding trial by jury. Following the creation of the Peacemaker Court, Navajo judges continued to look for ways to modify the courts so as to better express Navajo identity. Starting in 1985, the Navajo Nation Supreme Court began to regularly consult Navajo common law in reaching its decisions. Traditional Navajo justice did not involve a jury system; instead, all those affected by a dispute were involved in its resolution. Moreover, within the laws drafted by the US and adopted by the Navajo Nation, jury trials were only required in a limited number of cases.[25] Yet in *Duncan v. Shiprock District Court*, the Navajo Nation Supreme Court upheld jury trials on the basis of Navajo common law rather than rejecting jury trials or upholding them only to avoid further interference from US federal or state governments. The Court wrote:

> A jury trial in our Navajo legal system is a modern manifestation of consensus-based resolution our people have used throughout our history to bring people in dispute back into harmony. Juries are a part of the fundamental Navajo principle of participatory democracy where people come together to resolve issues by "talking things out." (quoted in Austin 2009, 74)

Thus the Supreme Court not only accepted the right to a trial by jury as outlined by the Indian Civil Rights Act, they also extended this right: "No person accused of an offence punishable by imprisonment and no party to a civil action at law…shall be denied the right, upon request, to a trial by jury of not less than six persons" (Austin 2009, 74).

Yet while the Navajo Nation Supreme Court ruled that jury trials were not in conflict with Navajo common law, the Court in a later ruling argued that jury trials should be modified. The Navajo courts, like US courts, had not permitted the jury to question witnesses. In 1995, in *Downy v. Bigman*, however, the Court wrote:

> A reformulation of the jury's duties to permit it to ask questions of the witnesses during trial is more reflective of Navajo participatory democracy. To maintain impartiality, all the questions will be channeled through the judge, whose authority to permit or forbid the question is discretionary. (quoted in Austin 2009, 75)

In this later decision regarding trial by jury, then, the Supreme Court in-

---

[25] The 1968 US federal Indian Civil Rights Act, which "tracks many of the constitutional restraints imposed on the federal and state governments by the U.S. Bill of Rights," allowed for jury trial, upon request, in criminal cases where the defendant, if convicted, could face imprisonment. The right to jury trial was not granted for civil cases (Austin 2009, 73).

augurated another new practice that reflected both traditional Navajo justice and the US justice system: jurors are now allowed to question witnesses during a trial.

In the creation of the Peacemaker Court and the introduction of jurors' questioning of witnesses, the Navajo Nation Supreme Court, though working to protect Navajo identity, did not equate this protection with resistance to any foreign influence or with denial of any change to its laws and practices. In each case, there was an acknowledgement of change and an engagement with these changes in ways that the judges of the Navajo Nation hope will protect the Navajo's defining values even as they reflect the practices of both Navajo traditional justice and the US judicial system.

It remains an open question whether the changes initiated by the judges have, in fact, served to better express the defining values of the Navajo, and if they have, whether they were the best possible way of doing so. As Derrida writes in *Rogues*, there is a certain "indecidability" linked with the logic of autoimmunity: once a change has been initiated, one can never really know whether this change was in fact the best way to maintain one's identity (Derrida 2005, 36). Nonetheless, these developments within the judicial branch of the Navajo Nation, insofar as they involve the acknowledgement of such changes and the effort to make them a matter of explicit reflection and action, reflect a form of autoimmunity that has the potential to be more constructive than one that denies any such changes.

Conclusion

I have argued that Fanon's analysis of changes to the Algerian practice of veiling and Austin's, Tso's, and Yazzie's analyses of changes to the Navajo Nation judicial system have not only provided additional examples of the phenomenon of autoimmunity described by Derrida but have also provided examples of how this phenomenon can be lived by a political body in ways that are potentially more constructive than destructive. To conclude, I want to briefly consider an implication of this argument for the political future of the United States. I think that the ongoing work of the Navajo Nation Supreme Court justices, only some of which I described above, serves as a compelling example of how the United States might itself engage with foreign political bodies, including the Navajo Nation. The political body of the United States is as susceptible to the autoimmunity Derrida describes as any other community: if the United States wants to continue realizing its defining values, it, too, must recognize that in certain respects its own laws and practices can be more foreign to it than those of foreign cultures and thus an openness to other cultures can be constructive rather than destructive. As it stands now, though, the United States is, at least with respect to Navajo common law, almost completely indifferent. The United States would do well to begin engaging as thoughtfully and seriously with Navajo common law and the decisions of the Navajo Nation Supreme Court as the judges of the Navajo Nation Supreme Court have engaged with the laws of the United States.

Works Cited

Arizona Rural Policy Institute. n.d. "Demographic Analysis of the Navajo Nation." Accessed February 28, 2020. https://gotr.azgovernor.gov/sites/default/files/navajo_nation_0.pdf.

Austin, Raymond R. 2009. *Navajo Courts and Navajo Common Law: A Tradition of Tribal Self-Governance*. Minneapolis: University of Minnesota Press.

Derrida, Jacques. 2002. "Faith and Knowledge: The Two Sources of "Religion" at the Limits of Reason Alone." In *Acts of Religion*, translated by Gil Anidjar, 42-101. New York: Routledge.

———. 2005. *Rogues*. Translated by Pascale-Anne Brault and Michael Naas. Stanford: Stanford University Press.

Fanon, Frantz. 1965. *A Dying Colonialism*. Translated by Haakon Chevalier. New York: Grove Press.

———. 1965. "Algeria Unveiled." In *A Dying Colonialism*, translated by Haakon Chevalier, 35-67. New York: Grove Press.

Meyer, Jon'a F. 1998. "History Repeats Itself: Restorative Justice in Native American Communities." *Journal of Contemporary Criminal Justice* 14, no. 1: 42-57.

Naas, Michael. 2006. "One Nation...Indivisible: Jacques Derrida on the Autoimmunity of Democracy and the Sovereignty of God." *Research in Phenomenology* 36: 15-44.

Tso, Tom. 1986. "The Tribal Court Survives in America." *The Judges' Journal* (Spring): 22-25, 52-55.

———. 1989. "The Process of Decision Making in Tribal Courts." *Arizona Law Review* 31: 225-235.

Yazzie, Robert. 1993. "Navajo Justice Experience–Yesterday and Today." In *Aboriginal Peoples and the Justice System: Report of the National Round Table on Aboriginal Justice Issues*: 407-414.

Zion, James W. 1983. "The Navajo Peacemaker Court: Deference to the Old and Accommodation to the New." *American Indian Law Review* 11: 89-109.

———. 2002. "Navajo Therapeutic Jurisprudence." *Touro Law Review* 18: 563-640.

9.

Effective Altruism and the Challenge of Partiality: Should We Take Special Care of Our Own?

Rosalind S. Simson

The advent of the recent social movement, "effective altruism," provides an opportune occasion for revisiting a long-standing debate in ethics about how people should weigh their obligations to humanity in general against their duties to those with whom they share bonds. As explained by its architect, Peter Singer, effective altruism maintains that, in order to live a minimally acceptable ethical life, people with resources to spare after satisfying their own basic needs must donate a substantial portion of those spare resources to trying to make the world a better place.[1] It directs each of these people to ask: How can I use my money, time, energy, talents, connections, etc. to make the biggest difference? Effective altruism organizations employ sophisticated social science methodologies to help individuals make well-informed and carefully considered decisions about such matters as which causes to volunteer for, which charities to donate money to, and which careers to pursue.

The concept of impartiality is central to effective altruism's prescriptions for how donors, in allocating their resources, should choose among possible recipients. Effective altruism sees all people as global citizens equally worthy of moral consideration. It therefore maintains that, in deciding whose needs and interests to prioritize, each donor should ask only such impersonal questions as: Whose needs are most urgent? Which interventions are most likely to have positive long-term consequences? Given my particular resources, whose needs can I address most effectively? What will be the probable effects if I bypass one worthy cause in favor of another? Will other people be able and willing to pick up the slack if I decide to devote my resources elsewhere? Absent from its long list of questions is: Do I have personal relationships with those in need? In the words

---

[1] Peter Singer, *The Most Good You Can Do: How Effective Altruism is Changing Ideas About Living Ethically* (New Haven: Yale University Press, 2015), vii. See section III below for further discussion of Singer's definition of effective altruism.

of William MacAskill, co-founder of the effective altruism organizations Give Well and 80,000 Hours, "What matters is not who does good, but whether good is done."[2]

Leaders of the social movement do not all share Singer's view of the cause's moral imperative. For example, MacAskill maintains that effective altruism does not stake out a particular moral position. He characterizes it as "an intellectual and practical project rather than a normative claim."[3] Although all effective altruists espouse the importance of impartially ben-efiting others and most donate at least ten percent of their incomes to charity, MacAskill says that effective altruism *per se* makes no demands on people. It neither criticizes them for the size of their donations nor asks them to justify the choices they make between addressing problems in the world at large and attending to their families, friends, and communities. As Julia Wise, a prominent effective altruist says, "I have lots of goals. I have a goal of improving the world. I have a goal of enjoying time with my children....You don't have to argue that your choice is the best way of im-proving the world if that isn't actually the goal."[4]

In this paper, I will understand effective altruism in the way that Singer does, and I will use the term to refer to Singer's view. It makes sense that in order to maximize the impact of effective altruism, leaders of the social movement characterize the position in a way that minimizes the likelihood of alienating potential recruits. Singer recognizes these practical considerations. He is upfront that he himself does not do as much good as he possibly could—the hallmark, he says of living a fully ethical life.[5] He also notes that effective altruists do not see much point in "feeling guilty about not being morally perfect."[6] Still, he sees effective altruism not only as an intellectual and practical enterprise but also as a prescription for how people ought to live. In other words, he sees it as endorsing a particular moral philosophy that has normative implications. My interest in effective

---

[2] William MacAskill, *Doing Good Better: How Effective Altruism Can Help You Make a Difference* (New York: Penguin Random House, 2015), 69. For a more com-plete list of questions that effective altruism considers relevant, see 201-4.

[3] William MacAskill, "Effective Altruism: Introduction," *Essays in Philosophy* 18, no. 1 (2017): 2.

[4] Julia Wise, "You Have More than One Goal and That's Fine," *Giving Gladly*, February 19, 2019, http://www.givinggladly.com/2019/02/you-have-more-than-one-goal-and-thats.html.

[5] Singer, *The Most Good You Can Do*, vii.

[6] Singer, viii.

altruism, like Singer's, is both philosophical and practical. Because effective altruism understands impartiality in a sophisticated way, it provides a useful context for philosophically evaluating impartiality as a moral position. Moreover, as an influential social movement, effective altruism underlines the real-life importance of this discussion. I believe that despite the desires of MacAskill and others to avoid moral imperatives, many of those contemplating effective altruism want guidance as to how to make principled decisions about when and why personal commitments ought to hold sway over the demands of impartiality.

I will accept without analysis Singer's statement of the requirements for a minimally acceptable ethical life. My project in this essay will be to evaluate both the impartiality advocated by effective altruism and the partiality critique that sees personal relationships as giving rise to special duties. Although effective altruism recognizes that sometimes the best way to make a difference in the world is to give special consideration to those with whom one shares bonds, I will argue that in many instances the demands of partiality and impartiality are in genuine conflict. I will make two principal claims. The first is that effective altruism fails to recognize that most people have a basic need to preserve close relationships with at least some individuals and that preserving these bonds requires attending to these individuals' interests before addressing effective altruism's impersonal questions. The second is that people with resources to spare after satisfying their own basic needs have both responsibilities to promote the overall good and some special duties beyond those related to basic needs. In the final section of the essay, I will offer several proposals for deciding which relationships give rise to special duties and, more generally, for accommodating competing considerations.

I. The meaning of impartiality and partiality

Before proceeding, it will be useful to clarify the concepts of impartiality and partiality as they apply to my project. Effective altruism does not claim that everyone with spare resources has moral obligations to the same people, nor does it deny that people's personal connections to others sometimes have bearing on how they ought to distribute their resources. Because it emphasizes the importance of taking individuals' particular situations into account, effective altruism is sensitive to some ways in which interpersonal relationships can affect moral responsibilities. For example, it recognizes that an adult son may have a distinctive duty to spend time personally caring for his ill, elderly mother if he is specially positioned to understand and address her needs. In Diane Jeske's words, the son may have "situationally-relative" reasons for needing to provide the care.[7] Effective altruism denies, however, that relationships *intrinsically* ever have bearing on individuals' moral obligations. If a government-paid aide, for example, could in all respects tend to his mother equally well, then effective altruism would say that the filial relationship would be irrelevant to the son's moral obligation to supply personal care.

By contrast, proponents of partiality maintain that, in assessing their duties to others, people with spare resources should consider not only the impersonal factors that effective altruism identifies, but also their own particular connections to those in need. Thus, partiality advocates typically see an adult son's relationship to his elderly mother as an important— though not by itself determinative—factor in assessing his moral obligation to provide his mother with personal care. The reason is that the parent-child relationship typically gives rise to special responsibilities, even if someone else could do the job equally well. In Jeske's terms, partiality sees people's reasons for prioritizing the needs and interests of those with whom they share bonds not only as "situationally-relative," but also as "agent-relative."[8]

Jeske also emphasizes that partiality advocates argue that some agent-relative reasons for privileging certain individuals are objective in the sense that it is not simply a matter of opinion whether particular relationships form the basis for special duties.[9] Clearly, not all interpersonal connections give rise to moral obligations. For example, people may wish to give favored treatment to co-workers, neighbors, and others with whom they have casual relationships but to whom they do not have special moral responsibilities. I will have more to say in Section IV about which types of connections among people do give rise to special moral obligations, but to convey the general idea it will be helpful for now to cite Samuel Scheffler's proposal for identifying these relationships: they are characterized by "ongoing bonds between individuals who have a shared history that usually includes patterns of engagement and forms of mutual familiarity, attachment, and regard developed over time."[10] Examples of relationships that

---

[7] Diane Jeske, "Friendship and Reasons of Intimacy," *Philosophy and Phenomenological Research* 63, no. 2 (2001): 331.

[8] Jeske, 331.

[9] Jeske, 332-334.

[10] Samuel Scheffler, "Morality and Reasonable Partiality," in *Partiality and Impartiality: Morality, Special Relationships and the Wider World*, eds. Brian Feltham and

partiality advocates often argue fall into this category are those among immediate family members, long-time close friends, and members of some close-knit civic and religious communities.

Finally, proponents of partiality recognize that not all the requests that people make of those with whom they share important bonds are based on needs or legitimate interests. Although people in relationships sometimes disagree about whether a particular wish qualifies as a need or even as a legitimate interest, the concepts of wishes, needs, and interests are distinct. For example, parents often wish that their adult children would practice the religion they raised them with, and it can put a serious strain on their relationship if the children refuse. But parents cannot reasonably expect to control the religious practices of their adult children. The debate between impartiality and partiality concerns whether people have moral obligations to prioritize the needs and legitimate interests of those to whom they have special connections—not whether they have moral obligations to do whatever those to whom they are connected insist is required to preserve the relationship.

II. Support for effective altruism's impartiality

Effective altruism is right to emphasize the intrinsic equality of all human beings and the importance of giving equal moral consideration to their lives and wellbeing. It is tempting to believe that if everyone attended to the interests of those with whom they share significant bonds, everyone's needs and problems would be efficiently addressed. However, effective altruism reminds us of the enormous disparities in people's resources. It underlines the injustice of allowing such factors as the family or community into which one happens to have been born to determine one's ability to maintain even a minimal degree of wellbeing.[11]

Effective altruism also properly underlines that, in a world with unequal wealth distribution, systematic bias inevitably results when people prioritize the needs and interests of those with whom they share relationships. The challenges people face are often linked to their social situations.

John Cottingham (Oxford: Oxford University Press, 2010), 115. Scheffler says, p. 129, that "reasons of partiality exhibit precisely the deontic characteristics that we associate with moral norms," and that our obligations to people with whom we share the sorts of relationships that he has identified can be viewed as "paradigmatic moral requirements."

[11] MacAskill devotes the first chapter of *Doing Good Better* to detailing the vast inequalities in wealth around the world.

For example, infectious diseases caused by poor sanitation are especially common in developing countries, whereas diabetes and heart disease are more prevalent in industrialized ones. When people with spare resources give priority to addressing the problems experienced by their friends, relatives, and community members, needy people who lack relationships with advantaged people typically receive little help. Moreover, the effects of this bias are multiplied, because the same sums of money typically make much larger differences in the developing world than in the industrialized one. For the cost of saving one very premature infant in a neonatal ICU in the US, for example, the lives of hundreds of impoverished children in various Asian and African countries can be saved simply by administering measles vaccines.[12]

Finally, effective altruists rightly point out that when relationship considerations influence decisions about where to donate resources, emotions often cloud rational judgment.[13] Many people prioritize giving to organizations to which they feel emotional ties. For example, they make annual contributions to their alma maters, because they look back with nostalgia on their college experiences, enjoy returning to campus for alumni events, and take pleasure in maintaining contact with former classmates, faculty, and coaches. At some schools—particularly ones with hefty endowments—more than half of alumni donate annually,[14] and most of these contributors make no inquiries into how their gifts are used. Of course, universities on the whole are worthy causes, and, undoubtedly, some individuals can best contribute to the general welfare by donating to their alma maters. The point is simply that effective altruism is right to ask prospective donors to look carefully at many types of evidence before deciding that a donation to the college they attended is the best charitable investment they possibly could make.

---

[12] For an analysis of the cost effectiveness of the measles vaccine prepared by an effective altruism organization, see Giving What We Can, "Immunisation," updated 2012, https://www.givingwhatwecan.org/research/other-causes/immunisation/.

[13] MacAskill gives several examples of situations in which people have allowed emotions to prevail over rational judgment on pp. 40-42 of *Doing Good Better*. Singer discusses this issue on pp. 85-86.

[14] Princeton University tops the list at about 60%. Josh Moody, "Ten Universities Where the Most Alumni Donate," *U.S. News and World Report*, December 18, 2018, https://www.usnews.com/education/best-colleges/the-short-list-college/articles/universities-where-the-most-alumni-donate. Of course, some of the people who donate to their alma maters do so for non-altruistic reasons—e.g., they hope to increase their children's chances of gaining admission.

III. Problems with impartiality

Most obviously, impartiality as conceived by effective altruism poses a threat to many cherished relationships. People enter into some relationships by choice and others because of circumstances. For example, they typically choose their spouses but not their siblings. But whatever the origins of interpersonal connections that people hold dear, valued bonds often cannot survive without people's commitments to "be there" for one another—i.e., to prioritize each other's interests in some instances in which an impersonal assessment of where one's resources could do the most good would lead to a different conclusion. Participants in cherished relationships frequently expect favored treatment and feel wronged if it is not forthcoming. For example, people often carry lifelong grudges against parents who seldom made time for them, even if the parents left them with excellent caregivers and spent their time away from family researching cures for cancer. Similarly, few people would remain members of a small religious congregation that declined to help them in a time of crisis—for instance, if they lost most of their belongings in a fire—even if the reason was that the members gave precedence to donating to the Against Malaria Foundation, a charity championed by proponents of effective altruism that distributes insecticide-treated bed nets to prevent malaria in populations at high risk of contracting the deadly disease.

Singer, of course, knows that people often expect preferential treatment from those to whom they feel connected. In fact, when he first defines effective altruism, he refers to spare resources as those left over after we "feed, house, and clothe ourselves *and our families*." (Italics added.)[15] However, he suggests that expectations of preferential treatment, though understandable, cannot be morally justified. He never mentions relationships with anyone outside of immediate family, and he has this to say even about the status of the parent/child bond: "Most parents love their children, and it would be unrealistic to require parents to be impartial between their own children and other children.…Effective altruists are real people, not saints, and they don't seek to maximize the good in every single thing they do, 24/7."[16] In a nod to practical realities, Singer thus acknowledges that it serves no purpose to dwell on human frailty, but he sees no moral justification for deviating from effective altruism's impersonal calculations. By contrast, partiality proponents maintain that protecting at least some

---

[15] Singer, *The Most Good You Can Do*, vii.
[16] Singer, 8.

sorts of cherished bonds is not only inevitable and morally permissible, but often even morally obligatory. In cases where special moral consideration is obligatory, those who fail to receive it are justified in taking offense.[17]

Defenders of partiality identify various reasons for valuing interpersonal relationships. One important reason is that caring relationships give people's lives meaning and purpose and so are crucial to almost everyone's ability to flourish.[18] This often remains true even when relationships bring people sorrow—for example, when a loved one dies.[19] Being the object of another person's affection also tends to make people feel valued. Caring relationships are therefore important sources of self-esteem.[20] Moreover, cherished relationships commonly provide people with a sense of security that derives from knowing that, whatever happens, they will not have to face the future alone. This feeling of security, in turn, tends to give people the confidence they need to take on challenges.[21] Finally, individuals' identities are usually bound up with their personal relationships to others—for example, with their statuses as spouses, parents, community members,

---

[17] Samuel Scheffler, for example, says "If I fail to act on compelling relationship-dependent reasons to attend to my son's needs, then, other things being equal, I have wronged him and he has a legitimate complaint against me." "Morality and Reasonable Partiality," 109.

[18] See, for example, Bernard Williams, "Persons, Character, and Morality," in *Moral Luck* (Cambridge: Cambridge University Press, 1981), 18; John Cottingham, "Ethics and Impartiality," *Philosophical Studies* 43 (1983): 97; and Scheffler, "Morality and Reasonable Partiality," 105, 115. Singer argues that people tend to discover that following the principles of effective altruism gives their lives meaning and purpose. *The Most Good You Can Do,* 92-104. I believe that this is true, but I strongly suspect that, although Singer does not address this point, the examples he cites are not about people who gave away so much to strangers that they did not prioritize the needs of those close to them.

[19] Susan Wolf makes this point in "Morality and Partiality," *Philosophical Perspectives* 6 (1992): 249.

[20] James Rachels makes this point in "Morality, Parents, and Children," in *Person to Person*, eds. George Graham and Hugh LaFollette (Philadelphia: Temple University Press, 1989), 223.

[21] For an extensive explanation and defense of this point, see John Bowlby, *A Secure Base: Clinical Applications of Attachment Theory* (London: Routledge, 1988).

etc.[22] Having a sense of identity helps people to feel grounded; without it most people feel anxious, empty, and adrift.[23]

Defenders of partiality also underline the failure of effective altruism's brand of impartiality to recognize the importance of repaying debts and keeping promises.[24] I will not address here the thorny issue of how people make promises and incur debts in the context of relationships—for example, whether parents implicitly promise care to their children and whether children owe debts to those who raised them.[25] For present purposes, it is enough to note that effective altruism's list of impersonal questions gives no special deference to bonds of trust that depend on keeping promises and repaying debts. Effective altruism looks forward, not backward, and asks: Given present needs and resources, which investments will make the biggest future difference?

Of course, it is entirely in keeping with effective altruism to acknowledge that people in most instances ought to keep their promises and repay their debts, because these behaviors tend to promote the general welfare. For example, those who habitually break promises and renege on debts often end up lonely and depressed, which tends to decrease their motivation to help others. Moreover, communities often work together to supply aid to the needy, and the distrust engendered by breaking promises and failing to pay debts undermines people's abilities to join forces to do this beneficial work. When the overall costs of ignoring commitments, and more generally of severing relationships, are greater than the overall costs of honoring commitments and maintaining bonds, effective altruists can agree that people ought to take the latter course. Historically, the difficulty of measuring the benefits of relationships and the costs of undermining

---

[22] Kwame Anthony Appiah makes this point in *Cosmopolitanism: Ethics in a World of Strangers* (New York: W.W. Norton & Company, 2006), xviii.

[23] Michael J. Formica, "Examining Our Sense of Identity and Who We Are," *Psychology Today*, October 25, 2009, https://www.psychologytoday.com/us/blog/enlightened-living/200910/examining-our-sense-identity-and-who-we-are.

[24] See, for example, Samuel Scheffler, "Relationships and Responsibilities," *Philosophy and Public Affairs* 26, no. 3 (1997): 189.

[25] For discussion of such questions, see Simon Keller, "Four Theories of Filial Duty," *The Philosophical Quarterly* 56 (2006): 254-74; and Elizabeth Brake, "Willing Parents: A Voluntarist Account of Parental Role Obligations," in *Procreation and Parenthood: The Ethics of Bearing and Rearing Children*, eds. David Archard and David Benatar (Oxford: Oxford University Press, 2010), 151-77.

them has posed a challenge to this kind of cost/benefit analysis, but effective altruism argues persuasively that contemporary science and social science can be helpful here. For example, a growing body of psychological and neuropsychological research has documented both numerous benefits of providing social support to others and the suffering that frequently results when people lack supportive relationships.[26] Effective altruists also often look to the burgeoning field of "health economics" for methods of quantifying emotional burdens.[27]

For a number of reasons, however, the approach of fine-tuning assessments to take account of the benefits of relationships and the costs of fracturing them is inadequate to rebut the partiality critique. First, effective altruism addresses people's obligations to attend to the needs of others using resources *left over* after satisfying their own basic needs. It fails to recognize that, because of the many ways that relationships contribute to wellbeing, maintaining at least some cherished bonds is for most people itself a basic need. Of course, Maslow's famed hierarchy sees the need for relationships as less fundamental than the needs for food, shelter, and clothing that Singer mentions, but this only means that people must eat before they can love. It does not mean that relationship needs are less important than lower level needs, and it certainly does not mean that the resources that people invest in protecting relationships are "spare."[28]

Second, effective altruism seeks to guide people's decisions about which of the world's existing problems to address. For instance, does it do more good in developing nations to administer vaccines to prevent measles

---

[26] See, for example, Tristen Inagaki and Edward Orehek, "On the Benefits of Giving Social Support: When, Why, and How Support Providers Gain by Caring for Others," *Current Directions in Psychological Science 26, no. 2 (2017)*: 109-113; Roy Baumeister and Mark Leary, "The Need to Belong: Desire for Interpersonal Attachments as a Fundamental Human Motivation," *Psychological Bulletin* 117, no. 3 (1995): 497-529; Debra Umberson and Jennifer Karas Montez, "Social Relationships and Health: A Flashpoint for Health Policy," *Journal of Health and Social Behavior* 51, no. 1 (2010): S54-S66; Lane Strathearn, "Maternal Neglect: Oxytocin, Dopamine and the Neurobiology of Attachment," Journal of Neuroendocrinology 23, no. 11 (2011): 1054–65.

[27] Singer explains this approach in detail on pp. 131-4 of *The Most Good You Can Do*. For discussion of some of the controversies surrounding this approach, see, for example, Scott D. Grosse et al., "Disability and Disability-Adjusted Life Years: Not the Same," *Public Health Reports* 124, no. 2 (2009): 197–202.

[28] Abraham H. Maslow, "A Theory of Human Motivation," *Psychological Review* 50, no.4 (1943): 370-96.

or antibiotics to prevent blindness in children suffering from trachoma? However, as previously noted, when people prioritize the interests of strangers over the interests of individuals with whom they share personal bonds, they often inflict harm on those close to them, thereby *creating* a problem that would not otherwise exist. For example, young children who are neglected by their parents sometimes develop attachment disorders. Preventing such disorders in one's own children is quite different from preventing measles or trachoma-caused blindness among children over-seas: the latter, unlike the former, are caused respectively by viruses and bacteria, not by one's choices about where to invest resources. Inflicting suffering may not always be morally worse than doing nothing to stop pre-dictable suffering from happening, but it often is. This consideration is entirely absent from effective altruism's impartiality calculus.[29]

Third, people need the characteristics fostered by interpersonal rela-tionships—i.e., self-esteem, security, and a sense of both identity and pur-pose—to be moral agents.[30] Interpersonal relationships are not the only bases for these characteristics, but they are critical ones. It is therefore un-tenable to view the value of relationships as entirely contingent upon the vagaries of how cost/benefit analyses happen to play out.

Lastly, the partiality critique challenges effective altruism's ability to explain the motivation for being the sort of moral agent who works to promote the general good. Citing Henry Sidgwick's nineteenth century argument, Singer suggests that we know based on reason that we ought to give equal moral consideration to everyone's needs. When we behave in a manner that we know is inconsistent with reason, we feel discomfort be-cause our self-respect is threatened, and this feeling motivates helping be-haviors.[31] The problem with this argument is that those who lack solici-tude for others typically feel no discomfort when failing to help them. In the words of Virginia Held, "unless the presumption of care is met, people seem not to be concerned enough about others to care whether their rights are respected or even recognized."[32]

---

[29] Singer rejects the claim that the principle "do no harm" has priority over the principle "do the most good you can." *The Most Good You Can Do*, 51.

[30] John Cottingham makes a similar argument in support of partiality toward oneself in "Partiality, Favouritism and Morality," *The Philosophical Quarterly* 36, no. 144, (1986): 365-7.

[31] Singer, *The Most Good You Can Do*, 81-83.

[32] Virginia Held, *The Ethics of Care: Personal, Political, and Global* (New York: Oxford University Press, 2006), 132.

Many believe that empathy—the ability to understand and in some cases even feel others' pain—is the characteristic that motivates caring behavior,[33] but psychologist Paul Bloom argues convincingly that empathy is not always enough. After all, some people who identify strongly with the suffering of others go out of their way to avoid personal interactions that might require confronting others' pain. Bloom instead argues that the necessary characteristic is compassion, which combines warm feelings toward others with the impulse to improve their situations.[34]

So how do people develop compassion? Research in developmental psychology has identified strategies for cultivating compassion in children.[35] Among these are: surrounding children with adults who are sensitive to the children's feelings and needs; ensuring that children personally witness acts of kindness; and encouraging children to practice helping behaviors, such as consoling an upset sibling or visiting a grieving relative. The Center for Compassion and Altruism Research and Education at Stanford University Medical School has developed an evidence-based eight week training program designed to promote compassion in adults.[36] Many of the program's precepts derive from a Buddhist practice called "loving-kindness meditation" designed to promote feelings of goodwill and concern for others. Participants begin by repeating a simple mantra, such as "may I be safe and protected." Over time they gradually add other people to the mantra in roughly the following order: a past cherished caregiver, a close friend, a casual acquaintance, a disliked or resented person,

---

[33] For example, Barack Obama has spoken repeatedly about an "empathy deficit" to explain the failure to respond adequately to a wide range of miseries experienced by people at home and abroad. See Ramesh Manocha, "Barack Obama and the Empathy Deficit," *Generation Next*, February 7, 2013, https://www.generation-next.com.au/2013/02/barack-obama-and-the-empathy-deficit/.

[34] Paul Bloom, *Against Empathy: The Case for Rational Compassion* (New York: HarperCollins, 2016), 139.

[35] Jim Taylor, "Five Ways to Instill Compassion in Your Children," *Psychology Today*, September 28, 2014, https://www.psychologytoday.com/us/blog/the-power-prime/201407/5-ways-instill-compassion-in-your-children?amp; Kristina Ponischil, "Cultivating Kindness and Compassion in Children," Center for Child and Family Wellbeing at the University of Washington, December 8, 2014, https://depts.washington.edu/ccfwb/content/cultivating-kindness-and-compassion-children-0.

[36] For information about the program, see The Center for Compassion and Altruism Research and Education, "About Compassion Cultivation Training," Stanford Medicine, 2019, http://ccare.stanford.edu/education/about-compassion-cultivation-training-cct/.

and finally, all people. This research has bearing on the impartiality/partiality debate, because these evidenced-based strategies all use observation of, and participation in, particular caring relationships as bases for developing the compassion for humanity that motivates people to become effective altruists. It therefore suggests that the value of interpersonal bonds far exceeds the instrumental factors that effective altruism recognizes.

IV. Accommodating competing considerations

I have argued that there are strong reasons both to embrace as well as to resist impartiality as it is conceived by effective altruism. Sometimes, as discussed earlier, it is not necessary to choose between impartiality and partiality, because prioritizing the needs of close friends, family, and community members turns out to coincide with doing the most good overall as determined by effective altruism. Clearly, however, this is not always the case. There are many instances in which partiality and impartiality point to different courses of action. An adequate account of moral obligations to others must address the issue of how much weight moral agents should accord the competing considerations.[37] There are no simple answers to this question, particularly because of the complexity of human relationships and the varying value that individuals ascribe to them. Nevertheless, I suggest that the defense of partiality discussed in the preceding section can provide a basis for formulating some proposals about whether and when relationship considerations should take moral precedence over obligations to promote the overall good.

One proposal is that, since bonding with others is for most people a fundamental need, individuals should set aside the resources required to satisfy their own basic needs for interpersonal relationship before undertaking effective altruism's impartial analyses of how to invest spare resources. Preserving a cherished relationship with another person does not

---

[37] Other authors have also addressed this issue. For example, Marilyn Friedman offers a "qualified defense of partiality, which makes a place for responsibilities or duties to distant others," in "The Practice of Partiality," *Ethics* 101, no. 4 (1991): 835. See also Virginia Held, "Care and Justice in the Global Context," in *The Ethics of Care: Personal, Political, and Global*, 154-68. Thomas Nagel also expresses support for this general approach in his review of Singer's and MacAskill's books on effective altruism. Thomas Nagel, "Ways to Help," The Times Literary Supplement, November 18, 2015, https://www.the-tls.co.uk/articles/ways-to-help/.

require *always* prioritizing that person's interests over either one's own interests or those of the general welfare.[38] Nor does it require that people maintain *all* their interpersonal bonds. The biggest challenge is identifying which relationships satisfy basic needs. I doubt that it is possible to specify clear criteria, in part because people differ in the number and types of close relationships they require for their own wellbeing, and individuals' needs for close relationships often vary over the course of their lifetimes. However, I suggest that my discussion in Section III of the value of relationships offers a basis for formulating guidelines that can help people to identify bonds that fall into this category.

To decide whether an interpersonal relationship satisfies a basic need and thus should be given priority over the obligations to humanity that effective altruism identifies, I propose that individuals try to answer the following questions as honestly as they can: Does this relationship give my life meaning and purpose? Is it a significant source of self-esteem? Does it help me to feel personally secure? Is it central to my identity? Relationships that satisfy basic needs: (a) do not undermine any of the four listed factors—e.g., they do not foster feelings of insecurity or erode self-confidence[39]—and (b) either significantly promote several of the listed factors or, if they promote only one or two, do so to a very high degree. There is one proviso, however, to this suggestion: individuals ought not to prioritize the needs of those with whom they share interpersonal bonds if those bonds are based on prejudice.[40] What does and does not constitute prejudice is, of course, a complex issue. Giving special consideration to a fellow white individual because of race is a clear example of prejudice. More controversial is allowing race to be a factor in prioritizing the interests of a fellow member of a societally disadvantaged racial minority. This is not

---

[38] For discussion of the importance of balance in this regard, see Bonnie Le et al., "Communal Motivation and Well-Being in Interpersonal Relationships: An Integrative Review and Meta-Analysis," *Psychological Bulletin* 144, no. 1 (2018): 1-25.

[39] Marilyn Friedman makes this point when she says that the moral value that partiality sees in relationships does not apply to relationships that are oppressive, abusive, or exploitative. "The Practice of Partiality," 820.

[40] Various authors have made this point. See, for example, Cottingham, "Ethics and Impartiality," 97, and Friedman, "Practice of Partiality," 819. It is important to recognize that avoiding relationships that are based on prejudice is very different from avoiding relationships with prejudiced people. For example, a son may legitimately prioritize the health needs of his ill, racially bigoted father, because his relationship with his father, despite the father's prejudices, is valuable in some of the ways listed above.

the place to pursue this issue. For present purposes, I will only say that prejudice, however it is ultimately defined, cannot be a moral basis for awarding people special consideration.[41]

Most people have significant interpersonal relationships besides those that satisfy their own basic needs, and I propose that at least some of these relationships give rise to special responsibilities. Again, the challenge is to decide which relationships fall into this category. I would argue that some obligations of this sort arise from debts and promises that people either knowingly and willingly agreed to, or unwittingly became a party to because of their actions. An example of the latter would be a debt incurred by negligently harming a stranger. Although there may be some instances in which it is morally permissible, and perhaps even morally obligatory, to break promises and to renege on debts, I suggest that, in general, special obligations generated by promises and debts should take precedence over duties to the general welfare.[42]

In a passage I cited in Section I, Samuel Scheffler describes other interpersonal bonds that give rise to special duties as ones that exist "between individuals who have a shared history that usually includes patterns of engagement and forms of mutual familiarity, attachment, and regard developed over time."[43] Drawing again on my discussion in Section III, I propose interpreting mutual "attachment" and "regard" in terms of the characteristics that confer value on relationships. The interpersonal relationships that I seek to describe here—i.e., ones that give rise to special duties but that are not necessary to satisfy one's own basic needs—are bonds that an individual, upon an attempt at honest reflection, determines: (a) do not undermine any of the four factors listed above; (b) promote at least one or two of the four factors to a significant degree; and (c) are not based on prejudice. Although I agree with Scheffler that bonds of this sort typically take time to develop, I do not think that the time element is a separate requirement. People sometimes can develop intense bonds in relatively short periods of time.

---

[41] In "Choosing Our Friends: Moral Partiality and the Value of Diversity," Sara Goering makes the interesting claim that "a theory of morality that allows or encourages partiality toward one's friends ought to encourage or even require the effort to cultivate a diverse group of friends." *Journal of Social Philosophy* 34, no. 3 (2003): 401.

[42] Of course, people sometimes knowingly and voluntarily make promises and incur debts that they ought not to have agreed to. This is an important issue, but I will not address it here.

[43] Scheffler, "Morality and Reasonable Partiality," 115.

So when should people prioritize the special obligations generated by relationships of these sorts over impartial obligations to humanity? There is no algorithm for answering this question, but I will make several suggestions that may help in weighing competing considerations. One is to use the factors identified above to think about how important the relationship is to the other participants in it. In particular, if *they* see the relationship as essential to satisfying *their* basic needs, this is extra reason to prioritize their interests. Another proposal is that, in weighing competing claims on their resources, individuals should consider not only their abilities to provide assistance going forward, but also assistance they have supplied in the past, either to the same individual currently in need of help, to other individuals with whom they share bonds, or to humanitarian causes—all factors ignored by effective altruism. I suggest that in deciding whether to give precedence to general or to special obligations when the relationships at issue are not critical to serving basic needs, people who have already made substantial contributions in one of these arenas should operate with a rebuttable presumption that they ought to prioritize the other. The reason that this presumption should be rebuttable is that there are times when a person's obligations in one arena should take precedence, regardless of past contributions. For example, consider a very elderly woman with few living friends whose closest relative is a nephew with whom she has not communicated in two years. Even if she has already donated generously to humanitarian causes, she probably still ought to use effective altruism's schema in writing her will.

A final proposal for accommodating conflicting considerations raised by impartiality and partiality is based on the recognition that governments everywhere use tax revenues to pay for services that benefit residents. Everyone who pays taxes therefore indirectly contributes to the wellbeing of innumerable strangers. In assessing past contributions to the general welfare, I suggest that people should take these contributions into account. Of course, it can be very difficult to know how much of one's taxes governments actually use for the general welfare, but these are the sorts of assessments that effective altruists are skilled at conducting.

A relevant question here is how much responsibility for the common good ought governments to take? Effective altruism addresses this question in only the very limited context of encouraging individuals to think about whether the best investment of spare resources might perhaps be advocacy work aimed at convincing legislators to change their goals, priorities or strategies.[44] But the question has much deeper implications. How governments collect and use tax money has a huge impact on the distribution of wealth in the world. It affects which people have spare resources and which people lack the means to fulfill their relationship obligations. It might seem appealing to propose that governments should take primary responsibility for impartially considering everyone's interests and thereby enable individuals to prioritize their relationship-based duties.[45] After all, governments have greater abilities than do individuals or private organizations to institute the societal changes most effective in reducing neediness. Moreover, by ensuring compliance with tax laws, governments can minimize the likelihood that some people will avoid contributing their fair share to the general welfare.

Nevertheless, there are reasons to resist assigning to government full responsibility for the common good. One problem is that governments derive a good part of their resources from taxes, and few governmental systems of collecting and distributing taxes are truly equitable. Moreover, there is a great deal of controversy over what an equitable tax system even is. Another concern is that governments in impoverished countries generally lack the resources to address more than a fraction of their constituents' needs, and it is difficult to make a strong case for affluent nations giving residents of impoverished ones the same consideration they give their own populace. One reason is that countries that donate resources internationally frequently have too little understanding of, or influence over, the policies and practices of recipient nations to ensure that all the aid is used effectively.

Of course, a possible solution, at least in theory, is a single world government—an idea proposed by some visionaries since ancient times but that has never taken root.[46] Despite its appeal in terms of equalizing access

---

[44] For Singer's views on the pluses and minuses of advocacy work, see *The Most Good You Can Do*, 157-64.

[45] For a defense of this general proposal, see George Lakey, *Viking Economics: How the Scandinavians Got it Right—and How We Can Too* (New York: Melville House Publishing, 2016). Marilyn Friedman proposes that a primary function of government is to impartially provide people with the resources they need to fulfill their care obligations to those with whom they share bonds. In this way she suggests blurring the impartiality/partiality divide. Friedman, "The Practice of Partiality," 830-31.

[46] For a contemporary discussion of this idea, see Alexander Wendt, "Why a World State is Inevitable," *European Journal of International* Relations 9, no. 4 (2003): 491-542.

to resources, however, there are some good reasons to resist this cosmopolitan ideal. Among the many legitimate concerns are that such a government would inevitably accrue too much power and that a monolith of this sort could not respond well to local needs.[47]

Ultimately, I believe that government must play a crucial, but circumscribed, role in the optimal solution. I will suggest here only a few key aspects of what that role should be. Governments must not require people to pay in taxes money that they need to satisfy their basic needs—including their need to maintain critical interpersonal relationships. People with wealth should be taxed at higher rates than those with less income. Governments ought to use tax revenues to equitably address the needs of all constituents, and to the extent possible, those of the global community. They should give special attention to enabling those with inadequate resources to fulfill their special obligations to others. And lastly, governments should ensure that wealthy people cannot avoid paying their fair share of taxes. For people with spare resources who live under governments that operate in these ways, paying taxes could satisfy a good portion of their obligations to the general welfare. As long as there are people in the world whose needs are still not met, however, individuals with extra resources who live in well-governed countries that give substantial amounts of humanitarian foreign aid still have some remaining obligations to contribute to the common good.

V. Conclusion

In this essay I have argued that to satisfy their own basic needs, most people must give at least some priority to the interests of individuals with whom they share distinctive bonds. Moreover, those with resources to spare after satisfying their own basic needs have both the kinds of impartial obligations identified by effective altruism and some special obligations that are not related to satisfying their own basic needs. Conflicts among these various obligations are inevitable, and an adequate account of moral duties to others must explain how moral agents ought to prioritize among competing considerations. I have offered various proposals that I believe make useful contributions to this project. I am hopeful that my discussion not only contributes to the philosophical debate, but also provides some

---

[47] See Appiah, *Cosmopolitanism*, 163 for discussion of these and other concerns.

practical guidance to those seeking to live in accordance with effective altruism's basic precepts while also taking seriously their responsibilities to close friends, family, and community members.

Works Cited

Appiah, Kwame Anthony. *Cosmopolitanism: Ethics in a World of Strangers.* New York: W.W. Norton & Company, 2006.

Baumeister, Roy and Mark Leary. "The Need to Belong: Desire for Interpersonal Attachments as a Fundamental Human Motivation." *Psychological Bulletin* 117, no. 3 (1995): 497-529.

Bloom, Paul. *Against Empathy: The Case for Rational Compassion.* New York: HarperCollins, 2016.

Bowlby, John. *A Secure Base: Clinical Applications of Attachment Theory.* London: Routledge, 1988.

Brake, Elizabeth. "Willing Parents: A Voluntarist Account of Parental Role Obligations." In *Procreation and Parenthood: The Ethics of Bearing and Rearing Children*, edited by David Archard and David Benatar, 151-77. Oxford: Oxford University Press, 2010.

The Center for Compassion and Altruism Research and Education. "About Compassion Cultivation Training." Stanford Medicine. 2019. http://ccare.stanford.edu/education/about-compassion-cultivation-training-cct/.

Cottingham, John. "Ethics and Impartiality." *Philosophical Studies* 43 (1983): 83-99.

———. "Partiality, Favouritism and Morality." *The Philosophical Quarterly* 36, no. 144 (1986): 357-73.

Formica, Michael J. "Examining Our Sense of Identity and Who We Are." *Psychology Today.* October 25, 2009. https://www.psychologyto-day.com/us/blog/enlightened-living/200910/examining-our-sense-identity-and-who-we-are.

Friedman, Marilyn. "The Practice of Partiality." *Ethics 101*, no. 4 (1991): 818-35.

Giving What We Can. "Immunisation." Updated 2012. https://www.givingwhatwecan.org/research/other-causes/immunisation/.

Goering, Sara. "Choosing Our Friends: Moral Partiality and the Value of Diversity." *Journal of Social Philosophy* 34, no. 3 (2003): 400-413.

Grosse, Scott, Donald Lollar, Vincent Campbell, and Mary Chamie, "Disability and Disability-Adjusted Life Years: Not the Same." *Public Health Reports* 124, no. 2 (2009): 197–202.

Held, Virginia. *The Ethics of Care: Personal, Political, and Global.* New York: Oxford University Press, 2006.

Inagaki, Tristen and Edward Orehek. "On the Benefits of Giving Social Support: When, Why, and How Support Providers Gain by Caring for Others." *Current Directions in Psychological Science* 26, no. 2 (2017): 109-13.

Jeske, Diane. "Friendship and Reasons of Intimacy." *Philosophy and Phenomenological Research* 63, no. 2 (2001): 329-46.

Keller, Simon. "Four Theories of Filial Duty." *The Philosophical Quarterly* 56 (2006): 254-74.

Lakey, George. *Viking Economics: How the Scandinavians Got it Right—and How We Can Too.* New York: Melville House Publishing, 2016.

Le, Bonnie, Emily Impett, Edward Lemay, Jr., Amy Muise, and Konstantin Tskhay, "Communal Motivation and Well-Being in Interpersonal Relationships: An Integrative Review and Meta-Analysis." *Psychological Bulletin* 144, no. 1 (2018): 1-25.

MacAskill, William. *Doing Good Better: How Effective Altruism Can Help You Make a Difference.* New York: Penguin Random House, 2015.

———. "Effective Altruism: Introduction." *Essays in Philosophy* 18, no.1 (2017): 1-5.

Manocha, Ramesh. "Barack Obama and the Empathy Deficit." *Generation Next.* February 7, 2013. https://www.generation-next.com.au/2013/02/barack-obama-and-the-empathy-deficit/.

Maslow, Abraham. "A Theory of Human Motivation." *Psychological Review* 50, no.4 (1943): 370-96.

Moody, Josh. "Ten Universities Where the Most Alumni Donate." *U.S. News and World Report.* December 18, 2018. https://www.us-news.com/education/best-colleges/the-short-list-college/articles/universities-where-the-most-alumni-donate.

Nagel, Thomas. "Ways to Help." *The Times Literary Supplement.* November 18, 2015. https://www.the-tls.co.uk/articles/ways-to-help/.

Ponischil, Kristina. "Cultivating Kindness and Compassion in Children." Center for Child and Family Wellbeing at the University of Washington. December 8, 2014. https://depts.washington.edu/ccfwb/content/cultivating-kindness-and-compassion-children-0.

Rachels, James. "Morality, Parents, and Children." In *Person to Person*, edited by George Graham and Hugh LaFollette. Philadelphia: Temple University Press, 1989, 213-33.

Scheffler, Samuel. "Morality and Reasonable Partiality." In *Partiality and Impartiality: Morality, Special Relationships and the Wider World*, edited by Brian Feltham and John Cottingham. Oxford: Oxford University Press, 2010, 98-130.

———. "Relationships and Responsibilities." *Philosophy and Public Affairs* 26, no. 3 (1997): 189-209.

Singer, Peter. *The Most Good You Can Do: How Effective Altruism is Changing Ideas About Living Ethically.* New Haven: Yale University Press, 2015.

Strathearn, Lane. "Maternal Neglect: Oxytocin, Dopamine and the Neurobiology of Attachment." *Journal of Neuroendocrinology* 23, no. 11 (2011): 1054–65.

Taylor, Jim. "Five Ways to Instill Compassion in Your Children." *Psychology Today.* September 28, 2014. https://www.psychologytoday.com/us/blog/the-power-prime/201407/5-ways-instill-compassion-in-your-children?amp.

Umberson, Debra and Jennifer Karas Montez. "Social Relationships and Health: A Flashpoint for Health Policy." *Journal of Health and Social Behavior* 51, no. 1 (2010): S54-S66.

Wendt, Alexander. "Why a World State is Inevitable." *European Journal of International Relations* 9, no. 4 (2003): 491-542.

Williams, Bernard. "Persons, Character, and Morality." In *Moral Luck.* Cambridge: Cambridge University Press, 1981, 1-19.

Wise, Julia. "You Have More than One Goal and That's Fine." *Giving Gladly.* 2019. http://www.givinggladly.com/2019/02/you-have-more-than-one-goal-and-thats.html.

Wolf, Susan. "Morality and Partiality." *Philosophical Perspectives* 6 (1992): 243-59.

List of Contributors

Susan Bredlau's work is grounded in the phenomenological tradition and focuses on the critical role of other people within our lived experience. She is the author of *The Other in Perception: A Phenomenological Account of Our Experience of Other Persons* (SUNY Press, 2018) and has published articles in *Continental Philosophy of Review*, *Medical Humanities*, and *Phenomenology and the Cognitive Sciences*.

Tony Chackal is a philosopher specializing in Social and Political Philosophy, Aesthetics, Critical Race Theory and Environmental Philosophy. He has published articles on the concept of place and environmental identity in *Environmental Ethics*, on street art and law in the *Journal of Aesthetics and Art Criticism*, and on autonomy and the politics of food choice in the *Journal of Agricultural and Environmental Ethics*. He has taught Philosophy at the University of Georgia, Missouri State University, and Slippery Rock University. Forthcoming publications include an article advancing a novel theory of collective autonomy and another on the nature/culture dualism in environmental aesthetics.

Pablo Munoz Iturrieta holds a doctorate in political philosophy from Carleton University (Ottawa, Canada). He is the author of *The Meaning of Religious Freedom in the Public Secular Sphere* (2020) and of the best-selling book *Atrapado en el cuerpo equivocado* (2019), which focuses on gender, identity, and civil rights issues. In the last few years, he has lectured in over 100 cities in 15 countries to thousands of people. Besides his research work, Dr. Munoz Iturrieta teaches philosophy, political science, and psychology courses to a large international audience via his online platform and is currently working on an online education program for the Spanish speaking world. He resides in Canada.

Matthew Brandon Lee holds a PhD in Philosophy from Notre Dame and is currently Associate Professor of Philosophy at Berry College (Mt. Berry, Georgia, USA). His research spans epistemology, philosophy of religion, and ethics. His papers have appeared in *Episteme*, *Philosophia*, *Philosophical Papers*, *Grazer Philosophische Studien*, and *Dialogue: Canadian Philosophical Review*.

Steven P. Lee is emeritus professor of philosophy at Hobart and William Smith Colleges (Geneva, New York, USA). As a researcher, he has written on various topics in social and political philosophy, especially just war theory. He has authored *Morality, Prudence, and Nuclear Weapons* (Cambridge, 1993), *Ethics and War* (Cambridge, 2012), *What is the Argument—Critical Thinking in the Real World* (McGraw Hill, 2002), and edited or co-edited several collections of essays.

Osman Nemli is an Assistant Professor of Philosophy at Vassar College (Poughkeepsie, NY, USA). His research interests are at the intersection between social and political philosophy, ethics, and aesthetics.

William A. B. Parkhurst is a PhD Candidate at the University of South Florida (Tampa, Florida, USA). Parkhurst specializes in the philosophical and methodological use of archival evidence with a focus on the continental tradition of philosophy (particularly Nietzsche). He has completed archival research fellowships at both the Linda Hall Library and the Leo Baeck Institute at The Center for Jewish History. His archival and philosophical research has appeared in flagship specialist journals such as *Nietzsche-Studien, Schopenhauer-Jahrbuch,* and elsewhere.

Gary J. Simson is Macon Chair in Law and Former Dean at Mercer University School of Law (Macon, GA, USA). He is also Professor Emeritus of Law at Cornell Law School and received his BA and JD from Yale University.

Rosalind S. Simson is Associate Professor of Philosophy at Mercer University (Macon, Georgia, USA). Earlier in her career, most of her teaching and writing was in epistemology. In recent years she has focused primarily on a variety of issues at the intersection of ethics, gender, and law, ranging from abortion to the environment to effective altruism.

About the Editors

Yi Deng is Associate Professor of Philosophy at the University of North Georgia (Dahlonega, Georgia, USA). Her teaching and research interests include ethics, social and political philosophy, Chinese philosophy, and global justice. Her recent work focuses on Kantian political philosophy and food justice.

Creighton Rosental is Professor and Chair of Philosophy and Founding Director of Ethics, Leadership, and Service at Mercer University (Macon, Georgia, USA). His research and teaching interests include history of philosophy, logic, and philosophy of art.

Robert H. Scott is Associate Professor of Philosophy at the University of North Georgia (Dahlonega, Georgia, USA). His teaching and research interests include ethics, phenomenology, environmental philosophy, and philosophy of religion. He is co-editor (with Gregory S. Moss) of *The Significance of Indeterminacy: Perspectives from Asian and Continental Philosophy* (Routledge, 2019).

Rosalind S. Simson is Associate Professor of Philosophy at Mercer University (Macon, Georgia, USA). Earlier in her career, most of her teaching and writing was in epistemology. In recent years she has focused primarily on a variety of issues at the intersection of ethics, gender, and law, ranging from abortion to the environment to effective altruism.